THE LIFE OF ÑĀṆATILOKA THERA

A Western Buddhist Pioneer

THE LIFE OF ÑĀṆATILOKA THERA

The Biography of a Western Buddhist Pioneer

Compiled and edited by

Dr. Hellmuth Hecker

and

Bhikkhu Ñāṇatusita

BUDDHIST PUBLICATION SOCIETY
KANDY • SRI LANKA

Buddhist Publication Society
PO Box 61
54, Sangharaja Mawatha
Kandy, Sri Lanka

First published 2008

National Library of Sri Lanka-Cataloguing in Publication Data

Bhikkhu Nyanatusita editor

The Life of Nanatiloka Thera: The Biography of a Western Buddhist Pioneer. Transl. by S. Analayo & Bhikkhu Nyanatusita.- Kandy: Buddhist Publication Society, 2008.- p.274; 21cm.

ISBN: 978-955-24-0318-7 Price Rs.

i. 294.3657 DDC 21 ii. Title
1. Biography—Buddhist monk 2. Buddhism

ISBN: 978-955-24-0318-7

Printed in Sri Lanka by

Creative Printers & Designers,
Bahirawakanda, Kandy.

CONTENTS

Foreword i

Introduction v

Part I: Buddhism in Germany 1

Part II: The Life of Ñāṇatiloka Thera 13

Chapter 1: Youth 13
Chapter 2: To the Orient, 1902–1903 22
Chapter 3: Ceylon and Burma, 1903–1910 24
Chapter 4: Europe and Tunisia, 1910–1911 30
Chapter 5: Island Hermitage, 1911–1914 35
Chapter 6: Sikkim, 1914 40
Chapter 7: Confinement at Polgasduva, 1914 44
Chapter 8: Internment Camp in Diyatalāva, 1914–1915 47
Chapter 9: Concentration Camps in Australia, 1915–1916 51
Chapter 10: Via Honolulu to Shanghai, 1916 54
Chapter 11: China, 1917–1919 56
Chapter 12: In Germany Again, 1919–1920 78
Chapter 13: To Japan, 1920 82
Chapter 14: To Bangkok via Java, 1921 86
Chapter 15: Back in Japan, 1921–1923 91
Chapter 17: Last years in Japan, 1923–1926 99
Chapter 18: Return to Ceylon, 1926 102

Part III: Biographical Postscript 105

Chapter 19: Ceylon, 1926–1931 105
Chapter 20: Flowering Period, 1932–1939 111
Chapter 21: Internment in Dehra Dun, 1939–1946 128
Chapter 22: Last years, 1946–1957 143

Appendix I: Life Sketch of Venerable Ñāṇaponika 159

Appendix II: The Literary Work of Ñāṇatiloka Thera 171

Ñāṇatiloka Bibliography 177

Appendix III: The Monk Disciples of Ñāṇatiloka 192

Endnotes 197

CONTENTS

FOREWORD

Ven. Ñāṇatiloka was one of the pioneers of Buddhism in the modern world and the first Westerner to become a Mahāthera, i.e. a Buddhist monk of twenty years standing. He was born as Anton Gueth in Wiesbaden, Germany, in 1878 and died in 1957 in Colombo, Ceylon, where he was honoured with a State Funeral. He had been a *bhikkhu* for fifty-three years.

As a young man, Gueth had been a gifted violinist and composer, but he renounced a promising musical career and travelled to Burma, where, in 1904, at the age of twenty-six, he became the second European (after the Englishman Ānanda Metteyya (Allan Bennett)) to be ordained as a Buddhist monk. Seven years later, in 1911, he founded the Island Hermitage in Ceylon, which was to become a focal point for the small but growing number of Westerners who were drawn to Buddhist monasticism in those early years. Through his extensive translations of classical Pali texts and his own lucid interpretations of the Dhamma, he became a key figure in introducing Buddhist ideas and practices to the West in the first half of the twentieth century.

Much of this work, however, was achieved under conditions of great hardship. As a German national, he was arrested, interned and deported by the British authorities during both world wars. During his exile from Ceylon, he was often forced to live in unsanitary and crowded conditions. He contracted both smallpox and malaria. Yet throughout these difficult times, whether imprisoned in camps in Australia and India or employed as a university teacher in Japan, he did not waver in his commitment to his monastic vocation and persevered in his scholarly work, often with minimal resources at his disposal. For those who have not experienced the turmoil and uncertainty of war and are accustomed to instant access of information through the internet, Ñāṇatiloka's accomplishments are all the more remarkable.

Living at a time when Europeans and Americans routinely ordain as Buddhist monks, it is difficult for us to appreciate the radical break that Ñāṇatiloka had to make with Western tradition. In the early years of the twentieth century, Christianity was still, for the vast majority of Europeans, the undisputed religion of the civilised world. No matter how sympathetic critics of Christianity might have been toward Buddhism—such as the philosopher Schopenhauer or adherents of the fashionable Theosophical Society—none of them would have considered becoming Buddhist monks. Irrespective of how nobly the Buddha was portrayed (as in Edwin Arnold's *The Light of Asia*), even to its admirers Buddhism still remained alien and exotic. By taking the highly visible step of being ordained as a Buddhist monk, Ñāṇatiloka abandoned his Christian identity. This required not only courage in the face of enormous cultural and religious prejudice but a willingness to embark on a journey into a field of human experience about which the Western world knew almost nothing at all.

The story of Ñāṇatiloka's life provides an inspiring example of one man's ability to put aside his cultural doubts and hesitations and embrace wholeheartedly a non-Western system of values, ideas and practices. In 1904, this would have been the spiritual equivalent of setting out into the heart of an unknown continent with meagre equipment and the sketchiest of maps. As with the explorers of uncharted lands, he would have had little idea of what awaited him or what obstacles he might encounter on the way. Yet what strikes one on reading his story is that the fanaticism or stubbornness one might expect in a trailblazer seem entirely absent in him. His manner is consistently unhurried, sensitive, patient and kind. The greatest hardships do not seem to deter him any more than his achievements appear to go to his head.

As the world's senior Western *bhikkhu*, Ñāṇatiloka attracted many disciples, through whose work his influence continues to be felt today, more than fifty years after his death. He was the preceptor of the eminent scholar and translator Ñāṇaponika Thera (Siegmund Feniger), author of *The Heart of Buddhist Meditation*, as well as Ñāṇamoli Thera (Osbert Moore), whose translations include the Buddha's *Middle Length Discourses* as well as Buddhaghosa's *The Path of Purity*.

The core of this volume consists of a translation of Ñāṇatiloka's autobiography, written in German when he was forty-eight. The remaining thirty-one years of his life, from 1926 until 1957, are presented as a biographical postscript, drawn from other sources. *The Life of Ñāṇatiloka Thera* offers a fascinating insight into the formative period of Europe's encounter with the Dhamma.

Stephen Batchelor
Aquitaine, France,
November 2008

INTRODUCTION

This work on the first German Buddhist monk Venerable Ñāṇatiloka is not intended to be a hagiography but a straightforward historical record. Its purpose is to introduce the life of a Western Buddhist pioneer, the first bhikkhu in modern times from Continental Europe. It presents the story of a man who encountered formidable hardships in his spiritual search, but nevertheless succeeded in creating a basis for successive generations of Buddhist monks: as a precursor, a teacher, a reliable translator of Buddhist texts, and a founder of monasteries.

Ñāṇatiloka's autobiography reveals his determination to become a Buddhist monk despite many obstacles and uncertainties, and then to remain a monk in the face of severe hardships. As a German national, Ñāṇatiloka had to spend several years in internment camps during the two world wars; after World War I he was also banned for several years from re-entering the British colony of Ceylon, the then current name for Sri Lanka, and from settling in other Theravāda Buddhist countries. He describes his failed attempt to set up the first Buddhist monastery in Europe, and his consequent success in establishing the first-ever monastery for Westerners, the Island Hermitage, situated on a small island in a lagoon in the southwest of Ceylon.

Ñāṇatiloka offers a window into a world which was still without passports and intercontinental plane travel; a world in which spiritual seekers from the West had to travel to Asia by ship, and once there, would meet with great discomforts, hardships, and a considerable risk of falling ill from then common and incurable diseases such as malaria and quite possibly dying from them, as happened to several Western disciples of Ñāṇatiloka. He writes about Asian countries and cultures, such as China and Japan, which have drastically changed since he was there. He gives a first-hand account of the terrible Great Kanto Earthquake, which hit the Tokyo area in 1923. He also describes life in the internment camps in Australia where he and his German disciples were interned during World War I.

This book can be regarded as an amalgam of various materials, written by different authors and obtained from different sources, but all relating directly or indirectly to Ñāṇatiloka. The book consists of three main parts. Part I is an essay on the early history of Buddhism in Germany by Walter Persian, a German journalist, co-founder of the Hamburg Buddhist Society (BGH) and later leader of the Buddhist Society of Germany (BGD). Part II is the autobiography itself. Part III is a biography of the later part of Ñāṇatiloka's life intertwined with brief biographies of some of his later disciples. There is also an appendix with the biography of Venerable Ñāṇaponika Thera, and another appendix with an extensive bibliography of all the works written by Ñāṇatiloka.

Persian's essay on the early history of Buddhism in Germany was earlier published in a Buddhist journal.[1] I have reproduced it in Part I to serve as an introduction to Ñāṇatiloka and his cultural background. The autobiography of Ñāṇatiloka, which constitutes Part II, does not cover his whole life but runs from his birth in Germany in 1878 to his return to Ceylon in 1926 after banishment. The biography in Part III, based on Dr Hecker's work, deals with the thirty years after 1926 and is supplemented by the accounts of some of Ñāṇatiloka's disciples and contemporaries.

Because Ñāṇatiloka did not finish the autobiography, it is somewhat unpolished and could have been improved upon in many ways. For example, he mentions nothing about how he, as a Buddhist monk, was treated by non-Buddhists in Europe. But, as Ñāṇatiloka writes at the very beginning of the autobiography, his purpose in writing it was merely to provide a few facts about his life. Nevertheless, despite these defects, the autobiography is intrinsically interesting and valuable as a source of information about the early Western adoption of Buddhism.

The German text of the autobiography was first published in *Der Erste Deutsche Bhikkhu*, edited by Dr Hellmuth Hecker (Konstanz, 1995) (From now on abbreviated as EDB). This is the first translation of it to appear in print. A draft translation of the autobiographical part of the Konstanz edition was prepared by S. Anālayo. This translation, partly modified as a result of suggestions from a number of proofreaders, was eventually passed on to me. I compared it with the German translation and made many corrections and improvements. For Part III, I further translated and added some of the biographical material found in the second part of *Der Erste Deutsche Bhikkhu,* an account of Ñāṇatiloka's life after 1926, intertwined with accounts and biographies of some of his disciples and other people who knew him. I also added other material not found in Hecker's work, such as the works of Eidlitz and Wirz, which I have translated from the German, and some notices, etc., I found in old Buddhist journals such as *The Buddhist Review.* Some of this material can also be found on the extensive *Neobuddhismus* website of Dr. Alois Payer at www.payer.de/neobuddhismus.

The focus is less on Ñāṇatiloka in the biographical Part III. This is because Ñāṇatiloka's life was not so eventful during this period and because there is no material by Ñāṇatiloka himself. To make this part more interesting, and to show the import and results of Ñāṇatiloka's teaching efforts, it has been supplemented with accounts of Eidlitz, Wirz and with brief biographies of later disciples of Ñāṇatiloka such as Ñāṇamoli.

The biography of Venerable Ñāṇaponika, written by Bhikkhu Bodhi, has been added as an appendix. I thought it worthwhile to include this because Ñāṇaponika and Ñāṇatiloka lived together for many years and Ñāṇaponika was Ñāṇatiloka's designated literary heir. Ñāṇaponika became an influential Buddhist writer and publisher as cofounder and long-time president of the Buddhist Publication Society. Appendix II consists of bibliographical information related to Ñāṇatiloka.

I was at first uncertain whether the whole of the autobiography should be published or not. However, in order to represent Ñāṇatiloka's story as he wrote it, I decided, after consulting others, not to leave out anything.

The original autobiography, in German, was not published until 1995. For some years it was at the Island Hermitage in Dodanduva, where it was written and typed out in 1948. It was then kept at the Forest Hermitage in Kandy, to which Ñāṇatiloka moved in 1951. The text had been written on thin airmail paper and the edges had been eaten by cockroaches, resulting in the loss of some words on several pages, especially the first two. In 1990 Bhikkhu Bodhi sent the manuscript to Dr. Hecker, who published it together with the great amount of additional biographical information he had gathered in a thorough and meticulous way.

The manuscript Dr. Hecker received lacked three pages, pp. 3-4 and 46. Dr. Hecker made up for these two pages by retranslating into German the partial English translation in *Forest Monks of Sri Lanka* by Michael Carrithers, who had seen those pages and partly translated them from German into English. Hecker briefly guessed at the content of the third missing in a footnote. The first two missing pages describe part of Ñāṇatiloka's adolescence, including his flight to a Benedictine monastery. The third missing page describes the repatriation from China to Germany in 1919.

In 2006 while going through the archives of the Forest Hermitage, I made two discoveries. First I found a partial English translation of the Ñāṇatiloka autobiography made by Ñāṇaponika in 1956. It is only of a part of the first chapter of the manuscript. These pages cover Ñāṇatiloka's youth up to his initial determination to go to India after he heard a lecture on Buddhism, that is, up to the second line of page ten of the German edition by Dr. Hecker. Then, sometime later, I came across three tattered papers in the Forest Hermitage archives. They turned out to be the missing pages of the manuscript. Making use of these discoveries, I compared the English translation with the translation of Ñāṇaponika and translated the untranslated passages into English. Two brief anecdotes about Ñāṇatiloka's time in Burma in 1907, which were attached as notes to Ñāṇaponika's translation, have also been incorporated.

Photographs of Ñāṇatiloka and his disciples, preserved in the archives of the Forest Hermitage, the Island Hermitage, the Hamburg Buddhist Society, and elsewhere have been added.

On behalf of the BPS, I would like to sincerely thank all those who, in one way or another, have made this publication possible—by proofreading, helping with the translation, doing research, scanning photographs, etc. As the editor, I take final responsibility for this work along with any errors that remain.

Bhikkhu Ñāṇatusita

PART I

BUDDHISM IN GERMANY

By Walther Persian, 1931[2]

Nearly all the Buddhists in Germany are adherents of the original form of Buddhism known as Theravada, nevertheless they may, and indeed often do, differ considerably in their views about minor points in the Teaching. For here we must remember that Buddhism has been introduced into Germany by way of literature and not through any missionary efforts on the part of the Buddhist communities of Asia.

A fairly large collection of volumes of belles-lettres in divers kinds have largely contributed to the spread of Buddhist ideas among Germans, and have aroused a general interest in Buddhism. Moreover, philosophy in Germany has already become imbued with Buddhist ideas.[3] Schopenhauer defended the religion of the Buddha with open enthusiasm already in the first third of last century and thus became the herald of Buddhism in and outside Germany. He considered Buddhism the most perfect religion as being not only an idealistic, but also a "pessimistic" and non-theistic teaching. Christianity of the New Testament appeared to him to be of Indian spirit, and therefore also of Indian origin. "It is in reality not Judaism, but Buddhism and Brahmanism, which in spirit and tendency, are related to Christianity. It is the spirit and ethical tendencies that constitute the essence of a religion, and not the myths in which they may be clothed. I therefore do not give up my firm belief that the doctrine of Christianity is somehow derived from both those ancient religions." After such utterances of Schopenhauer, it is not all surprising that, by reason of its inner superiority as well as its overwhelming number of adherents, he considered Buddhism the sublimest religion on earth.

Further, since the French translation of the *Oupnekat,* i.e. the Persian version of the Upanishads, which through Schopenhauer had become fashionable, the number of treatises and articles on

Buddhism grew steadily. Here it must be mentioned that in those writings the Northern, especially the Tibetan and Chinese sources, were exclusively used, and that the most important scholar J. J. Schmidt had placed Buddhism in a time before Brahmanism. Even for Schopenhauer there did not yet exist any marked distinction between Buddhism and Brahmanism. Schopenhauer's philosophy is nothing but a systematic synthesis of Buddhism with Brahmanism. His ethics are Buddhist, but his metaphysics Brahmanical.

Koeppen's monumental German work on Buddhism (1859) is entirely based on Northern sources of Bhutan, Nepal, etc. In this work the author calls the ethics of Buddhism negative, a morality of renunciation, not energy.

One therefore can understand the attitude of Max Müller, the great German scholar at Oxford, one of the most indefatigable pioneers in the field of Buddhism. For the first time, at the philological congress at Kiel in 1869, Müller fought against the idea that Buddhism was nihilistic and emphasised the fact that Buddhism and Sankhya were to be kept strictly apart.

In the following decades, influenced by the Northern sources, a mystical conception of Buddhism came into prominence. Influenced by this so-called esotericism, the philosopher Philip Mailaender, a day after the publication of his book *The Philosophy of Deliverance* in 1876, put an end to his life by shooting himself.

However, not only was the scholarly and philosophical world influenced by Buddhist thought, but also art. And it was one of the greatest in the sphere of art whose soul had listened to the profound voice of Buddhist wisdom: Richard Wagner. Out of the deepest inner need, Wagner had caught hold of the Indian doctrine of deliverance. "You know, how I instinctively have become a Buddhist," he wrote in a letter (22 February 1859) to Mathilde Wesendonck.

Though various points in the teachings did not find his approval, it is nevertheless certain that his great enthusiasm, born in the gloomy fifties of last century and having become quite dominating also in later years, in the happier period of his life, never disappeared from him entirely. On the 16th of May, 1856, Wagner conceived the idea for the opera *Der Sieger* (The

Victor), in other words the Buddha. A rough sketch was found 30 years later among his posthumous works. With this Buddhist conception of the world, he put himself on the side of Schopenhauer, whose philosophical standpoint he quite openly follows in his later works. Most characteristic of his Buddhist spirit is the double conclusion of the *Götterdämmerung* ("The Twilight of the Gods"). At first Bruhnhilden's song ended quite optimistically and full of life in the verse:

Bliss in delight and woe
Love alone may bestow.

Then the optimism changed into that Buddhist insight, that even love itself is woe. The Norse-German Valkyr proclaims this last consummation of Buddhist wisdom:

Know ye wither I fare?
From the home of desires I am departing.
Leaving vanity–home for ever.

The open gates
Of endless becoming
Close I behind me:
To the holiest, the Chosen Land
From wishes and vanities far,
To the end of world-migration,
For ever released from rebirth
Does the Knowing One fare.
The Blissful end
Of things everlasting
Know ye how I did find it?

Deepest woe
Of mourning love
Opened my eyes
Ending saw I the world.

This great enthusiasm for Buddhism, which had received its first impulse through Schopenhauer, was gradually dying off, when Eduard von Hartmann's *Philosophy of the Unconscious* proclaimed that Buddhist pessimism and ascetic pessimism were a heroic kind of pessimism.

It must be further mentioned that pessimism thus popularised became at that time the fashion also in literature, especially in lyrics, as testified by three bulky German anthologies of pessimistic lyrics, published in the Eighties of the last century. Their titles, translated into English, are: *Pessimistic Song-book* by Otto Kenner, *Sources of Pessimistic World-conception* by Max Seiling, *Voices of the World-woe* by Fereus.

At the same time a further impulse in the Buddhist direction was given by Oldenberg's work *Buddha, seine Lehre* etc. though its author was not himself a Buddhist. Published in 1881, this book, more than any other book of his time, contributed towards the rapid popularising of Buddhism in Germany. The highly artistic description of the Buddha's personality and teaching has remained unexcelled, not only with regard to its critical lucidity, but also with regard to its style. Oldenberg tries to prove that Buddhism is throughout ethical, and that all metaphysical speculations and theories were rejected by the Buddha. Further he shows that, for the Buddhist, ethics are only the means to reach the goal. Buddhist morality is however, according to Oldenberg, decidedly egocentric, negative and quietist. But it should not be left unmentioned that he, just as Max Müller, defends it against the common accusation of being pessimistic.

Even the philosopher Nietzsche, although himself a Hellenist, says in his *Antichrist* that Buddhism is a hundred times more realistic than Christianity: "Buddhism is the only positivistic religion we know of in history." [4]

It was in those years that Buddhism in Germany turned into an open fight against Christianity. The *Dhammapada* translation (1885) from the English by the "German Buddhist" Theodor Schultze showed already such tendencies. These polemics had, correctly speaking, already started with Rudolf Seydel, who, whilst attracting widest attention, emphasised the fact that the Christian gospels owed everything which was not Judaic, especially their poetical part, to Buddhism. This is a theory which in our days is strongly advocated by Mathilde Ludendorff, wife of the famous German general, in her book *Deliverance from Jesus Christ*.

The above-mentioned Schultze, a remarkable thinker and ardent fighter for Buddhism, wrote amongst others a book with the title *Vedanta and Buddhism* as ferment for a future regeneration of religious consciousness within the domain of Indo-European culture. Schultze, moreover, defended Buddhism against the attacks of a well known Indologist, Leopold von Schroeder, who complained of the absence in Buddhism of that devout childlike piety and affection found in Christianity, whilst Schultze on the other hand demonstrated that just therein consisted the superiority of Buddhism. Schultze called Christianity today a merely nominal religion. And instead of calling Buddhism atheistic, he emphasises its freedom from God. Instead of the egoistic Christian love he advocated the Buddhist *maitri,* i.e., the universal feeling of good-will towards all creatures. Jesus, he says, is usurping the love of his disciples for himself and thus lays claims that Christianity is a belief for children, for the poor in spirit, whilst to the mature man of today only Buddhism could give satisfaction; that the Christian paradise is subjectively idealistic and only suitable for children, whilst the Nirvana of the Buddhist is an objectively realistic metaphysics capable of bestowing peace on the mature mind.

This Buddhanising movement found its most rigorous opponent in the Jesuit Dahlmann, who again attacked Buddhism for its so-called weak side, which already Oldenberg and Max Müller had defended, as shown above. In spite of his and other attacks, Buddhism gained more and more ground in Germany.

Side by side with the scientific inquiries, Buddhist thought spread more and more through the religious need of the German people. There are many Germans, who—without stimulation and encouragement on the part of Buddhist communities in Asiatic countries—are finding a greater satisfaction for their religious feelings in Buddhism than they ever hope of being able to find in Christianity. They are not only of the intellectual classes, but consist to a great part of people engaged in the social struggle of life, who, beside their own hard professional work, are often intensively engaged in studying the teachings of the Buddha. Here one should well distinguish between theosophy, occultism, pessimism, or so-called parlour-Buddhism, on the one side, and those admirable, heroic men who have renounced the worldly life and are resolutely following the noble path of Homelessness.

Then there are those devout and upright laymen, imbued

with the deepest reverence for the Buddha and his doctrine, in whose houses the peaceful image of the meditating Buddha occupies the place of honour, which in many a Christian home is occupied by the mournful image of the suffering saviour on the cross.

It may here be mentioned, that, whilst at first most of the German works on Buddhism were based on Mahayana, the Germans at that time began to show a keener interest for the original Theravada Buddhism as followed in the Southern countries of Asia.

About that time a little Buddhist anthology was published (1892) by Karl Eugen Neumann, the gifted son of Richard Wagner champion Angelo Neumann, and one year later followed his translation of *Dhammapada.* After studying Indian philosophy and Pali, Neumann had at that time become the most influential translator of Buddhist texts in Germany. His translations of sacred Buddhist scriptures represent a monumental life work. Being himself imbued with the genuine sentiment and spirit of Buddhism, Neumann succeeded in suiting his translation to the spirit and style of the German language. With his essay on the *Sārasaṅgaha,* a 14th century Pali Text, Neumann fell in line with the great translators. Thereafter followed translations of the *Majjhima-Nikāya, Thera-* and *Theri-gāthā, Suttanipāta* and *Dīgha-Nikāya.* What Neumann has accomplished can only be understood by one who has read his neat little volumes on the Buddha's discourses. Due to his translations many of those sympathetic towards Buddhism could join together to form large or small associations.

Thus a great sensation was created when Dr. Karl Seidenstücker published *Der Buddhist* in 1905, the first German, nay the first European, Buddhist magazine. In 1903, at Leipzig, a Buddhist Mission Society was founded, proclaiming as its goal and aim the publication and propagation of Buddhism, and the promotion of "Buddhological" research in the lands of the German tongue. For the realisation of this goal the following activities were planned: (1) publication of Buddhist books, treatises and pamphlets, (2) publication of a magazine, (3) holding of lectures on Buddhism.

In 1906 the Buddhist Mission Society, now called the "Buddhist Association," convened the first Buddhist Congress in

Germany. Favoured by the general development of the Buddhist movement in Germany, several new magazines came to life: *Die Buddhistische Warte, Buddhistische Welt, Der Buddhistische Pfad, Neubuddhistische Zeitschrift, Brockensammlung, Weltspiegel* (Dr. Grimm), *Der Buddhaweg und wir Buddhisten* (Martin Steinke Tao Chun), which through the unfavourable conditions during and after the War, had to discontinue publication.

In 1908 the German Pali Society was founded by Walter Markgraf, a pupil of Ñāṇatiloka, with Ñāṇatiloka as its Honorary President. Thereafter, Dr. Bohn called the "Bund für buddhistisches Leben" (Union for Buddhist Living) into existence. But due to the War both came to an end. The above mentioned Markgraf had further started the first Buddhist publishing house in Breslau, which after the War was succeeded by the Schloss Verlag. Now called Benares Verlag, it is the only Buddhist publishing house in Germany which publishes, besides historical works and scholarly translations of Pali texts, a series of good introductory works to the world of Buddhist thought as well as books on allied subjects. The most prominent collaborator of this publishing house is the well known German Buddhist monk, Ñāṇatiloka of Ceylon, besides Wilhelm Geiger (*Saṃyutta*, Vol. I) and Karl Seidenstücker (*Pali Buddhismus, Khuddakapāṭha, Udāna, Itivuttaka*, etc.).

In 1903 Ñāṇatiloka became a Buddhist Sāmaṇera, and the following year a Bhikkhu, the first Bhikkhu of the European Continent. Since then he gradually came in close contact with the Buddhist movement in his native country. Now, whenever Buddhist scholars are spoken of his name above all deserves to be mentioned. His works would require a special bibliography of their own to do him full justice. His name sounds almost like a myth in Germany, where hardly anybody exactly knows who he is and from where he comes, though in many "Buddhological" works he is mentioned as an eminent scholar.

Through his works the German outlook with regard to Buddhism became considerably widened. His numerous translations from the originally Pali texts—which he has translated more than any other author—are not merely to be valued as an eminent philological contribution. At the same time they are also born of his deepest and innermost being. Amongst

Ñāṇatiloka's chief works are *Aṅguttara-Nikāya* (in 5 vols.), *Milinda-Pañha* (in 2 vols.), *Puggala-Paññatti, Visuddhi-Magga,* , etc.

Even that most rigorous critic Dr. Dahlke says already in 1920 (*Neubuddhistische Zeitschrift*): "Ñāṇatiloka may be considered one of the best experts of Buddhism in our day... His translations belong to the best of our literature and are to be recommended to all..."

In the preface to his translation of the Majjhima Nikāya, K. E. Neumann says that "he who knows Pali needs no borrowed light... when the sun is shining we do not need the moon." This utterance has found no small measure of fulfilment through the labours of Bhikkhu Ñāṇatiloka. He was the first to prepare in the German language an intelligible Pali Grammar, and an anthology of Pali texts together with a Pali dictionary for the benefit of the earnest Buddhists of his native country. With diligence and study they are now able to read the original teaching of the Buddha in the Master's own words.

With ever fresh vigour we find the venerable Elder of the Order still pursuing indefatigably his work, highly honoured by the whole Buddhist world, especially in Germany.

Of the above mentioned late Dr. Dahlke, the founder of the Buddhist House in Berlin, who unfortunately died much too early, it may be positively said, that his books are the best scholarly and orthodox expositions of Buddhism. They are without doubt also intellectually and spiritually the most prominent publications. Dahlke, who claims to be a Buddhist and not a mere philosopher or interpreter, from the very outset categorically denies the existence of any metaphysical and transcendent speculations in the Buddha's teaching.

To Dahlke, the Buddha's doctrine is pure individualism. Dahlke's starting point is Buddhism considered as a world-conception ('Weltanschauung'). The aim of his work is the proof that on the "golden middle-path"—midway between belief and science—the Buddha's doctrine provides a satisfactory, logical and wise world-conception, from the sources of which genuine morality and ethics are streaming forth. That this evidence has been proved is Dahlke's merit. To appreciate his merits fully however, one never should forget that he was the founder of the famous Buddhist House in Berlin, and that till the last minute of his life he sacrificed all his health and wealth in order to complete and safeguard his work. Thus during that most difficult period from 1923–27 he was working all day in his capacity as a doctor with the single object of financing his work.

The Buddhist House stands on a hill. One enters the premise through the door of the "Eight-staged Path," the crossbeams of which, decorated with Indian ornaments, are supported by two little elephants. Then, in 8 landings—symbolising the 8 stages of the Holy Path—the stone steps lead up to the summit of the hill. In the main building Dr. Dahlke carried out his profession as a homeopath, and people from near and far came flocking to him to regain their health. There, beside the dwelling apartments, was a huge library, the biggest of its kind in Europe. In the first storey one is, so to speak, overwhelmed when one sees in the twilight of a niche the mystical glimmering of the image of the Buddha from Kalawewa in Ceylon. Behind the wide main buildings rises the temple proper, the two pinnacles, one resting upon the other, being surrounded by a row of longitudinal sky-light windows all around the hall, show the upward curve so characteristic of the religious buildings in the Far East. The walls are only pierced by a single door. There are no other windows besides the already mentioned sky-light windows. The interior forms a small room with coloured mosaic floor and ochrous walls of sandstone. In the simple but worthy-looking hall in the front, we find a Buddha relief embroidered with flowers, on both sides of which there are stone tablets inscribed in golden letters with sayings from the Dhammapada and other books. Here, still today, on Uposatha days they hold their religious meetings. But the outsider can scarcely form any idea of that solemnity of Dahlke when he explained the doctrine of his Master, the Buddha. From this temple hall he then led the devotees and visitors to the front platform, when far in the horizon the first segment of the full-moon appeared. From here also the other architectural works can be seen, the Ceylonese portion, two further entrance gates, the "Door of Refuge" and the "Door of the Wheel." Here and there are scattered smaller buildings, and quietly concealed in the wood we notice the hermit-cells.

In the same city of Berlin there has existed for more than ten years another Buddhist circle, the "Community round the

Buddha" with Martin Steinke (Bhikkhu Tao-Chun) as its leader, who, like Dr. Dahlke, hold on full-moon days regularly meetings with lectures and subsequent discussion. It publishes the well-conducted bi-monthly paper *Der Buddhaweg und wir Buddhisten*. This group of men, all of them being real Buddhists, do not tolerate any religious adulteration or outside dogmas or mixing up with politics, but try to realise the goal as preached by the Buddha in living according to his doctrine. They moreover do not engage in any so-called missionary work or propaganda, being well aware of the fact that it was not by such propaganda that Buddhist thought found favour and spread in Germany, but that it was solely due to Buddhist literature, especially to the works and translations of those indefatigable Buddhist scholars.

There is still another Buddhist circle, the "Loge zu den drei Juwelen" (Lodge of the Three Jewels), with its seat at Munich. It enjoins on its members the ethical principles of the Buddhist doctrine, which they should observe in daily life. The founder and leader of that group is Dr. Georg Grimm, author of the well-known book *The Doctrine of the Buddha, or the Religion of Reason*. This book has had an enormous success. Apparently this is due to the fact that the author is attempting a compromise between Buddhism and Western philosophy, and at the same time, with penetrating and absolute devotion, he sets forth the liberating truth of Buddhism as the only perfect and absolute truth.

Thus, whilst the philosophers as Schopenhauer, Nietzsche and Hartmann, and the music-dramatist Richard Wagner, were foreshadowing the truth of Buddhism, whilst the scholars as Max Müller, Oldenberg, Karl Eugen Neumann, Ñāṇatiloka Thera, Karl Seidenstucker, Paul Dahlke, Max Walleser and many others were striking at very roots, whilst the interpreters as Paul Dahlke, Kurt Fischer, Georg Grimm and many others were suiting it to the capacity of Western thinkers, last but not least, the poets as Gjellerup (*Pilgrim Kamanita*, etc.) and many others contributed their share in popularising Buddhist ideas amongst all classes of Germans.

Here we may mention that in Germany there is many a sincere Buddhist who does not wish to join any Buddhist society or meeting, but who, whilst keeping far aloof from all society, like a real disciple of the Buddha, is striving for the realisation of higher life as proclaimed by his master.

Such a case is reported in the Hamburger Anzeiger of the 6th of July, 1928, under the heading "Buddha in the Heath": "A man with name Ludowic Stoehr in his 31st year left his native land Silesia, and emigrated to the Heath of Lüneburg (near Hamburg). Near Töppingen, in the Soltau district, he erected for himself a little hut, and fitted it up in the most primitive way. He then built a little fireplace, made a table, a chair and an unwieldly bedstead. On a board there are lying five big well thumbed volumes of the Dialogues of Gotamo the Buddha, the standard work of Karl Eugen Neumann, These are his spiritual tools. His livelihood this hermit gained by working in the harvest season with the farmers of the Healthland. At first those health-dwellers treated this taciturn person with distrust. True, his hands were coarse and hard, his face open and robust, but there seemed to be some mystery about this man with the white, backward-bent forehead. However, to the busy peasants only one thing counted: work. And Ludowic Stoehr showed himself a man of work. He would not work for hard cash, but for a loaf of bread, or a jug of milk, and he turned hay over, lifted the sheaves up, or loaded potatoes. It was only the want of food and drink that took him to the society of men. At any other time he would be sitting in solitude and listening to the voice of the great Indian sage whose teaching he followed. Whenever a stranger attracted by the smoke blowing from the little chimney-flue into the evening-air, unexpectedly entered his hut, he found a cheerful, open-hearted person bidding him welcome. It is said that Ludowic Stoehr was the heir of a peasant farm, and that after returning home from military service he found his mother, a widow, married again, and that his stepfather had a design to make away with him as heir of the farm. Walking already at that time in the Buddha's footsteps, he left house and home and went into the silence of solitude, choosing the wide silent heath as his abode. Now, a short while ago this little Buddha has died. A farmer found him lying lifeless before his hut with legs crossed."

Thus, this man had spent a whole lifetime in solitude, during the severe cold winter nights walking up and down in his hut, free from Christian superstitions, without bible, without God, whom Buddhists thousands of miles away from him would call a holy disciple of the Buddha and who really was perhaps one of them. And like him there may be many others.

Now, as to the question, whether Buddhism in Germany ever will penetrate and influence the thinking of the great masses, the editor of Neumann's *Dīgha Nikāya* translation writes this in his preface:

"There will come a time when nobody any longer will regard the Buddhist doctrine as something Asiatic, just as little as they do with regard to Christianity. And yet, Christ though nearer in space has never set his foot on European soil, just as little as the Buddha did. The universally valid points of his teaching have in the course of centuries brought about this that every European nation hears Christ speaking as if he were of their own nation. Sooner or later also the Buddha will be conceived by Germans only as speaking German. The external world of India, today still something foreign, will not appear to them any more oriental than the surroundings of Christ, or it will have become more familiar than the latter, or even as such as not be noticeable any more. And the plastic arts, which have not yet begun with forming the allegories and image of the Buddha, will learn to conceive them without their Indian form. And thus–also the Buddha will have become an object of European art, not in the form of nauseous copies of old-Indian models, but in quite an independent and indifferent formation conceived from within. The Buddha's influence upon the law and customs of the West can't be discussed until Buddhist thought will have permeated generations and, in defiance of a flood of antagonistic books[5], become the property of the West."

PART II

THE LIFE OF ÑĀṆATILOKA THERA

The innermost part of man remains inexpressible. So, in looking back on my life, I shall content myself with giving just a few outlines of my outer and inner experiences.

Chapter 1: Youth

I was born on 19 February 1878 in Wiesbaden, a famous and beautiful health resort in the heart of Germany. My full lay name was Anton Walther Florus Gueth and my patron saint was Antonius, the hermit. My father, Professor Anton Gueth, was a professor[6] and later the principal of the municipal Gymnasium[7] of Wiesbaden and a privy councillor. He was born in Hangenmeiligen and was the son of the landowner and mayor Anton Gueth. My mother's name was Paula; she was the daughter of Auffahrt, the District Administrator, from the town Hersfeld in the province of Kurhessen.

I had two brothers and one sister, being the fourth and youngest of the family. My eldest brother, Armin, a lawyer, died in 1938. My other brother Oswald, who was four years older than me, was an engineer and also a professor for some time at the University of Washington. He acquired US citizenship, but after resigning from his teaching position at the university he came often for longer or shorter periods to Germany. He had a house in Wiesbaden where he lived during the Second World War, even though he was an American. My sister, Ria, also lived in Wiesbaden and was married to Doctor Symanski, the principal of the local Gymnasium.

Our father, who was somewhat feared by us, was very strict, but just. In spite of his occasional outbursts of temper, he had a very empathetic and soft character. Among the children of the family, I think I was the one who understood him the best. Daily, in the evening, he would go for walks to the forest, sometimes together with our highly learned mathematics and physics teacher or with our doctor, but most times he would go alone. If he had company on his walks then, when coming back, he would remark that his walks would lose, rather than gain, in internal quality by having company. I shared this characteristic of loving solitude with him. His sensitivity is also shown by his remark that calves have beautiful eyes–something that we as city people did not really understand. He was obviously referring to the boundlessly mild and childlike expression in the eyes of these animals.

I have never forgotten a short episode that influenced me again and again in my later work, which occurred when we sat down on a seat during one of our walks in the forest. My father had asked me what I was learning at that time during mathematics lessons at school, and I told him about certain formulas that we were learning. He then told me that he did not understand what I had said, and could I not tell him how these formulas had come about? I, however, was not able to do this. This appeal to develop my own lucid imagination and understanding had, and still has, a very strong influence on my character, forcing me to give up all stereotypes and clear away all adherences to formulas, slogans, and empty concepts, and to try to gain a vivid picture and clear overview of all things. How far I have been able to do this in my translations and other work, I do not know; this is up to the judgment of the reader.

In Lausanne, Switzerland, I once was asked by a journalist from a Christian journal whether I believed in God. I gave him this laconic answer: "I don't know. Please first explain to me what you mean by the concept of 'God'." Much later, when I was interned in India during the Second World War, another question was put to me by a German as to whether I believed in a "soul." I asked him in return what he meant by that expression. Surely, I believed in God, if understood as the law of the Good acting in man, and also in a "soul" if it meant to signify the unconscious life processes. One should always insist on such clarifications of terms, otherwise people will misunderstand each other in their discussions. What is important is the meaning and the content, not the words as such. If one uses words without clarifying them, two people might mean the same thing but use different words, or they might use the same words and yet mean something quite different. If one does not clarify what one is talking about, one's conversations may end up without either person having understood the other.

Our mother, who was very much beloved by all of us, was gentle and understanding. Occasionally, she quite suffered from the temper of our father. She must have been very beautiful in her youth and even in her old age she was an imposing figure. During her boarding-school time in Kassel she had studied piano and singing under Reiss, the orchestra director of the Royal Court Theatre. She once told us that King Ludwig of Bavaria,[8] the close friend of Richard Wagner, had been quite interested in her in Bad Kissingen and had invited her to a ball. She told us that she got married to our father because...[9] [he had] a strict and, even then, quite jealous nature, and therefore did not allow her to sing anymore in front of other men and also... This caused her a lot of suffering. Nevertheless, she turned away a somewhat foppish cousin[10] who was wooing her too. He later married an Italian princess or countess and settled down in the Ponikl castle in Steiermark.

When the revolution broke out in 1848, her father, the district administrator, was threatened by a crowd of people which had gathered in front of his house to claim food. Although the town was surrounded on all four sides, he and his family managed to escape in a cab. When the Crown Prince of Hessen lived as a prisoner in Kassel during the war with Prussia, my grandfather tried to free him, but was not successful.

My father died in 1913, two days after an operation for cancer, and truly peacefully so, while my mother sat on his lap and was discussing with her and my sister a journey they were planning to take to Switzerland. Four years later, in 1918 before the end of the First World War, my mother also passed away. She died because of negligence on the part of a doctor.

My education in Europe was this: I went to secondary school from 1884 to 1888; then to the Königliche Realgymnasium (Royal Gymnasium) from 1888 to 1896; from 1896 to 1898 I had private tuition in music theory and composition, and in the violin, piano, viola and clarinet; from 1889 to 1900 I went to the Hoch'sches

Conservatorium (Advanced Music Academy) of Frankfurt to study the theory and composition of music as well as to study the violin and piano; and from 1900 to 1902 I went to the Music Academy of Paris to study composition.

My childhood and early school period were happy and without any illness. Already before my tenth year of my life, the desire to eventually dedicate myself completely to a spiritual life had arisen in me. I even wanted to go to Africa to convert the "savages" and was prepared to suffer a martyr's death there. I had been brought up a Catholic, and it was thus under the influence of the Catholic teachings received from a priest that I said things such as "Whoever mourns at the death of a close relative, particularly at the death of a small child to whom heaven is assured, such a one does not have true faith." One will have to admit that the utterance of my precocious years was logically quite correct. My father, however, was a Catholic only in theory, not in practice. His routine was to attend mass just once yearly, usually the so-called "loafers' mass" at 11.30 pm.

Since early childhood I had a great love of nature, of solitude in the forest, and of religious philosophical thought. I liked especially to contemplate the nature of God, the vastness of the starry sky at night, the brotherhood of all living beings, and other topics of that kind. My great aspiration was to live as a hermit or as a monk. Therefore I had a great respect for everything that had to do with monks. I would imagine myself standing in church once and preaching on the impermanence and vanity of the world, and how all those who listened to me, convinced of the meaninglessness of all worldly things, would pull off their jewellery and other ornaments on leaving church.

I secretly wished that my older brother, Armin, who was studying law at that time, would become a monk, and indeed, some time before he finished his studies he determined to enter the Capuchin order. Nevertheless, in a short time, he gave up his somewhat impetuous plans. I myself was becoming more and more religious, but I was also rejecting all external ceremonialism more and more. I did not kneel down anymore in the church, I did not take the holy water, and I did not cross myself in public. I also stopped hitting myself on the chest while saying "mea culpa," and all those things. On the other hand, for some time I went to church every evening when nobody else was there and absorbed myself in the book, *The Imitation of Christ*, by Thomas à Kempis. That book, which I had received from my religion teacher Dr Wedewer at my first communion in my twelfth or thirteenth year, was always in my coat pocket. However, the attraction to the solitude of the forest has run like a thread through my entire life. And today, too, I live in the forest-solitude of my island.

In 1897 I put into action my longstanding plans to escape to a monastery. Leaving behind a letter to my parents, I said goodbye to my best friend at the train station and took a train to the village Schwalbach. From there I walked through the snow, through Holzhausen, Ems and Koblenz, to the beautiful and secluded Maria-Laach, the famous Benedictine monastery. After I had rapped thrice on the door with the knockers, I waited with a beating heart until it was opened and they let me in. I then handed over the letter of recommendation written by my religion teacher Dr Wedewer. In the end, however, I stayed only a very short time in the monastery as I found that the kind of subordination and lack of freedom was not to my taste. I quickly returned to my weeping parents.

From then on my former belief in a personal God gradually transformed into a kind of pantheism. The prevailing atmosphere of Weltschmerz (world-weariness) at the end of the last century took possession of me, and I began to flirt with suffering. My musical compositions breathed this same melancholic spirit to a great degree.

It was approximately in my fifteenth year that I began to feel an almost divine veneration for great musicians, particularly composers, regarding them as the manifestation of what is most exalted and sublime. Once I had gone with my mother to listen to a violinist and I was so touched by the performance that I said that whoever could play in such a way had to be a noble person. Later on I became good friends with many violin players. During the symphony concerts at the Royal Theatre and the Municipal Spa (*Kurhaus*), I listened to the world's best artists, like Sarasate,[11] and many others, all of whom I adored. How happy I was when they sat down next to me behind the stage curtain (from where I was allowed to listen) during the breaks. I also adored musical

Wunderkinder (child prodigies) such as Edgard Wollgandt and Carl Schuricht,[12] the later *"Überdirigenten"* ("leading orchestra conductor"), and made them my most beloved friends through my persistent patience.

With Wollgandt, the student Joachims, and a good friend of the then already famous Max Reger,[13] I played in about 1894 for the first time the superb Haydn quartets under the direction of the later musical director Pochhammer from Aachen. Following this I often played in quartets or piano trios. I played the piano trios of Beethoven with my father and Mr. Kaiser (cello), who later became the provincial school councillor. For a longer time I played in the municipal Kurhaus Orchestra and the Royal Theatre Orchestra. In 1897 my first composition (for strings) called *"Legende"* ("Legend") was played by the Kurhaus Orchestra. I also played with the Gymnasium Orchestra, in which I directed, my composition *"Jubiläumsmarsch zur Hundertsten Geburtstagsfeier Kaiser Wilhelms I"* ("Jubilee March for the Hundred Birth Anniversary of Kaiser Wilhelm I"), my *"Concert Waltz"* and a gavotte. Further, I composed in this time the *"Heroische Ouvertüre"* ("Heroic Overture") for orchestra, the *"Seven Musical Sketches,"* songs, etc.

My idea of love, invigorated by religious enthusiasm, was clearly expressed in my musical composition to a poem by Hoffmann von Fallersleben: *"Ich liebe dich in Gott / und Gott in dir. / Wo du bist / bist du bei mir.,"* etc. ("I love you in God, and God in you. Where you are, you are with me.")

With great enthusiasm I studied the score of Beethoven's *Ninth Symphony*. It was a copy bound in red plush with marginal notes in Richard Wagner's own hand. Felix Mottel had inherited it from Wagner and presented it to his pupil, Professor Gerhard, who was a friend of mine.

At about the same time I conceived a great love for philosophy. I read my first work, Plato's *Phaedo*, together with one of my few friends while seated on a bench in a forest. Descartes followed, later came Kant's *The Critique of Pure Reason*, von Hartmann and others. But above all, I thoroughly studied the *Collected Works of Schopenhauer* in six volumes.

I also had a great interest for languages, foreign countries and peoples. Moreover, I had a great love for walking, which took me through various parts of Germany. Even in the hot climate of Ceylon and India I did not lose my liking for walking. My first great walk I made in my first year at the Gymnasium. I walked to the National Monument in Rüdesheim and back in one day. It was about sixty kilometres–my normal minimum for a day trip. In 1899, during my vacation at the Music Academy of Frankfurt, I made my great hiking tour to Switzerland and Italy. I walked sixty kilometres a day and finished near Turin, Italy. A man who pretended to be a photographer joined me in Locarno. In a hotel in Milan he stole all my belongings during the night, but was caught while returning to Switzerland by train. He was sentenced to one year imprisonment and a sixty lira fine.

From about my seventeenth year onwards, I completely abstained from alcohol and smoking which I considered to be damaging to body, mind and virtue. I have been true to this principle under all circumstances, at home as well as in Maria Laach, the Benedictine monastery where, besides choice fish and meat, beer and wine were always served.

In 1898 I went to Frankfurt and attended the Hoch'sches Konservatorium (Advanced Music Academy) where I studied music theory, composition, violin, and piano. It was during that period, in the beginning of 1899, that I became a vegetarian for ethical reasons and it was in a vegetarian restaurant that I had my first encounter with the Dhamma.

Paradoxically as it may sound, the reason for my entrance into the monks order and the 'reason' (in Pali we would speak of upanissaya) for my conversion to Buddhism, my travel to India, my entry into the Buddhist monkhood, and finally my nationalisation as a Sinhalese, was my love for oat porridge. I had been talking about diet with a music lover who was from a vegetarian family and I mentioned to him my love for oat porridge, upon which he told me about the vegetarian restaurant where I could get oat porridge any time.

In the vegetarian restaurant I once heard the well-known Theosophical lecturer Edwin Böhme[14] give a talk on Buddhism. That talk made me an enthusiastic Buddhist, although at first more from an emotional response than because of rational understanding. The following day I told my violin teacher, Professor Bassermann, about the talk and he presented me with the *Buddhist Catechism* by Subhadra Bhikshu.[15] He also recommended me to read the Life and Work of the Buddha translated by Pfungst.[16] When he gave me the Buddhist Catechism he said that I should not go mad and think of becoming a Buddhist monk. Bassermann himself, however, was rather enthusiastic about the Indian hermit lifestyle.

By then my goal to travel to India to enter into the Buddhist monkhood was clear to me, although I was not at all certain about how to take the next step in order to achieve it. Travelling to India seemed to be a financial impossibility to me. From where would I get those thousands of German marks necessary for such a voyage?

In 1900 I was offered a job by a well-known composer in Vienna as a solo viola player with his concert orchestra, but I declined. Instead, I went to Paris, where I was able to study composition at the Music Academy through the help of Massenet.[17] I was thus able to study under the famous symphonist, opera-composer and organist at St. Sulpice, Maître Charles-Marie Widor.[18] I was regularly playing viola in his symphony-orchestra in the Palace of Countess de Bearn, but I also played elsewhere. During the vacations of 1908, which I extended up to December, I first played in Lille and went from there with the orchestra to Malo-les-Bains near Dunkerque. Then, on an invitation for a concert tour to Algeria, I left for North Africa via Paris and Marseilles. The absurd, tragic-comical adventures that I had in the different cities in Algeria with the hysterical, alcoholic artist-couple who had employed me are beyond description, and I would rather keep them to myself. During my stay in the town Bône in Algeria I took daily lessons in Arabic from an Arab, and after a short period I was able to write a fairly well composed letter in that language.

At the end of 1901 I returned to Paris and through my Rumanian Jewish friend Konrad Bercovici[19] –apparently identical with the author of gypsy stories now well known in America–I struck up a close friendship with another Romanian Jew, Aleku Zingher. With them I was reading Tolstoy, Plato, and others. We also read the book that has left the deepest and most transforming influence on my life and thought, *The Dietetics of the Soul* by Feuchtersleben.[20] It helped me to understand very clearly that all mental suffering is only conditioned by our own wrong way of thinking and that it is therefore great foolishness to get irritated or angry. The Buddha taught exactly the same thing when he said that through the complete eradication of all desires one will find freedom from all suffering.

Another friend, Johannes Scarlatesco,[21] also a Rumanian, but was, alas, very anti-Semitic. I had met him already during the first hours at the Music Academy. Apparently, he was an illegitimate child of a Rumanian prince and a protégé of Carmen Sylva,[22] for whom he composed some songs. He was a highly educated man, philosophically schooled, and highly gifted as a poet, philosopher and composer. He was quite attached to me. By the way, he was the first person who confessed himself a Buddhist to me, and that on the first day of our meeting immediately made me his closest friend. Even after I had destroyed all bridges behind me, he got my address in Egypt from my parents and sent me a letter there. He should be about seventy eight years old now.

In Paris I got acquainted with the famous composer Mozkzowski,[23] for whom I had a letter of recommendation from the Belgian violin virtuoso Ysaÿe.[24] I have to say though that I did not feel at ease with him, as he appeared to be possessed by tremendous artist's conceit. How different was Charles-Marie Widor, who was informal and very likeable. He would even explain and whistle the scores of his newest Storm-symphony to me while walking on the street.

My heart was urging me more and more to finally realize the plan that I had already made in Frankfurt, that is, to go to India and become a Buddhist monk there. As a first step for the realization of this plan, I took an engagement as a violin player in Thessaloniki, which at that time still belonged to Turkey, with the idea of continuing on from there in stages to India. At that time, I still thought that I would need many thousands of marks for such a journey. Of course, my parents were not to know anything about my real plans.

In May 1902 I took leave from my two Romanian friends with tears in my eyes and travelled by train via Marseilles to Thessaloniki. My two friends promised me that they would follow me later on, but that never happened.

Chapter 2: To the Orient, 1902–1903

In Thessaloniki there was only one person who had an appreciation for Buddhism to some degree—he was the eminent Violin virtuoso, Professor Drucker.

Once, just outside of Thessaloniki, I was attacked by robbers with knives in full daylight. Just as I about to give them some money out of my pocket, the military police appeared and the robbers ran off. Thereupon the police officers organized a chase on foot and on horse to capture the robbers. They searched the whole area up to the mountains and finally caught the robbers who were punished with one year prison. In Thessaloniki I also experienced my first earthquake, after which we had to sleep outside for fourteen days. My mother, who had read about the earthquake in the newspapers, was worried and sent me a letter asking me to come back to Germany immediately.

Finally, after about nine months, that is, towards the end of November 1902, when it was starting to get really cold, I was able to leave Thessaloniki after I had resigned and I travelled on to Egypt. In this way I came a little closer to my goal. Taking my chances, I left with just a couple of hundred francs in my pocket.

First, I sailed to Constantinople (Istanbul). From there I sailed with the Austrian Lloyd via Smyrna (Izmir), Mitilini (Mytilène), Samos, Alexandrette (Iskenderun), Cyprus, and Tripoli to Beirut. It took about fourteen days. From Beirut I took a ship to Haifa, from where I thought I could make a side-trip by horse to Jerusalem.

Until Constantinople I had to sleep with Greek and Turkish peasants on some bags in the hold of the ship. Squeezed in like a sardine in a can, I had to sleep without being able to stretch out my legs. On the next leg of the journey to Beirut, I slept first on some stacked boxes, then on a table on the deck. From Beirut to Haifa I was accommodated in the midst of a herd of sheep. Just as we were about to reach the coast with the landing boats, a terrible storm broke out and for the next three weeks no ship was able to land, so I was forced to stay on board. Due to the cholera which had broken out in the area I had to cancel my journey to Jerusalem, therefore I just made a short trip to Nazareth, where I stayed for three days in a Catholic monastery.

On the way back I was travelling in the company of two Greek priests. We travelled in a horse carriage, but unfortunately it got stuck in the mud so often that we were walking more on our feet than travelling by carriage. At times we even had to pull the carriage ourselves.

In Haifa I met Gustav Nagel,[25] the "nature man" and later Reichstag candidate. He immediately came and greeted me with the words, "How are you doing, compatriot?" I lived a few days with him and must admit, putting aside a few whims, that he made a really sympathetic impression on me.

I had to wait three weeks until my luggage was given back to me at the customs, although every day I went to press them to release my things. Then, one day, a man who was working there approached me and said that if I would give some baksheesh to the director, they would hand out my things immediately. I made him repeat what he had said and then took him to his director. I told them that I would go and complain to the German Embassy, upon which they immediately gave me all my things without receiving one penny of baksheesh. In Thessaloniki I had exchanged my huge travel basket from Paris for a large wooden suitcase covered in deer hide. This, in turn, I exchanged in Haifa for a thick blanket in which I put all my things. Rolling this ball-like bundle in front of me, I went on board.

On the 31 December 1902 the ship arrived in Alexandria. As we were coming from a cholera infected area, we had to stay for eight days in quarantine–all of us together in one large room. From there I went on to Cairo, where I arrived with just twenty francs in my pocket. Luckily, I was able to find work immediately as a viola player with the Belgium orchestra playing at the Ghezira Palace. However, after one month the hotel was closed down. The police had found out that roulette had been played, which was forbidden at that time in Egypt. Nevertheless, the next day, by way of telegraph, I had already secured new work for myself as a violinist in Port Said. Thus I was able to move a little bit closer towards India.

In Port Said I resigned after a couple of weeks and continued travelling with an Italian-Austrian violinist from Trieste. We went to Bombay, where we gave concerts as a duo in a café. I had to change all the musical scores I had, so that it was possible to play them for two violins; I played the first and he played the second.

Once we had enough money (which must have been about July 1903), we continued travelling from Tutikorin (Thoothukudi) to Ceylon. In those times the disagreeable institution of the passport did not exist yet, nor did one have the need for a visa, except for Russia and Turkey.

Chapter 3: Ceylon and Burma, 1903–1910

During my short stay in Ceylon, I visited the Malvatta monastery at the Kandy Lake. It is the most famous monastery in Ceylon. There I met the Elder Sīlānanda, who was the monastery librarian. He immediately said that he was prepared to accept me as a monk. He spoke excellent English, something hard to find among monks at that time. I replied that I wanted to discuss this first with a Scotsman I had heard about. He was called Ānanda Metteyya[26] and was living in Burma. As Sīlānanda did not know the exact address of Ānanda Metteyya's whereabouts, he sent me to the proctor, Richard Pereira, in Bambalapiṭiya,[27] the father of Dr Cassius Pereira (the later Kassapa Bhikkhu who entered the Saṅgha in 1947). There, I got the address of Ānanda Metteyya, who had actually become a monk just a year or two before. I also got the address of my future chief supporter in Burma, Mrs Hlā Oung.[28]

I had very little money left so I travelled in the most primitive way via Tutikorin and Madras, where I slept on the ground or on a bench in the railway station, to Rangoon. Even today, I travel in the most primitive way on a train, third class, or even fourth class if it is available. On board a ship, I sleep on the deck without a cabin or bed. I have never been in any way interested in comfort.

In Burma, for the first fifteen days, I lived in the villa of the very kind Mrs Hlā Oung who was held in high esteem among the Burmese. She was a descendent of a Talein (Mon) prince and was married to the Indian Treasurer Mr Hlā Oung, who lived mostly in Calcutta.

I came to know Ānanda Metteyya there and also his friend and supporter Dr Rost,[29] who was the chief doctor at the government hospital and later a colonel[30]. With great interest I read the wonderful book, *The Soul of the People,*[31] which brilliantly describes the character, as well as the customs and the way of life, of the Burmese people. In Mrs Hlā Oung's house I also learned to memorize the threefold refuge in Pali and the ten rules for novices which I had to be able to recite when I entered the order. I would also like to mention that, whilst there, I transcribed a song that a young Burmese lady had sung to me, to piano accompaniment, which due to the unclear rhythm caused me some problems at the performance.

I was accepted as a novice in the monastery at the Ngda Khi Pagoda under Venerable U Āsabha Thera in September 1903. I then lived for one month in a single room with Ānanda Metteyya. Later on, I went to the nearby Kyundaw monastery, which was then still bordering the forest. After about four or five months (in January or February 1904), I received full acceptance into the Sangha under the name of Ñāṇatiloka.[32] I became bhikkhu under U Kumāra Mahāthera. Thus, in the history of Buddhism, I was the first continental European to enter the Buddhist Order.[33]

In Burma I was very impressed by the beautiful golden Shwe Dagon Pagoda and the very friendly people that daily made flower offerings and paid their respects to the Buddha, the lofty teacher.

Ānanda Metteya advised me not to learn Pali, but rather to intensively study Burmese, but I did the very opposite as I really wanted to study Pali intensively and abstain from learning Burmese. After four years I could not only speak Pali quite well, but had at the same time, without any special effort on my part, acquired a working knowledge of colloquial Burmese. Burmese is a very simple language, related to Chinese and closely related to Tibetan. It is a mono-syllabic language and I consider it to be one of the easiest languages of the world to learn. It was fairly simple to learn because of the friendliness of the Burmese and their willingness to communicate, especially the children.

My preceptor (*upajjhāya*) had a thorough knowledge of the Abhidhamma and was able to recite by heart the six enormous volumes of the Abhidhamma text called *Paṭṭhāna* (Conditional Relations). Strictly speaking, I learned Pali as well as the

Abhidhamma without any teacher. True, often it was not easy to do that alone, but after some time I could discuss difficult points of the teaching with great ease in Pali with Burmese and Sinhalese monks. This greatly helped my understanding. Already in 1907 I gave an unprepared talk in Pali about the Four Noble Truths to a large crowd at a Pagoda near Moulmein.

In 1904 I went by sea to Singapore with my Sinhalese helper. There, I stayed at first with an Irish monk of dubious reputation, U Dhammāloka, and later on, for about a fortnight, with a very friendly, and married, Japanese priest.

In order to avoid having to continue waiting in Singapore for the ship that I was expecting, I went to Kuala Lumpur, capital of the Malaysian state of Selangor. There I lived for about a month in a Sinhalese temple which was at that time unoccupied. From there, by invitation from some Sinhalese, I visited the Batu caves, which are about five kilometres out of town. The entrance to both caves is on a bare slope of an otherwise forested mountain. The first cave that one reaches when approaching from below is light, dry, and quite high, like a giant cathedral. It is open in the front and the back and the floor is smooth, as if it is made for walking up and down. In some of the natural niches and holes higher up, we found bamboo bed constructions left over from Buddhist monks that had lived there a few years earlier.

The other cave is about twenty to forty metres broad. It is very high and long, and has a relatively small entrance, about ten metres wide. Soon after entering this cave, we had to light the torches that my Sinhalese friends and some Chinese, who came with us, had brought along, which were bottles filled with petroleum with a wick. Then we continued with more courage. From time to time we were confronted by deep holes, hundreds of metres deep, in which, without the help of the torches, we would have certainly met a terrible death.

Continuing on the gradual down-sloping path, we heard a sound that grew stronger and stronger, somewhat similar to the sound of the sea at the beach. We were all somewhat frightened. We then found that we were walking deeper and deeper in bat-faeces, eventually reaching up to the level of our knees. At the same time, above us, we could see millions and millions of bats flying around in the air. After having passed this bat cave, the path went down over boulders. It was difficult for me to climb in my monk's robes, so I stayed behind, with one lighted torch in my hand, waiting for the return of the others. I saw how the others were continuing downwards and after some time, far away, I saw them walking upwards again and finally disappearing towards the left.

I was getting tired from waiting and thought of leaning against a boulder close by, but only at the last moment did I discover, right on this boulder, a huge snake, asleep fortunately. Turning around I saw that on almost all the boulders around me were coiled-up snakes of a light green colour. When, after about half an hour, the others finally returned, I was able to breathe more freely again.

At the end of 1904 I left Rangoon, together with my Indian friend, the monk Kosambi Dhammānanda[34], who had visited India during my absence. We went together to Upper Burma, where we lived in a cave in the Sagaing Mountains. There we practised concentration and insight meditation under the instructions of a monk who was reputed to be a saint (*arahant*). Dhammānanda later disrobed and became a professor at Calcutta University and Harvard University in America. He wrote a Pali commentary to the *Visuddhimagga (Path of Purification)* and a number of other important books.

In 1906[35] I went to Ceylon in order to dedicate myself to a thorough study of Pali and the Scriptures. In that same year I had already started with my translation of the *Aṅguttara Nikāya* (*Gradual Sayings*), the first part of which was published in 1907. *The Word of the Buddha* had already been published in 1906 and has since been translated into many languages.

I came to know the Siamese prince, Prisdang Jumsai, in 1906.[36] He had earlier been the Siamese Ambassador for Europe. After his return to Siam (modern-day Thailand), he attempted to overthrow King Chulalongkorn and put himself on the throne. He had to escape and eventually came to Ceylon where he entered the Sangha.[37] In Colombo he had been put in charge of the famous Dīpaduttarārāma Monastery in Kotahena. Together with him, I settled down on the small island of Galgodiyana near Mātara, which he called Culla-Laṅkā ("Small Lanka"). We lived in small huts made of coconut leaves.[38]

One day a 20-year-old Dutchman visited us who was the son of a rich merchant from Amsterdam by the name of Bergendahl. He was a very shy but good person who had the intention of becoming a monk. Later a German, by the name of Stange, came. He was accompanied by a Pole, who later went by the name of Dr Sobczak.[39] I accepted Bergendahl and Stange as novices under the names of Suñño and Sumano.[40] A lot of celebrations had been arranged.

After some time, Suñño went to India where he visited Miss Annie Besant,[41] the president of the Theosophical Society at Adyar near Madras. During his stay at Adyar he had a series of dubious hallucinations due to his pathological mental condition. He took these hallucinations for real, but he soon let me enlighten him about them. Even as a child Suñño had problems with claustrophobia. (Concerning other pathological cases among my students, I prefer to remain silent, although this would be an interesting field of investigation for a psychiatrist.)

Sumano, on the other hand, soon suffered from consumption. This condition probably had been present before he became a monk. Thus he had to leave Ceylon and return to Europe. The German ambassador advanced the money for the journey by ship (which was only one hundred and eighty rupees at that time). The Siamese Prince acted as a guarantor for that money.

I also left Ceylon soon after Sumano's departure. On the invitation of my parents, I returned for a three-month visit to Wiesbaden. Sumano was living in Steiermark with a Buddhist doctor who looked after him in an exemplary manner. With the beginning of the cold season, Sumano returned to Ceylon on the recommendation of the doctor and I left with him.

We both departed by sea from Genoa and, on arrival in Ceylon, we stayed in the Maitreyya Hall in Colombo. This was a place where I stayed often and was supported by Proctor Richard Pereira. Later we went to Hatton in the high country. Near the railway station we stayed in the Buddhist School, the upper storey of which was a residence for monks. Here I contracted bronchitis, which continued for many years. This was due to the fact that during one very cold night I gave my only blanket to Sumano. Because of his consumption, he had to be especially careful.

At that time in 1906 my first work, *The Word of the Buddha,*[42] had just been published and a copy had been sent to me. At the end of 1906 I returned to Burma alone, where I continued to work on translating the *Aṅguttara Nikāya* while staying in Kyundaw Kyaung and in Maymo in the high country.

Twice I had encounters with snakes there. The first time it was just after I had finished reciting the Snake Protection Verses.[43] While walking up and down I had, without noticing it, stepped over a much-feared cobra. The second occasion was when I was coming back from taking my bath in the evening. Together with a young prince who was acting as my attendant, I was walking through a small forest. The boy gave a loud shout when I placed my sandal on a big python. When I noticed the snake, I let myself fall to the ground in front of it.

On my return to Kyundaw Kyaung, Mrs Hlā Oung built a dwelling place for Ānanda Metteya and me. It was in a quite secluded area. Sīlācāra,[44] to whom I had given novice acceptance, was living with me, too. Soon after, Walter Markgraf came, whom I had also accepted as a novice and he thus became my fourth European monk-disciple. Of these four, only the Scottish Sīlācāra is living today (1948), the other three having been dead for over thirty years. Sumano died in January 1910 near Bandaravāla,[45] Markgraf (Dhammānusāri) died in 1914 during the war, and Suñño died in 1915.[46] Sīlācāra has written a series of Buddhist works, and is well known as an author. Sumano was known because he wrote *Pabbajjā* (*Going Forth*)[47]. Markgraf became a Buddhist publisher and also wrote works on Buddhism. In addition he founded the German Pali Society (Deutsche Pāli Gesellschaft), of which I became the Honorary President.

In 1907 I was asked to give a talk in Burma to a large gathering in Pali on the Four Noble Truths and I didn't even have a chance to prepare myself in any way. The talk was given on a platform in front of the Pagoda of Moulmein and a Burmese Pali expert who was present acted as interpreter.

One day, at the beautiful Shwe Dagon Pagoda at Rangoon, a young Burmese man addressed me and exclaimed: "Oh, our religion is certainly the best in the world! Isn't it?" I replied, "Do you know all religions of the world?" I soon found out that he did not even know well his own religion, the Buddha-Dhamma.

Certainly, I also believe that for those who are ripe for it, the Buddha's Teaching is the best and the only way to liberation. However, I don't appreciate vain boasting which, just as in this case, goes along with ignorance.

Another time I went through the streets of Rangoon sitting in a horse-drawn carriage. Dhammānusāri was with me and happened to see a fishmonger selling fish. He called out to him: "How can you kill living beings? Is it not forbidden?" The man replied, "Oh, I am a Christian."

Sāmaṇera Dhammānusāri only stayed in robes for half a year. Inner unrest drove him back to Europe. Thus he has been able to do more than he would have if he had remained a monk. During this time, Ānanda Metteya went to England on a Buddhist mission and Markgraf was planning to open a Buddhist Monastery in the southern part of Switzerland.[48]

At this time, I had been in contact with the publisher of *Coenobium: Rivista Internazionale di Liberi Studi*[49] from Lugano, Mr Enrico Bignani (a friend of Garibaldi,[50] with whom he had escaped to Switzerland). He had found a beautiful solitary alpine hut for me. It was at the foot of Monte Lema Mountain, 20 minutes behind Novaggio, and was about 800 metres above sea level. I departed for Europe.

Chapter 4: Europe and Tunisia, 1910–1911

In Germany a small Buddhist group had formed to support monks.[51] One of the regular donors of this group was the poet who composed *The Pilgrim Kamanita*.[52] Soon after my arrival in Lugano, I initially stayed with Mr Bignani, who became a very good friend of mine. Whilst there, I was also visited by Subhadra Bhikshu (Zimmermann) as well as by my brother and others. The *Buddhist Catechism*[53] by Subhadra Bhikshu was actually the first book that I had ever read on Buddhism.

As for the Alpine hut on the mountain, I actually had to pay ten francs a month. I suffered a lot because of cold and snow, which I had to traverse with my sandals. Besides the cold, the food was also very one-sided, so that, in addition to my persistent bronchitis, a terrible furunculosis developed—my head, face, and chest were covered with boils, so that I could not sleep well. It was here, seated amidst the snow, that I worked on my *Pāli-grammatik* (Pāli Grammar) and on translating the Abhidhamma text called *Puggalapaññatti* (*Human Types*). However, my primitive situation improved considerably when the new, long-expected monk candidate arrived: Ludwig Stolz[54] (the later Venerable Vappo) who was an expert in the field of food and was a good cook, too.[55]

My stay in Europe was discussed in all the newspapers and caused a big sensation.[56] All sorts of reporters from Switzerland, Italy and Germany, etc, came to see me and took photos and so on. I also received a number of rather fantastic letters from mediums, psychopaths and similar kinds of persons. A number of people wanted to come and stay with me—a French Count, a twelve year old schoolboy from Milan who had run away from home, and an Austrian who told me that he had already accomplished quite a lot (which was exactly the reason why I did not take him). A female medium implored me to give spiritual support to her and her medium-addicted son; she even came from Germany to visit me after I had already left, unfortunately. Even an Italian female schoolteacher asked me to get her a denture through propitiation of the gods![57]

I was often visited by an English colonel who personally knew the Theosophist Blavatsky,[58] and also by my brother Armin. Both were living in the hotel behind the village from where it was just a ten-minute walk up to my Alpine hut.

Because of the incredible cold[59] and the difficult life caused by it, I decided to go further south, together with Stolz, possibly even to North Africa, to establish a monastic settlement there. First, at the invitation of the lawyer, Professor Costa, who was practicing occultism, we went to Costa's hometown near Turin. He was thinking of starting a settlement for monks there. The monks would be able to get the necessary supplies by producing harmoniums. Shortly afterwards, he tried to introduce us to his woodworking mill on the other side of Turin to make us earn our requirements.

After some time I decided to continue and find my luck further south. Thus we arrived in Rome. There we stayed in a hotel close to the railway station and visited the famous music professor Alessandro Costa,[60] who was also well known for his

Buddhist writings. He showed us his concert hall with the giant organ built for him by Frau Herz. He was a lovely, very gifted, and philosophical person. In Rome I also visited St Peter's Cathedral. Then we continued on to Naples, and from there took a ship via Palermo to Tunis.

Mrs Alexandra David-Néel[61] had been told of our arrival. At that time, she was busy with writing a Buddhist work and had been corresponding with me. Only with difficulty were we allowed to enter the country, as we did not have a passport or visa. After a stay of eight days in the house of Mrs David-Néel and her husband, who was a civil engineer, we continued, partly by train and partly by camel, to Gabès.

In Gabès we fairly soon found a house on the edge of the city, close to an oasis. The following day I went to the local authority, who was evidently not very happy about our stay. We were staying in a kind of storage room resting on pillars, situated immediately beside a public toilet, which, from the bottom, had no wall separating it from our room. All the faeces flushed by, close to our eyes and nose, and caused a nauseating smell.

One day a group of policemen came on horses and told us that we had to leave Tunisia. As we actually felt quite at ease with the Arabs, who clearly had a lot of trust in us, it was not easy for us to leave the country. We decided to travel to Lausanne, where Monsieur Bergier had earlier invited us to stay at his Buddhist hermitage called "Caritas," which he had built near the city. We left Gabès and travelled by ship to Tunis, once again visiting Mrs David-Néel,[62] and then travelled, via Marseille, Lyon and Geneva, to Lausanne.

Monsieur R.A. Bergier seemed to be a real Parisian and a lovely person.[63] He came to meet us at the railway station and offered us lunch in his home. Then he brought us to Caritas on the Rue d'Echallens. Every Sunday, many people passed nearby and admired the exotically looking two-level small house with a flat roof and golden Buddhas. They read the teachings of the Buddha which were written in red and golden letters on the walls.

During my stay in Lausanne, where I was supported in an exemplary manner by Monsieur Bergier, I was visited by many people, including our friend Bergier, the typesetter Millioud,

Pastor Vionnet, the Mayor, an Egyptian, a theosophical president from Geneva, reporters, and so on. A recording on a phonographic wax plate of my recitation of the Metta Sutta was kept in memory of me in the archives of Lausanne.

I also accepted the invitation of a German lady to visit her orchard near Bergamo, where Mr Ferrari, the close friend of Professor Costa, was in charge. Mr Ferrari, along with his friend Professor Costa, wanted to convince me to use the land belonging to Costa near Perugia to start a monk's settlement. However, every monk would have been obliged to work there for ten hours per day! Even in an unbiased person such plans would have aroused strong suspicions of menial exploitation. In any case such kind of arrangements are not possible at all for a Buddhist monk. Thus, together with Vappo, I went via Milan and Turin to Aosta in the beautiful area of Piedmont to meet Vappa at the house of Mr Evaristo Cuaz, with whom I was exchanging letters and who was interested in Buddhism. On our departure the next morning he broke down in tears as he would have liked to follow me, but he was married.

We climbed the St Bernard mountain. I walked barefoot on the icy ground and my robes were very thin. I arrived at the monastery in the evening, shivering with cold. I went to bed right away but kept on shivering for half an hour, while others tried to warm me up by giving me a massage. The next day, in the early morning, we went down the mountain on the Swiss side. We arrived in Martigni, from where we could take a train back to Lausanne.

After some time the glass painter Bartel Bauer[64] found me, after unsuccessfully looking for me at Assisi and Perugia (north of Rome). My little booklet, *The Word of the Buddha,* had a strong impact on him and had convinced him of the truth of Buddhism. As a consequence he definitely wanted to leave behind the worldly life. In case I should refuse him, he had decided on living as a wandering ascetic in Germany, where he would beg for his daily alms. He was living with Mr Millioud and I trained him every day in Pali. I made him memorise some pages of Pali conversation and then I sent him to Ceylon where, without knowing a word of English, he had only his five pages of Pali conversation to get along with. Of course, I first accepted him as a novice under the name of Koṇḍañño.[65] And thus, clad in yellow robes, he departed as the first monk to be accepted into the Sangha on European ground. This all took place towards the end of 1910. Koṇḍañño had just left when Friedrich Beck and a young German called Spannring turned up.[66]

On arrival in Ceylon, Koṇḍañño was welcomed by one of my supporters while he was still on board the ship. This supporter, who was later to become Sumedha Bhikkhu, then accommodated him in a hall built upon granite pillars in Galle.[67] The hall was called the Koṇḍañño Hall after him. Vappo and I, too, were preparing our luggage for the journey back to Ceylon. A huge crate with books had to stay back and be sent to Ceylon later on.

At that time, we were invited by the theosophist Dr Migliore, a friend of Professor Costa, to visit his orange-plantation at Santa Marta a Vico near Naples. He pretended that he wanted to make it a Buddhist settlement. That was, if I am not mistaken, in January 1911.[68] I remember only too well the two dangerous and huge dogs there, which were fed on dried blood only. Our one-month-long stay there was not fruitful at all. From there I made a visit to the Vesuvius volcano and another one to Capri. After leaving our luggage with the Norddeutschen Lloyd shipping company, which would load it onto our ship during our stopover in Naples during our journey from Genoa to Colombo, we left Naples and went to Lausanne. It was here[69] that the monk-candidate Spannring met us, and some days later the naturalised American, Friedrich Beck. Beck, who was a friend of Markgraf, was to become Bhikkhu Bhaddiyo.[70]

During these journeys there were always people who asked me for spiritual help. For example, one day a medium came to me, telling me that again and again the devil was taking possession of him. He asked me to help him get out of this terrible situation. I told him that he should develop loving-kindness towards all living beings. If he were thus to suffuse the whole world with love, no devil would ever be able to do anything to him and all terrible visions would disappear.

Another request for help came from a female scientist from Poland who was a friend of ours. She had started writing a book on chemistry, but was unable to finish and publish it due to her inferiority complex. On our departure, when Monsieur Bergier, Vappo, Bhaddiya, Spannring, and I had gone to the railway station and boarded the train, this Polish lady came and presented me with a departure gift of a beautiful collection of flowers. Earlier, she had made a yellow satin robe. Then, by way of Milan, we went to Genoa where we boarded the ship to Colombo.[71]

Chapter 5: Island Hermitage, 1911–1914

In Colombo we were welcomed by our supporter, the teacher Weeraratna, who later went on to become Bhikkhu Sumedha. On the train journey to Galle we had to get out at Kalutara and continue our travels by oxcart, which was actually pulled by people. We stopped in front of a big monastery where I had to give a talk on the Dhamma in front of a big crowd. From there we continued by train to Galle, where Koṇḍañño was eagerly waiting for us at the railway station.

In the Koṇḍañño Hall we were received by a great number of supporters, in particular the director of the Mahinda College, as well as the Buddhist author and well-known lawyer A. D. Jayasundera. Koṇḍañño had made himself quite at home. Although in the beginning, when he still did not know any English, he had to sit like a mute Buddha-statue in front of those who came to visit him, with the other monks he could at least have some form of conversation, because he had memorised those five pages of Pali conversation.

At that time, every evening we would go together with Weeraratna to the beach to take a bath. I gave daily lessons in Pali and Dhamma. Vappo was accepted with great celebrations as a novice in the monastery close by. Beck and Spannring stayed on as eight precept laymen. Later on Spannring had to go back to Germany for some reason.[72] On the other hand, if I remember correctly, I only made Beck a novice under the name of Bhaddiya[73] after we had moved to our island.

The supporters had constructed a small mud hut for Koṇḍañño in the jungle, not far from the hall. I often stayed there with him. One day he told me that once, when he was staying in a monastery (Dāgalla) near Dodanduva, he had gone by canoe with some other monks to an island that was completely covered by jungle. He thought that this island would probably be quite suitable for a hermitage.[74] I immediately decided to investigate the matter in order to procure this island for us. My supporter Weeraratna knew a man in Dodanduva who could give us some more information about the island which was called Polgasduva[75]. He was Coroner Wijeyesekera, whose father, the notary Mendis Wijeyesekera, had formerly been the owner of this island.

We went to visit him by ox-cart. At first we were received quite formally and obviously with some suspicion. However, the idea of an island hermitage was well liked by the population, so it was decided to give it a trial. We went by canoe to the island, where on the east coast we found a suitable landing place. Soon we started exploring the island. Some strong men with axes were able to open a small path through the jungle. As a welcome sign we saw cobras slithering by to the left and right, but the worst thing was the attack by the big red ants that rained down on our upper bodies from the branches above, where they had made their nests.

Slowly we continued until we reached about the centre between the east and west coasts of the island. We were told that a clearing would be opened up here and five simple wooden huts could be built, each provided with a path leading to it from this clearing.

After some days, that is, shortly before the beginning of the annual monk's rainy season retreat of 1911, we were able to move to the hermitage. The huts were ready and a well had also been dug. I have since then called it the "Island Hermitage" and it has become well known to Western Buddhists under this name. Thus the Island Hermitage was founded on 9 July 1911.

Though we were already living in the huts, we had not yet received proper permission from the owner. This finally was procured by Monsieur Bergier in 1914, when he bought the island from its owner—a Dutch Sinhalese.

At that time the island was still completely covered by impenetrable shrub-jungle. But this jungle has slowly changed during the years, becoming a forest. This happened when the smaller trees and bushes died out as the higher trees became higher and bigger. For this reason, today the island is much more airy, shady, and cool than it was in the beginning.

On the island there were many kinds of animals. Among the venomous snakes were especially the cobras and the very dangerous *tik polonga* (Russel's viper), due to its hot temper. In the period from 1926 to 1938 fourteen dogs died due to being bitten by these two types of snakes. The snakes would not have done anything to the dogs if the dogs had not kept attacking them again and again. Also there were small, but very poisonous, snakes such as the *karawela* (krait). Also there were the large, but harmless, *gerendiya* (ratsnake), which could be taken in the hand, and the slim and swift bright-green tree snake called *aesgulla* ("eye-devourer"). The python (*pimbura*) also visited us often as it is a good swimmer, like most snakes.

No snake attacks people or dogs without being provoked. Once, a huge cobra came out from under a chair on which I was sitting and kept on calmly circling around me for at least ten minutes in its defensive posture, with its neck high up and its hood open, then it disappeared. Actually, the only reason it did this is because I had greeted her a little bit too loudly.

There were about a dozen mouse-deer (*miminna*) that were quite cute. They often came to our eating-hall to be fed; but, while they dared to play with the cats, they were killed off by the dogs.

Also there are large monitor lizards (*kabra-goya*), which on superficial inspection look like crocodiles. These monitor lizards are at home in water as well as on land. A smaller kind of monitor lizard (*thala-goya*) only lives on the land. And there are mongooses (the so-called "snake-killers"), fish-otters, hares, other lizards, chameleons, forest rats and bats. Countless flying foxes (*māvarulā*) go at night to eat the fruits from mango trees and other fruit trees. Moreover, there are innumerable smaller and bigger birds, including honey birds, hawks, herons, kingfishers, parrots, owls, etc. Of course, the cosmopolitan crow is not absent here too. Finally there are the unloved animals, such as scorpions, large and small centipedes and the mosquitoes. Luckily, there are no malarial mosquitoes here.

There are many fruit trees on the island; beautiful mango trees, coconut palms, cashew nut and papaya trees, jackfruit and breadfruit trees, and a number of wild fruit and berry bushes.

Concerning the dogs and cats that live on the island, they had all been put there secretly, probably by people who were not able to feed their animals any longer or who wanted to get rid of them for some other reason. In this way, we sometimes had up to sixteen dogs. In any case, no one had to suffer hunger here, not even the animals.

On 8 October 1911 the painter Karl Hilliges[76] and the pharmacy owner Viktor Stomps[77] from Westfalen made their arrival. Soon after, they both took the eight precepts. Since there was at that time still a strong pull to Europe, Stomps, left on 29 October. At first he only got as far as Egypt, and then finally to Italy, where he stayed with Professor Costa. There, he very soon realized that it was better over here and announced his return to us. However, Hilliges, who I made a novice with the name of Mahānāmo on 4 November 1911, returned for good to Europe on 26 December with the ship called the Bremen. According to Koṇḍañño, he claimed to have reached the four absorptions (*jhānas*). He was dedicated to Theosophy, extremely arrogant and, when one was discussing the Dhamma with him, he could become very vehement and dogmatic. He used to complain that the food given by the faithful Sinhalese was too abundant and rich. Stomps, the later Mahānāmo,[78] was the other way—very slow and relaxed, almost phlegmatic. He showed irreproachable and modest behaviour throughout the years.

I think it was about the end of 1912[79] that Mrs Alexandra David-Néel came and stayed with our chief supporter, Coroner Wijeyesekera. She started to learn Pali under my direction, sitting in front of me in the forest, but soon she had to go to the cooler hill country because of migraines.

On 12 February 1912 my hut was completed. It was just behind the highest lake bank of the island and could only be reached by a small path through the jungle. All the huts that were constructed before the First World War were made out of sun-dried bricks with chalk and the roofs were covered with locally made tiles. The wood used for constructing the two windows and the door was of the best kind, jackfruit, and the floors were mostly covered with tiles.

On 9 May I was visited by the first European Buddhist, C. T.

Strauss,[80] and his friend Anāgārika Dhammapāla.[81] On 1 May, the elderly American Franklin received the novice acceptance under the name of Assaji. On 23 June, the American diplomat and adventurer, Henry Clarke, arrived. He stayed for a short while on the island as a white-robed layman.[82] On 16 February 1913, the foundation stone for the construction of the dining hall was laid by Mrs Jeremias Dias of Panaduva. On such occasions a big festival hall was always temporarily erected in which the many monks who were invited gathered and were given food. Often there were up to three thousand people present on the island and the whole lake was then covered with big sailing boats from morning to evening. Even special trains were arranged.

I think it was in 1913 that I, together with the teacher Cooray and the Ceylonese-Dutch Ñāṇavipula (who later became a monk under my guidance), started a mission for the so-called "outcastes" (*rodiya*). First we established a mission for those in the area of Kadugannāva. We changed the school hut that had been constructed by Christian missionaries into a Buddhist one and then the outcastes built us a little dwelling place. Later on we built a stone dwelling place a little higher up on the steep slope of the mountain. We did this with money which we had gathered by a collection.[83]

Some of these outcastes lived and studied on our island. The thirteen year old Rājasingha, son of the chieftain Hulavaliya, was accepted by me as a novice after my journey to the Himalayas in 1914.[84] Today he is the forty-eight year old Ñāṇāloka Thera (Elder) and still one of my faithful students. He is loved and respected by all. However, earlier there were a lot of reproaches because of our caste egalitarianism.

On 24 May 1913, Viktor Stomps received his novice acceptance and got the name Mahānāmo. On 3 June, Koṇḍañño returned from Burma. On 8 July, Dr Arthur Fitz[85] arrived. On 11 July, an outrigger canoe was donated by Joanis de Silva. On 18 August, an outrigger canoe was brought by the Abangama supporters in a big procession and donated. On 27 September, Dr Fitz was accepted as novice Soṇo. On this occasion thousands of people came to the island and extra trains, etc, were arranged. The German ambassador Freudenberg was also present at the ceremony.[86]

Chapter 6: Sikkim, 1914

In April or May 1914 I travelled to Madras, Calcutta, Darjeeling and Sikkim, with the intention of proceeding to Tibet. I was accompanied by a young Sinhalese boy of about fourteen years old. His name was Aperis and he was the son of the switchman from Dodanduva.

At the Darjeeling station we were questioned by a British secret police agent and told not to proceed to Tibet. Usually these kinds of people start out by greeting one very kindly and seem to be very happy to know you, then they ask where you come from, etc. I usually said that they were welcome to continue asking me questions as that is their job, whereupon they usually became ashamed and told me that they don't want to trouble me any longer.

In Darjeeling I was staying in the Lama monastery Bhutiya Banti, where the Tibetan Schempa offered to become my supporter. I visited the British Deputy (Government Officer) and his wife and was received in a very hearty manner. Once I had received a pass to Sikkim, I telegraphed Vappo to come to Darjeeling as soon as possible with the young Sinhalese Rājasingha (the later Ñāṇāloka.)

In the meantime, I had started to learn Tibetan. An aristocratic lama from the area of Simla wanted to come with us on the journey to Sikkim and Tibet, and then wanted to return to Ceylon with me as my student. As he knew Hindustani, it was not difficult for him to learn Pali.

Vappo telegraphed me of the time of his arrival. I went with my lama to the station to receive him, but I told the lama not to greet Vappo by using the reverential 'tongue-greeting'. He was, however, so used to it that he couldn't stop himself, so, in a respectful manner, he stuck out his long tongue towards Vappo.

From the monastery we had an indescribable view. Below us we could see a whole world full of valleys, small towns and villages. Above this the mountains stood out with great clouds around them. If we happened to look even higher up, we saw, reaching high above the clouds, the Kangyinching, a peak always covered with snow. It is the second highest mountain in the world.

After a while we departed. With the help of a carry-pole, we ourselves carried the luggage in turns until Manjitar by the Tista River. This was actually not too difficult as most of the path led downwards. Half an hour before we were ready to cross the border to Sikkim via the Tista bridge, we were stopped by armed people. A man and a woman, who said that they were the police, said that we had to pay money in order to cross the bridge. Because they were threatening to attack us, we gave them a little baksheesh and then we went on.

We spent the nights in rest houses. In the evenings, our two boys bought potatoes, dried bread, sugar and other things for our breakfast the next morning. We usually ate only in the mornings, as only then did we have the possibility to cook something in the rest houses. We had milk, jam and cake that I had brought along from Ceylon. We consumed those, too, if it was before twelve and if we could stop somewhere where there was water.

We then hired someone to carry our luggage. Each day it would be someone else. The porters were only asking for four cents (anna) a day, even though they sometimes had to walk for a distance of 30 kilometres, and then had to cover the same distance again when turning back. I usually gave them a little more, although they never asked for that. We did not really see the villages, since the rest houses were usually situated in the forest. Apart from the Himalayan people and the Tibetans, one would often find huts inhabited by Gurkhas from Nepal.

The famous scholar Kaji Sandup, with whom I had been in contact by letter, had announced our arrival in Gangtok, the capital of Sikkim. (His two brothers were to become my students in Ceylon later on.) In Gangtok we found accommodation in the Tibetan school. There I could converse with the teacher in English. The next morning the Mahārāja,[87] who had heard of our arrival at night, sent a servant with some food and a letter to me. In his letter he first excused himself for not having been able to send me a horse, as he did not know the exact details about my arrival. He then invited me to visit him.

On my visit to him, we were offered tea in a silver pot and cakes on a silver plate, while we conversed about various things. Here I also learned that Mrs Alexandra David-Néel, and also Venerable Sīlācāra (with her support), were living twenty kilometres away in Tumlong, near the Tibetan border. It is to be mentioned at this point that the people in Sikkim speak Tibetan, and the Mahārāja, too, was a Tibetan.

My journey by horse to the monastery near Tumlong brought me through thick clouds. Knowing this, I had put on thick clothes as well as shoes and socks. The path went down the slope of the mountain. On the left side of the path one could look down into immeasurable depths, while on the right side of the path there were overhanging rocks. If the horse had obeyed me, I would have banged my head against these rocks. However, I had to obey the clever horse, which always insisted on walking along the very outer edge of the path.

When I arrived at the monastery, I met Sīlācāra. I immediately handed over the horse to him as I knew very little about horses. If I remember rightly, Mrs Alexandra David-Néel was clothed in a kind of (Buddhist) layman's robe. All the windows in the monastery were made of paper instead of glass, just as in Japan. I had no opportunity to speak with the monks because they normally live with their families earning their living through agriculture and similar works and only come to the monastery on moon days (*uposatha*).

As far as I could see, Mrs Alexandra David-Néel was living quite comfortably there. She sent a porter to Gangtok daily, apparently to get new provisions of food. The cook, a good-looking young man from the Gangtok School and apparently identical with her later adopted son, had learned, under her instruction, how to cook French cuisine very well.[88] I stayed only one night in the monastery and returned to Gangtok the next day by horse.

Superstition here was incredible. For example, one day the teacher Dowgyal Kadji and I were talking about the superstition of the Tibetans and I spoke about the so-called "hail priests," who, standing in the fields, were to destroy the hail gods by whirling around a sword. If no hail came and the corn grew well, then these hail priests would get a special reward from the government; hail, on the other hand, meant facing punishment. The teacher interrupted me and said that although it was true that there was much superstition, in this case, the hail priests was no superstition–it was true!

The father of this teacher was an alcoholic. The whole day he turned around his silver prayer wheel, even when he was drinking. On the return journey I saw huge prayer wheels at the monastery of Rumtek. There were six of them, as high as a man's height, in front of a shrine room. My two Sinhalese boys, loudly laughing, started to make them all move while reciting "*Om Mani Padme Hum*." I immediately stopped them because I wanted to avoid upsetting the local people.

Here in the school–morning, lunch and evening–we were served the famous "brick tea," named after its being packed in brick form. This tea was mixed with salt and butter and then put in a big piece of bamboo to be whirled. It had a flavour somewhat similar to meat broth.

Before my departure I visited the British Political Officer, whose bungalow was in a large English style park. Although I was walking barefoot (I had not been using sandals since leaving Ceylon), he was very welcoming, and he discussed Buddhism with me for about two hours. On my departure he gave me a free pass for all the rest houses.

As the Himalayan passes were still blocked with high snow and I was also running out of finances, I decided to return to Ceylon. After some smaller adventures, we returned to Darjeeling and from there to Calcutta, where we stayed for some days in the monastery residence built mainly by monks from Chittagong.

At this point we had to get rid of the lice in our clothes, which all of us were plagued with, having caught them in the Tibetan beds. From the morning onward, we washed all our clothes again and again and hung them out in the sun to dry. Really, there aren't any Tibetans without lice. In Darjeeling, Shempa told us once that a Tibetan Lama had come to visit him. While the Lama was talking with Shempa, he was again and again passing his hand over his face and then carefully into his coat. Somewhat surprised, Shempa asked him why he was doing that. The Lama replied that his face was not the proper place for these creatures.

At this point we were faced with a new problem: how could all six of us–that is Vappo, myself, the two Sinhalese and the two Tibetans–go to Ceylon? We had only money enough to pay the journey for one person. Thus I went to Bhikkhu Siddhattha and asked him to advance the necessary money for me, but he replied that he was receiving from Dhammapāla only twelve Rupees per month and so he was not able to lend me any money.

Vappo tried the German Ambassador, but without success. When I was coming back towards the monastery, on my way I met the Chittagong monk Puññamaṇḍa[89], whom I knew since my stay as a novice in Burma. He told me that recently seven hundred and fifty Rupees had arrived for me from Switzerland, by way of Dodanduva. Just as in Gabès and in Naples, this was due to my "protective angel," Monsieur Bergier. Actually, it appears to me that all the difficulties I have encountered in my life have always turned out to be blessings in the end.

In Ceylon the two Tibetans caused quite a commotion because of their brown clothes and their round hats ornamented with shells. Some months later, during my stay in Kadugannāva, the eleven or twelve-year-old younger brother of Puṇṇaji, called Serki, was put in my charge by a monk. In my absence during and after the First World War, Serki became one of the top Sinhalese poets with the name Mahinda.[90] I am not sure if he still knows Tibetan well.[91]

Chapter 7: Confinement at Polgasduva, 1914

The following recollections of the period 1914–1917, which I have written before the end of World War I, are somewhat overly extensive in relation to the whole, but this doesn't do any harm.

In August 1914, the First World War started. Coming back from the Galduva monastery that Robert de Soysa, a former supporter in Mātara, had donated to me, I was arrested in Ambalangoda by a detective, just as I was standing in front of de Soysa's house wishing to say goodbye to him before catching the last train to Dodanduva.

On my request I was allowed to stay the night at the big monastery near the railway station. I had to promise to report the next morning to the police and then to take the early morning train to Colombo, together with the other German monks who were expected to come from Dodanduva. We were to sign a declaration of neutrality there. Although at first thought I was not being watched in the monastery, it seems that the police stayed close by throughout the night.

The next morning I went to the police station and from there to the railway station, continuously followed by the police. My supporter, the lawyer de Soysa, came with me to the train, the other monks were already there. He looked at me despairingly with tears in his eyes, as if he feared that we were all going to be shot or hanged.

On arrival in Colombo we went together to the Police President in the Fort[92]. He was very welcoming and even offered us chairs. This was not to happen again during our later confinement—from then on, we never saw chairs or beds or tables.

After taking down pertinent dates and our names, we were to sign a neutrality contract with the Ambassador.[93] As it was already 11.30 a.m. and we, as monks, couldn't eat after twelve, the Police President was kind enough to send us to a nearby restaurant, where we ate at the government's expense. Then we all went by cab to the Embassy and signed the document, which we then brought back to the Police President. Until our return to Dodanduva, we stayed at the main police station at Maradāna. The very friendly native police officers there offered us soft drinks. At four o'clock, we took the train back to Dodanduva.

From now on we had to report to the local police station twice daily, mornings and evenings. The area we were allowed to use went from the Dodanduva bridge to the Gintota junction and to the sea. All German monks had to live on our island. All other Germans, even the Catholic priests, were in a camp at Ragama.[94]

Vappo was arrested in Kandy, Mahānāmo in Bandaravāla, and Koṇḍañño on the island Culla-Laṅkā near Mātara, where I had been living earlier on with the Siamese prince. Soṇo was kept in custody on a ship. The German Ambassador was not willing to be a guarantor for him since Soṇo was an Austrian. Later he was brought, like all the others, to the Ragama camp. On request by the Governor, Sir Robert Chalmers,[95] and after I had given my agreement, Soṇo was allowed to live on the island after being brought there by the police. Also Dr Sobczak, whom we had already come to know on Culla-Laṅkā and Ankenbrand[96], was brought to the island by the police.

Due to his American citizenship, Bhaddiya was left alone during all these events, even though his passport had expired a number of years previously. In addition, on the island there were the Sinhalese novice Ñāṇāloka, the Tibetan novice Puṇṇaji (the former Purpa Töndrup), the Lepcha[97] novice Subāhu (Jempa Rinzin), as well as Puṇṇaji's younger brother (the previously mentioned Serki), our old helper, Vaturāla, and one or two Sinhalese boys.

After two or three weeks the order came through that only German Buddhists should stay on the island. All non-Germans had to leave the island. However, we were able to get permission for the novices to remain.

No one who was living on the island was allowed to leave it. The police came daily to check and to bring us the food that was given by our supporters. No one else was supposed to visit the island, still some supporters and friends often came to the island together with the policemen, sometimes even by themselves. However, all this was to come to an end and we, just like the Christian priests, were eventually brought to the Ragama prison camp. According to the police, it was due to the jealousy of the Catholic priests.

It was about midnight of the night between the 1 and 2 November when, while everybody was deep asleep, the bell in our dining hall suddenly rang. Everybody jumped out of bed in surprise even though we were expecting this. After some minutes, we saw people coming towards the dining hall with lanterns in their hands. There the police were waiting and they informed us of our future destiny. Within one hour we had to leave the island. What to do with the library and the many books in Puṇṇaji's house? Without thinking too long, I packed my most important works—about ninety leather-bound canonical Pali texts and commentaries in Burmese script—into the huge box given to me by Monsieur Bergier.

After finishing this job and being about to carry the box to the boat, the police told me that nobody was able to carry this box. It was stormy, raining and the waves were too high to be able to bring the box by boat. Thus I had to take a small parcel only. In it was only that which was most necessary for the continuity of my work. In order to protect the books in the big box from termites, I took two new big towels, soaked in petroleum, and put them over the books.

Soṇo had become so excited by the arrival of the police that he became hysteric and had to stay back under surveillance of some policemen. The rest of us took our things and possessions to the boat and crossed over to the railway station. There the police inspector phoned Galle, asking whether Soṇo could, for the time being, stay back at the police station in Dodanduva. Waiting for a reply, we missed the morning train and had to wait until the afternoon. We were then marched through the village street to the railway station guarded by the police, who, if I remember correctly, had bayonets fixed on their guns, while the population of the village looked on.

Chapter 8: Internment Camp in Diyatalāva, 1914–1915

On our arrival in Maradāna, a huge crowd had already gathered.[98] We had to change to another train, which within one hour got us to the Ragama camp, whereupon all our things were searched for weapons, newspapers, etc. Then we were taken to a corrugated-iron hut, separated from the other huts by a fence. There were sufficient beds with mosquito nets and also tables and benches. Everything was still done in a very friendly and courteous manner.

Major Robinson, whom I had already met in Burma, was very welcoming, just the way only a European can be who has been living for some time among Burmese Buddhists. His companion and representative, a lieutenant, was also very nice and courteous. They may not have been war heroes, yet they were good-hearted and kind people, and that is much more important.

I took the left corner at the entrance of our barrack, and hung up some yellow robes as a partition. The food was cooked and brought in a very respectful way by the people, just the same as happens in all monasteries. However, some of our monks seemed to think that, from this point on we needed no longer follow the monastic rules, especially those who were not taking them very seriously anyhow. Among these, the faith in the real teaching was quickly disappearing. They were left with only their vegetarian ideas and one could already see that they would eventually leave the order. Their daily talk was about politics, war, the military, readings from Maupassant, and so on. If one quoted the Buddha, even as a senior monk, one was laughed at, and accused of blind faith.

Soṇo's nervousness was getting worse by the day and he seemed to be on the brink of madness. He had the idée fixe that we were all going to be shot. One late evening I therefore had to call on the camp doctor, a South Indian, who knew the hysterical ways of Soṇo from his earlier stay in Bandaraväla. Finally the date was set for our departure to the Diyatalāva camp, which was in the cooler highlands. In Ragama, especially in the corrugated-iron barracks, it was incredibly hot. If I accidentally leaned against the corrugated iron walls, it felt as if my arm was being burnt.

On the day of our departure we were awakened at about half past three in the morning. We jumped out of our beds and packed our field beds and bed sheets according to the regulations. Our luggage had already been sent the day before. At five o'clock we were marched in a single line down to the train, during which all the internees, with the exception of us monks, were singing "Die Wacht am Rhein" ("The Guard on the Rhein"), then we boarded the train. Since we monks were regarded as socially low class, due to our being on an equal footing with the dark-coloured Sinhalese, we were only allowed to travel second class, while the Colombo Germans went first class.

The train was watched by Punjabis with bayonets fixed on their guns. During the train journey we were not allowed to leave the train, so that many of us had to urinate through the windows, which must have made a terrible impression on the Sinhalese. On many stations there were huge crowds that had come to see us. At the station of Kadugannāva, where the train stopped for some minutes, my novice Ñāṇāloka was waiting to see me for the last time. Also some of the outcaste people from Kadugannāva were on the railway station to give me their respectful greetings.

The only sustenance we were given to eat on this day was some bread and cold tea before our departure, at 4.30 a.m., and during the journey another piece of bread partly covered with butter and partly with meat paste. On our arrival at the

Diyatalāva camp[99] in the evening at seven, we did not get any more food, although we had just come from a very tiring twelve-hour journey. We were also quite weak due to insufficient sleep the night before.

We were brought to a corrugated-iron barrack at the outer edge of the camp and were given one third of this barrack; the rest of it, just separated by a thin wooden wall, was filled with noisy sailors, who were shouting and fighting the whole day long. Most of the Emden[100] sailors were staying in this camp.

Next, we had to recover our luggage. As there was nobody to help us, we carried it ourselves. (But all this is nothing compared to what happened to us later on our journey to Australia.)

There were nine iron beds with mattresses, and every bed had three black covers and white blankets. There were no chairs, but we had brought some deckchairs from the island. While the exhausted Soṇo was resting on his chair, a fight broke out among the sailors in the next compartment. The loud shouting stimulated an attack of desperation in Soṇo. He started to run around in circles, like a madman, throwing his clothing off and shouting, "Help, Help!" while thrashing his arms about. I called the German doctor, Dr Heinemann, whom I knew from Ragama. When Soṇo saw him coming close, he lashed out in all directions and ran away. The Commander jumped after him and grabbed him from behind with both arms and lifted him up. Then he was taken to the camp hospital on the hill.

After some weeks an attempt was made again to accommodate Soṇo into the camp. For this purpose two small compartments had been separated by a wooden wall from the soldier's guard room, one for Soṇo and one for me, as I had taken on the responsibility for him. But on the second or third day, I had to tell the Commander that I was not able to watch over him any longer, for he was constantly trying to kill himself and throwing himself out of the glass window. I could not leave him alone even for a short moment, because again and again I had to hold him down. While he was in hospital later, he told me one day that he had secret communications. He was hearing voices and these voices were telling him that soon we were all going to be shot.

On the second day we all woke up with a good appetite, hoping to see some food soon, but all our waiting was in vain.

There was no organization. We just got some dried bread from somewhere. Nobody told us where or how to get food. Upāsaka Siemer begged for some dried bread crusts, and that was all we got for our lunch. Some Sinhalese servants, who had come here earlier with the Colombo Germans, heard about our problem and brought us some rice and vegetables late at night.

The next day was not much better; no one seemed to care about us. After that, every morning we got a piece of raw meat and one loaf of bread per person. However, four of us were vegetarians; and in any case, how could we cook it? We had no fireplace, no containers, no wood, or matches. Thus we put three big stones on the floor, borrowed a container from somewhere, and we cooked a bread broth, that is, bread in water. However, as soon as a heavy rainstorm came, everything was washed away.

I telegraphed my supporter, Richard Pereira, and to Bastian asking them to help us get some potatoes, rice, lentils, and a cooker. After some time we received some vegetable tins, jam, milk tins, and rice. That way we were able to continue for some time. The four vegetarians had only a small barrack to use as a kitchen, and the others cooked on a small burner.

On 12 December, my former student, Aperis, came. I had helped him to become a typesetter, and he was working at the Mahābodhi Press. He had been given holidays to come and help me in the camp. He stayed with us until March, then Ñāṇāloka came and he cooked food for us until our departure to Australia.

One day during my stay at the Diyatalāva concentration camp, I was threatened with immediate execution by the Commander if I dared to say another word against his administration. This happened because I had openly complained about the brutality of one of his Punjabi soldiers who had seen a Sinhalese monk wishing to talk to me over the barbed wire. The Sinhalese monk did not know about the camp rules and also did not understand the Punjabi language. The Punjabi soldier had hit him with his rifle butt and put him in prison overnight.

During the time of our stay in the prison camp in Diyatalāva, Bhaddiya died in the Gonamātara monastery, about three kilometres from the camp. I had frequently stayed at this monastery during earlier days because of the pleasant climate.

The old abbot was a very good friend of mine. We were not allowed to go to the cremation ceremony. On one occasion only, Vappo and I were allowed to visit the monastery, escorted by four Punjabi soldiers with fixed bayonets on their guns.

I also gave a talk on Buddhism in a large auditorium. Another time, one of my songs, *"Bettlerliebe"* ("Begger's love"), was performed at a concert.

Chapter 9: Concentration Camps in Australia, 1915–1916

In July 1915 we were brought to Australia by a troopship called the "Kursk."[101] As long as the ship was in the harbour, it was continuously surrounded by airplanes or steamboats. On this ship all class differences disappeared as we were now in the hands of Australians. All of us, without any kind of distinction, were sent into the hold, where we were to sleep in hammocks. Moreover, also without exception, including Buddhist and Christian monks and priests, everyone had to clean the toilets, which were used by the Australian soldiers as well.

Twice, morning and evening, at the sound of a trumpet, we had to come up to the upper deck for the roll-call. From six in the evening to six in the morning we were not allowed to go to the upper deck. After seventeen days our ship arrived in Sydney, with its beautiful harbour. As there were no porters we had to carry our luggage ourselves. I still remember well how the poor Catholic priests, one of whom had died on the journey, were toiling with this dreadful task, which they were not used to. After arrival, we were taken to the railway station and then on to Liverpool by train.

During the train ride, all compartments had remained completely closed, causing some of our monks to become sick and to vomit because of the dense cigarette smoke in the car. One of my main difficulties when being too close to others is the way that smokers, without any kind of care for their own health or the health of others, indulge in their habit. From Liverpool station, we were marched under close surveillance for about eight kilometres until we reached the prison camp.[102] Our arrival there was such a great disappointment that I was reminded of what Dante wrote when he saw the hell realm: *"Lasciate ogni speranza, voi ch'entrate"* ("Abandon all hope, you who enter here").[103]

Sitting on the grass in front of the camp, we prisoners were each given an old potato bag filled with a little bit of straw, to sleep on. We were also given a tin plate, a cup, knife, fork, and spoon, and three blankets. Due to being in the southern hemisphere, the month of July is the coldest month in this sub-tropical part of Australia.

With our arrival, the camp had three thousand inmates; later on the number grew to six thousand. Most of the inmates were shady characters and criminals.[104] They were mainly Australian Germans, with some Germans from Singapore, Hong Kong and Ceylon, the Emden sailors, as well as many others from different countries. All were accommodated in double barracks without windows and with very thin walls. Each barrack had a low corrugated iron roof and took a hundred people. On the completely open front side of each barrack, there was a sheet of sailcloth that could be pulled down in case of rain and storm. The room for each of us was just enough to put down the potato sack for sleeping and our sandals. Evidently there was no space for tables, chairs, nor any space to put luggage or boxes. If somebody wanted to have more space, he could go to the forest under the surveillance of guards and cut himself some wood for constructing a hut for two or three people.

During the nights it was terribly cold and windy. I used a bag that Vappo had made for me out of my covers, pulling up the upper end and putting it under my head as a pillow. The toilet conditions were terrible. The "toilet" was just a one and a half foot high stick, parallel to the ground, behind which were buckets. It was completely out in the open, with no protection against the cold wind, weather, and rain. It was well within view of others and this was the reason why I went there only at night. However, in the dark of the night it was difficult to find the way to get there and I could not use my sandals because they would have gotten stuck in the mud, so that I had to go barefoot. I would then go back to my homemade sleeping bag with my feet full of mud.

Luckily, after some time, together with about hundred and fifty prisoners from Ceylon, Singapore and Hong Kong, we were brought by ship to a new prison camp near Trial Bay,[105] north of Newcastle. This was an old abandoned prison house, beautifully situated on the top of a promontory surrounded by the sea. From morning to evening we were able to spend our time at the beach. As Vappo was getting my lunch every day, I was able to use the entire day until sunset for my literary work. The conditions got even better when a Russian, who was quite interested in Buddhism, made a little hut for me in my favourite place—a sort of beach hut. His example was soon followed by others and some eventually constructed real villas. During my stay in Trial Bay I studied Greek under Professor Grubner from Bonn and in return I taught him Pali.

The most incredible escapes were thought out during the Australian internment. For example, some prisoners from the Liverpool camp escaped by digging underground tunnels from their tent until they had reached outside of the barbed wire. However, after some months out in the bush, surviving only with difficulty by hunting, they came back on their own to the prison camp. In the Hong Kong camp a tunnel reinforced with cement had been made. One evening, after a theatre performance, all the inmates—including those inmates who had been acting and were still wearing their costumes—left with their travelling suitcases, and so on, through this tunnel, but when the leader had reached the exit of the tunnel and had thrown out his suitcase first in order to follow himself, there was a gunshot outside. Everybody immediately hurried back to their tents and barracks. The whole plan had been betrayed—and by a German at that.

In Trial Bay three friends were planning to escape, i.e., Count Carl von Cosel[106], Vappo and myself. Deep inside the jetty, made of stacked giant rocks, on which a guard was continuously going up and down, we had secretly constructed a large boat made of canvas with a sail made out of our yellow robes. Cosel had also stacked there a large amount of food in tins such as chocolate, milk, and dried bread. The most difficult part of our escape would be to go over the imposing wall of the prison camp at night as the whole wall was patrolled by guards. We had thought of constructing a sort of slide with the canvas, just as it is used when a house is on fire. Later on Count von Cosel also tried to get some of the German naval officers involved, so that when a large sailing ship would be moored in the bay, and the prison wall would have been passed successfully, the officers could hijack the ship and sail with the prisoners to America.

Chapter 10: Via Honolulu to Shanghai, 1916

Before we could put our escape plan into action, permission was given for all priests and monks to return to Germany via America. This was partly due to my many petitions. The condition was that we would pay for the journey ourselves. Shortly before, I had contacted the Governor of Ceylon and asked him to let me live in Ceylon—even in a prison camp. He had replied in a friendly way, but told me that at present I was not welcome.

Now I was suddenly allowed to return to Germany. I, however, had not the slightest intention to do that. I decided to first go to Honolulu and once there, try to go and live in a Japanese Temple. Should that not work, I would visit and ask the famous Buddhist philanthropist, Mrs Mary Foster, who was the friend and staunch supporter of the Buddhist preacher Dhammapāla of Ceylon, to enable me to travel to China and the Chinese Shan area bordering Burma in Yunnan. There I could stay in one of the Theravāda monasteries.

As I was without any money in Australia, I sold my nice Underwood typewriter—a present from Bhikkhu Sīlācāra—to the German camp commander Kosak for five pounds. Furthermore I received two hundred pounds from a Siamese German to whom I had taught Pali. Thus, on 15 November 1916, I left Sydney together with Sobczak and some other Germans. We embarked on the American ship, the Sierra.

The American Ambassador was acting as a representative of the German interests at that time.[107] He stayed on board until shortly before our departure and forcefully tried to make me take off my yellow monks' robes because he thought that with that kind of dress I would not be allowed to land in America. This, however, was not the case at all.

Spa at Wiesbaden, mid-19th century

Kaiser Wilhelm II

Maria-Laach, Benedictine monastery

"Peoples of Europe, protect your sacred goods!" Lithograph ordered by Kaiser Wilhelm II, pointing to the approaching "yellow danger."

Karl Neumann

Schopenhauer

Richard Wagner

F. Zimmermann

E. F. von Feuchtersleben

Karl Seidenstücker

Paul Dahlke and Suriyagoda Sumaṅgala

Maître Charles-Marie Widor

Gustav Nagel

Fritz Stange/Suma

Ānanda Metteyya, Burma, 1901–02

Ānanda Metteyya

Mrs Hlā Oung

Ñāṇatiloka & Bergendahl, Culla-Laṅkā, 1906

Sīlācāra, Dhammānusāri (Waltgraf), Ñāṇatiloka, Rangoon, Burma, 1907

Prisdang Jumsai/Jinavaravaṃsa, Culla-Laṅkā, 1906

ṇḍañño, Ñāṇatiloka, ?, R.A. Bergier, in the Caritas Vihāra, 1910

R. A. Bergier, 1909

Alexandra David-Néel

Caritas Vihāra, Lausanne, around 1910

Sidkeong Raja of Sikkim

David-Néel, Sidkeong, Silācāra on yaks in Sikkim, 1914(?)

Bhaddiyo going through Dodanduva, 1912.
By David-Néel.

German monks disembarking in Australia, 1915

Vappo as prisoner of war in Austral

Trial Bay Goal, Australia, around 1915

Prisoners of war at Trial Bay Goal.
Pictures by Dutoit.

The Kursk, which brought Ñāṇatiloka to Australi

In the meantime, Lenga (Yasa) and the two Bauers (Koṇḍañño and Vimalo), who were also leaving with us, had taken off their robes a long time earlier, and had earned some money. Vappo and Mahānāmo, having no money, were thus unable to leave, and stayed in the prison camp until the end of the war.

On the 27 November 1916 we arrived in Honolulu. I immediately tried to find accommodation in one of the Japanese Temples, but I was refused with kindness and regret every time. The reasons were that the Japanese monks are usually married and live together with their wives and children. In addition Japan was at war with Germany. Thus, together with Sobczak, I went to Mrs Mary Foster.[108]

We were received in the kindest manner and the lady promised me her full support. Thus I gave my five pounds to Sobczak and let him continue his journey to America. I was accommodated in the Hotel Majestic. At Mrs Fosters' I met a German lady named Dishins and I was invited to her house for lunch where I met the German Ambassador.

Through the German Ambassador I sent a letter, seven pages long, to Count von Bernsdorff,[109] the German Ambassador to the USA, in which I described the situation of the Buddhist monks in the prison camp. I also asked for help for travel expenses to China for myself, Vappo, and Mahānāmo. On 28 December I got a telegraphic reply that the ambassador would lend me the money for the travel expenses to China. (I found out later that these eight hundred marks travel money had been repaid by my mother.) The very next day, a ship arrived which was travelling to Shanghai, and this was the ship I travelled on.

As a German I was not allowed to land in Japan, although I would have loved to stay in a monastery there and to give Pali lectures at the University. (This did happen some years later.) I decided to continue to China and try to stay in a monastery in the Shanghai or Beijing area.

Because of repairs, the ship had to stay in port for a few more days. I found it difficult to stay on in the second class because it rather resembled the steerage deck. Further, in the next cabin there were seven Japanese babies, two Japanese male adults, and one Japanese lady. I just could not get any air and could not sleep throughout the night because of the babies' crying. (A few of the babies died here.) So I asked for first class accommodation from the Ambassador.

Finally on 1 January 1917 we departed. The passengers in the first class were, for the most part, Presbyterian missionaries with whom I had numerous conversations about Buddhism. They tried without success to get me to participate in their mediocre Salvation-army singing. One of the missionaries, by the name of Reisschauer,[110] was apparently a German American. He was about to write a book on Japanese Buddhism. Among the other passengers were an obdurate anti-German, young Dutchman, the friendly nephew of the famous Chinese General Li-Hung-Tschang, and some young German people who were going to meet their partners in Shanghai and get married there. There was also a huge American lady who, by means of her fatness and the dancing abilities of her pretty daughter, earned a fair amount of money. In the Chinese steerage deck there was a lot of commotion until far beyond midnight. Everywhere there were electrically illuminated casino tables with heaps of dollars, as well as delicacy food-stands, and so on.

Passing by Japan, we were able to see the beautiful snow-covered Mount Fuji. Day by day it was becoming colder. While stopping over at the three Japanese ports of Yokohama, Kobe, and Nagasaki, our papers were inspected by the police.

Chapter 11: China, 1917–1919

Shanghai

I arrived in Shanghai on 21 January 1917. The city, particularly the Chinese part, made a fantastic impression on me. I was taken by two rickshaws—one of which was loaded with my luggage—to a Chinese hotel where no one understood a word of English. It was almost impossible for me to communicate. While walking through the huge town, I did not meet a single European during the whole day.

On my way I was harassed by beggar women and children who were wearing clothes made out of little pieces of cloth. Because of the many pieces of thick cloth sewn together they looked almost like balls. They were very insistent, throwing themselves in front of me on the ground again and again, even after I had called a policeman for help and then, to proceed quickly, I took a rickshaw. Again and again they kneeled down and were repeating the words *"Ching, ching, chow, chow"* ("Please, please, food, food"). Finally a young English-speaking Chinese man arrived who took me with him. As it was New Year's Day, I would not have gotten any food in the hotel. No one cooks on those days (just as in Ceylon), so he took me to a restaurant. To the amusement of all the others in the restaurant I had to try to use chop-sticks, like it or not, under the tutelage of my young guide.

The Chinese were beautifully dressed, both genders wore the same kind of fur-coated trousers with an accompanying jacket, a coat with flower designs, a round hat, and felt shoes. In winter all the clothing articles of the Chinese are well-lined with cotton wool, the same as in Japan. As I was only wearing an under-trouser and an under-jacket under my thin robes, I suffered badly from the cold. I suffered to such an extent that even the Chinese laughed at such thin clothes while I was walking through the streets of the huge town observing the unusual people. Almost everywhere, in almost every street, one could see prostitutes, who were standing in a row amidst the people passing by. This was certainly one of the most curious or remarkable days of my life; everything just seemed to be like in a dream.

In the evening, I was told by an English-speaking Chinese person in the hotel that it was possible to proceed by water to Canton. One could travel by steamboat up to Hankow, and from there by another steamboat to Honan, and from there, in six days, by a sailing boat, for a fare of six Chinese dollars, to Canton. There and then I decided to take this journey.

The next morning I went to the German Bank, in order to find out how I could exchange a draft that I had for four hundred and thirty Chinese dollars, (which was equivalent to the two hundred and ninety dollars that I had paid for this draft in Honolulu). Although, I had heard that the Hong Kong Shanghai Bank, which was the holder of my draft, would not give out any money to Germans, I was advised by the German Bank to try it anyway. Fortunately, the Englishman who was serving at the Hong Kong Shanghai Bank did not recognise me as a German and did not ask for my nationality. So I was able to go to the shipping agent and buy a first class ticket to Hong Kong. (I had tried my best to get a ticket for the third class; however, that was not permitted to Europeans.)

By ship to Hankow

The ship was to depart at two o'clock in the morning. Snow was falling when I went on board in the evening. The water of a little pond that I had to pass by was completely frozen. It was Chinese New Year and everywhere one could hear firecrackers, which, together with gunpowder, are an invention of the Chinese.

Lying in my cabin, I heard German passengers saying "Adieu" to their friends on land. The next morning at breakfast I met a young German ship engineer who was working at an engineering school near Shanghai. He was travelling with his wife for the New Year holiday. He had brought a toboggan and wanted to go snow sliding in Kyukyang. They both seemed pretty naive and childish people, the like I have not met for years among Germans. We were the only first class passengers, so that the entire salon was at our disposal. On 23rd and 24th January we had terribly cold days and the cold was biting my face. The German engineer lent me his coat because of my thin clothing.

Both the banks of the Yangtze River were quite flat and barren. The river was sometimes so broad that one could not even see the other shore, but soon one could see small snow-capped hills and even some mountains further away. Here and there, one could see monasteries on top of hills. Each time we reached a town, we would hear New Year firecrackers; they were placed like garlands along a bamboo stick so that they would ignite each other. Soon after, beggar families would come rowing out in big oval pots normally used for washing. They tried to beg from the passengers, using small begging bags put on long sticks.

On the morning of 26 January we ran onto a sandbank from which we could not get off. The ship was stuck about two and a half feet deep into the sand. The ship's engine was working so hard that the turbines caused waterfalls. Other ships tried to pull us off the bank. Every means was tried but it was all in vain. However, at about six o'clock that evening the ship suddenly became free from the sandbank, so we continued on our journey.

Far away one could see black and yellow-coloured mountains. On the shore there was a small mud hut village. Here, near Kyunkyang, the two Germans, who had become good friends with me during the last two days, disembarked. Thus I had to continue my journey lonely and alone, without a home, without being understood, and with an uncertain future. Such a good bye, under such uncertain circumstances, hurts.

Many porcelain merchants came on board. Gong music was heard from the shore and many people were brought in palanquins. The ship was supposed to arrive the next morning at 9.30 a.m. in Hankow! A jovial Russian from Siberia came on board who first appeared to me as an English sports hunter. He was a former Greek Orthodox priest. I wished to learn my first Chinese expressions from him, but he only taught me pidgin expressions like "*chow*" (food). He also tried to help me understand the incredibly complicated money system in China, which I actually never really understood, so it's better to say nothing about it.

At 8 o'clock in the evening the ship ran aground on a sandbank again, and some were even saying that the ship might have to go back to Shanghai. However, on the morning of 27th January the tow boat told us that we would probably be able to pass the island in front of us on the left side, which we succeeded in doing.

Conversation during lunchtime was getting more and more friendly. On my left there was an engineer from England, on my right was the Captain, a Scot, who had lived for a long time in Burma and Ceylon. Opposite me was the Russian from Siberia, and to the left of him, the First Officer, who was also from Scotland.

Passing Wutchang on our right side, we saw a seven-storeyed pagoda. Now and then some green spots could be seen, probably rice fields. The winter appeared to be over soon.

Despair in Hankow

On the evening of 27 January 1917, after a journey of about five days, we arrived in Hankow.[111] I was brought by rickshaw to one of the Chinese hotels, which, I was to find out, were all more or less brothels. Ladies of every possible age and size were sent to my room to catch me; however, as I stayed as cold as ice, they sneaked out of the door feeling ashamed. Until three or four o'clock in the morning there was terrible tumult and screaming, so that it was impossible to sleep there.

In the morning I looked for another place to stay, but I had unpleasant quarrels with the owners of the small hotels. The main cause of which was my lack of knowledge of the Chinese language and, above all, Chinese customs. Finally, however, I found somewhere to stay in a place situated in a dirty alley. I was probably allowed to stay there only because I gave the owner ten dollars immediately. To get to my so-called room I had to climb up a ladder to reach the thin, crooked wooden floor, which was suspended in the air. Nothing was to be seen of a table, mirror, mattress or similar things and it was terribly cold. When going to sleep, I put my wallet under my head, ready for a robbery at any time. However, what could I have done anyhow in case of an attack? Quite possibly this area of town was where the criminals were living anyway.

I got a terrible cold: coughing, sneezing, spitting, pain in the chest, pain in the head. It all became worse due to the terrible cold weather, against which I could do nothing as I had no thick clothing. Thus I lay down to sleep at four o'clock in the afternoon, and slept until eight o'clock the next morning.

I had visited the Consul on my first day, but he had been very reserved at our encounter and had asked me to come back the next day. When I came back the next day he was not in so I came again the day after. Finally, after going back and forth for a long time I was able to get a good map of the Yangtze area, although until shortly before that he had told me that he did not have such a map. Subsequently, I was brought to another room with two young Germans, who were to help me get my personal data together for making a Chinese pass. One of them had heard of my monastery project in Switzerland, and he had also heard about me from the schoolteacher Schäfer, who was a former student of my father with whom I was well acquainted in Wiesbaden and who had visited me in the Maitreya Hall in Colombo in 1905.

The young German told me that because of the dry season the Yunnan was only passable by boat up to Itchang, thus I determined to stay in a monastery here until it was passable again. The young German would have preferred to bring me to the monastery himself, but he had no time; he could only give me a letter of recommendation to the Chief Police Officer of the German colony, Grabe.

This Chief Police Officer then sent me to the monastery, along with a Chinese police officer as a translator and another police officer as a guide. He asked me to just visit the monastery and then come back to him. First we went by rickshaw, then by horse carriage, and then by boat, and finally we walked through fields and villages to the monastery. The first thing I noticed was the sixty golden Arahants, each with a different symbol in the hand. Then I saw some huge Buddha statues. When we arrived a ceremony was being conducted and all the monks in their robes were singing and at the same time hitting gongs. This reminded me strongly of a mass in a Catholic church.

A congenial young monk received me and brought me to the reception room. Somebody brought tea and sugar, dried fruit and similar things. Later on an elderly monk came. He looked somewhat like a knight from the Middle Ages, with the pointed hat he was wearing and a long beard. The behaviour of the monks was very refined and cultured, which reminded me very much of behaviour in a Sinhalese monastery.

I asked the Abbot for permission to stay in his monastery and I was told that after three days someone would come and give me a reply. This, as was to be expected, did not happen. Nothing could happen without permission from the Chinese authorities, and these were afraid of Germans, who at that time were often suspected of being spies or secret agents.

For three days, Police Officer Grabe gave me accommodation in a cell in the German police prison and sent me food and tea three times a day. This was actually the first German who had really helped me during my whole odyssey. Until then I had the thought: "The darker the skin, the whiter the heart; but the whiter the skin, the darker the heart."

Next day I thought of trying to go by steamboat, via Itchang, to Canton, but no boat could go from Itchang to Chungking (Chongqing), due to the dry season. Because the China Navigation Corporation was British, I tried the Japanese

Corporation. However, because of the dry season the Japanese boat would go only to Yotscho and that on early Sunday morning. Moreover, even this was not sure because the repairs that had to be done on the boat might not have been finished by then.

I almost collapsed on the road because I had not eaten yet, and I was still quite sick due to my cold. My head was hot with fever and my coughing was tormenting me. I went quickly back to bed. Oh, how much I suffered there: in a foreign land, without a home, without a friend, without money, without knowledge of the language, sick with a bad cold and no warm clothes. How long was this to continue? If I only knew Chinese, then I would not even hesitate to walk the two or three thousand kilometres to the Shan countries. Concerning the luggage: I thought I would much rather throw it all away, apart from my manuscripts.

A change of luck

The next morning I got a third-class ticket on a Japanese steamboat which was supposed to bring me to Yotscho. I had already placed my luggage on the wooden platform in my cabin when there was a change of fate. In the afternoon, Mister Clément,[112] whom I took to be a Frenchman, invited me to visit him. On arrival I talked to him in French; however, he turned out to be a German of Huguenot descent. He was a somewhat theosophically inclined Buddhist who was trying to realize the Higher Life together with his wife. When he told me that, I remembered that I had already heard about him and his celibate, divine marriage from Sumano.[113] He also knew Sobczak from Kassel. He told me about a certain Wagnerian who had retreated to a monastery in the Taishan mountains and was living as a hermit, although I also heard that he got married to a Japanese woman there.

Here I decided to take up again my original plan to travel to the Shan area. The Cléments suggested that I could leave my luggage with them. In the evening the old captain, Rhode, whose sailing boat was moored in the harbour, came for a visit. He immediately invited me to come to Itchang and stay for some time in his house until his return. After that he would be able to help me to continue to Chungking. However, when Rhode had left, Clément advised me to first get healthy again and to wait for the cold season to pass. Until then, I should stay with him. Without any hesitation I immediately accepted his kind offer. My luggage was brought back from the ship and the ticket returned. Now I was living like a prince and able get over my terrible cough and weakness.

How often everything turned out to be good for me in the end! At first, though, I certainly had to pass through a trial. In fact, I might have died miserably if I had left with that steamboat, since during the next few days it snowed a lot and the whole river was covered with ice.

Clément and his wife also asked me to invite the other two monks, Vappo and Mahānāmo, to stay with them and later on to go and live in a secluded mountain hut they had in the summer resort of Chikusan.

Now that I had time, I was able to get better maps from Shanghai for my further travels. I was also able to get a Chinese pass for south-west Yunnan, and to learn a little Chinese—those expressions that were most necessary for future travelling. I had these expressions written down in Chinese characters, so that I would be able to show them in case my pronunciation was not understood. This was indeed required, since each Chinese province has a different pronunciation, sometimes even a different language! I was thinking of leaving with just a backpack, a small gas cooker (given to me by Clément), and some clothes. Books, manuscripts, and similar things could be sent after. I was keen to get news about Vappo and Mahānāmo. I thought that Vappo could come with me to Yunnan, while Mahānāmo could stay with Clément.

As the steamboat from Itchang to Chungking would only start in April, I decided to wait until then. This was a good decision as the cold continued for quite some time, even on the last day of February it was still snowing heavily. On Sundays Clément and I often made excursions with his large sailing boat, which had a galley and two sleeping cabins. At night time we would sleep on the boat. On one occasion I was steering the boat and on our return going upstream I had to manoeuvre it continuously. As we had forgotten to bring petroleum for the lamps, in the darkness we ran the danger of being hit and capsized by one of the steamboats.

At Clément's house I came to know the editor of the Daily News, a German by the name of Nevel. He helped me to get the necessary maps and gave me a book by Dingles who had gone from Chungking to Burma, via Yunnan Fu. The book by Hackmann, who took the route via Tatschin Fu to Burma, was the one that I intended to follow as a guide for my own journey. There was only one part of the journey that no other European had done before me, the stretch from Suwe Fu to Ningyan Fu, crossing wild, autonomous areas. I got a Chinese pass without any kind of difficulty through the help of the German Embassy.

During my stay with Clément, I was struck with shooting abdominal pain together with heavy diarrhoea. It might have been appendicitis, but I was able to heal this myself by keeping the abdomen warm and by putting on a "Priessnitz-compress" for two to three days. These were the last days of March and there still was no news of ships going to Chungking.

The arrival of Sobczak

Clément received a letter from Sobczak, which he showed me. Sobczak did not know that I was staying with Clément. He was writing from Shanghai, which he had reached from America. He left America because he was afraid that it would declare war on Germany. He thought that I was still in Honolulu. His idea was to go via Hankow to Tibet. We immediately wrote back to him informing him that I was staying with Clément. I asked him to come so that we could do the journey to southwest Yunnan together, and find a Theravāda monastery in the Shan area.

As soon as I had sent off the letter, I came to learn that the ships had resumed going to Chungking and I telegraphed Sobczak asking him to give me his decision by way of telegraph. Some days later I got a telegraph from him saying that he was going to come, but his departure from Shanghai was delayed. He had gone up to Nanking by train; there, someone had brought him by mistake to a British boat, which had treated him as a German prisoner and put him out in Wuhu. From then on everybody took him to be a German spy. I was told by the

Embassy that I was also being regarded as a spy and that the British authorities in Shanghai knew about my stay.

Finally Sobczak arrived. The Japanese maid announced his arrival in less than flattering words. A Chinese officer from the Foreign Police Office accompanied him. I was told that I would need a new pass for Tenyush in southwest Yunnan and I also needed to issue a draft of a hundred dollars.

Shortly before we were going to start our journey, the police officer came back. Interestingly, of the three police officers that came to visit us one after the other, the first one spoke German, the second one French, and the third one English. We were told that for the time being we could not depart because it was considered too dangerous. Why? He did not know, but on the way to Chungking there were many robbers and the like at this time.

After the suspension of diplomatic relations between China and Germany,[114] the German settlement was handed over to the Chinese, and the Ambassador left China. The Acting Deputy Ambassador, Janowski, told me that the British Ambassador in Hankow thought that Sobczak and myself were "suspicious elements" and "agitators," and he was putting pressure on the Chinese authorities not to give us permission to go to West Yunnan.

This news struck me like lightning. Would I have to give up all the plans that I had had for so many months? However, I was not willing to give up so easily. We decided, on the recommendation of the Deputy Ambassador, to just get a pass up to Chungking, which we got without any kind of difficulty. Yet I had not given up my hope to continue to Yunnan. I bought myself a foldable bed and a Japanese compass with a sundial. These things were necessary if we were to pass through wilderness areas. Clément had already offered me his foldable gas cooker and a mug.

I would have loved to take Vappo along as well, but since my departure from Australia I had not received any news from him. I supposed all the letters I sent him from Honolulu and China had been intercepted. Day after day, night after night, I longed for the end of this fatal, unfortunate war that was costing me some of the best years of my life!

Departure to Itchang

On 20 April Sobczak and I finally left on a Chinese steamboat bound for Itchang. Arriving on board with our third class tickets, we had a long quarrel with the ship's officer before he allowed us to stay. We were European and were only supposed to use first class tickets. On the ship we were allocated the foredeck. There, I immediately made friends with the ship-boy with whom I was able to communicate fairly well in Chinese. The Chinese language seemed extraordinarily easy to me as it had almost no declensions or conjugations. I kept on talking to everybody in order to improve my Chinese, and everybody was friendly and helpful.

Between Hankow and Itchang there was nothing in particular to see, everywhere the land was rather flat and only in the far distance there were some small hills. For the first time, after many years, I saw camels. In several of the villages where we stopped, gunboats were moored and the soldiers on them were shooting to salute us. For food we were given rice with some vegetables twice a day. The Captain and officers of the ship were English. It was not possible to enter the toilet as the floor of the toilet was filled with excrement up to the highest possible level. Apparently it had never ever been cleaned and one could only use it by squatting right at the entrance. I had never seen such a degree of filthiness before—not even in Algeria.

After four days we reached Itchang, where we were taken ashore by boat. With our luggage being carried behind us we went to the house of Captain Rhode, as he had given me permission to live there in Hankow. On the way we were stopped by soldiers. They checked our passes and asked us to wait. Soon the District Officer came. He was very polite, handing us his visiting card and asking us to follow him to his office. Then he asked me for my visiting card, but as I did not have one, I could not give it to him. Again the passes were checked, and we were told in pidgin English that our ship would continue to Chungking in about eight days time.

Then he brought us, together with the soldiers, to the house of Captain Rhode. The housekeeper there thought he could make some money from us, but I told him that we were not to pay anything for our stay. Every day he cooked rice, vegetables, and eggs into a pancake covered with onions, together with unpleasant, weak, unsweetened tea. For this meal he charged us ten pence on the first day, the second day thirty, the third day forty, and from then on fifty pence.

Two soldiers, who slept at night outside our rooms, had to be with us all the time wherever we went. Whether we went for a walk on the massive inner city rampart, or to the market, everywhere they were following us, serving simultaneously as military escorts, guards, protectors, translators, guides, servants, and carriers. It has been a custom for a long time that any European who goes far into the inner parts of China has soldiers for protection. Since China had interrupted diplomatic relations with Germany, Germans were given this 'protection' even more. It had been announced throughout China that Germans were to be especially treated with attention and care.

Continuing to Chungking

Already on the second day, when I was walking up and down on the flat roof of our house, I saw a ship coming with a Chinese flag and suspected that it was the ship we were waiting for. The next day we drove out to the ship and made inquiries. The ship was to go to Chungking in two days time, that is, on 25 April, at four o'clock in the morning. Thus the day before it was due to leave, we took our luggage on board and without any kind of difficulty got third class tickets, for which we nevertheless had to pay twenty dollars each this time. The third class compartment was just one room and it was filled to the brim. Since our tickets did not entitle us to a bed, we were given a place to sleep in the corridor of the second class. Our foldable beds thus turned out to be very useful on this occasion. They did again later on, too, and still even later, on the boat that was to bring us back to Europe.

The missionaries from the China Inland Mission and one other lady were the only white people aboard this ship. However, we did not want to have any contact with them.

I did not have a thick blanket for sleeping; therefore under my yellow robes I wore a shirt, three sweaters, a vest, a jacket and short Manchester trousers. Sobczak had surrounded his foldable bed with his robes in order to be protected from other people looking at him.

Waking up the next morning I saw steep rocky mountains with sparse vegetation close to both banks of the river. The countryside was incredibly beautiful. In many places the mountains ended right in the river so that it was not possible to look very far. The river winding around the rocky mountains could only be seen as stretches appearing to be lakes. In the areas where there were rapids, passages and steps had been cut in the sides of the gorge. We saw how the poor fishermen, in order to pass the dangerous rapids, were pulling their big house- and sailing-boats with long ropes while walking along these paths and stairs. In many respects this area reminded me of the Alps or the Himalayas.

In the evening we arrived at Kweifu, a small town surrounded by a wall and situated on a high slope. This area was apparently a centre for comb production. The many traders who came to the boat had, besides pomelo fruits, nothing to sell but wooden combs. Sometimes the rocky mountains retreated somewhat and large, towering mountains covered with grass and trees displayed themselves to us.

The food that I ate on the ship along with the poor Chinese was quite good. However I used a spoon as I was not yet proficient with chopsticks. Twice daily we were given rice with vegetables fried in oil, and sometimes pork in oil and a sort of lentil soup with shark-fins. In the evening at six we were all given rice soup. From Itchang we had brought along thirty-six cooked eggs, for which we had paid a cent each. In remote areas, however, one could get a dozen eggs for a cent.

On the second evening we reached Wan Hsien where, on the opposite side of the river, one could see beautiful corn and vegetable fields. It reminded me of a dream I had while in the prison camp at Trial Bay where I was walking towards a village passing through cornfields and gardens, and the people were speaking to me in some foreign Mongolian language. They were prostrating themselves in front of me and telling me that they wished to support me. Would this beautiful dream become reality in the fertile Red Basin area behind Chungking?

From time to time we saw seven-storied pagodas and on top of the mountains beautifully situated monasteries. The dirty and loamy appearance of the Hankow area had by now been replaced with the lush green of the cornfields and the mountains. The only thing I found displeasing in this countryside was the ever-same yellow colour of the Yangtze River. On another mountain-top opposite Wang Hsien, there was a small city that looked like a fortified mountain palace.

On our ship there were some Chinese Jewish ladies,[115] possibly from the Kweifu area, where there are a lot of Chinese Jews. In Wang Hsien I saw many men, as well as women, using the same kind of turban-like black cloth around their forehead, similar to these Jewish ladies.

The whole journey from Itchang to Chungking took four days altogether. At night-time the ship would stop and drop anchor, mostly because of the dangerous rapids. Thus the ship covered the whole distance in forty-four hours. It was one of the best of steamers, and it had been constructed by Germans.

Before we left the steamboat an important-looking Chinese man, who was fluent in English, asked for our names. When I asked him who he was, he told us that he was an officer of the Foreigners' Department. However, he was probably an English spy, because nobody knew of him at the Foreigners' Department.

Waiting in Chungking

When we left the boat, I was clothed in my yellow silk robes and Sobczak had also put a yellow robe over his European dress. He followed me after a quarrel with the boat people about the payment for our boat transport and luggage. This was a real hassle which happened repeatedly. I asked the people who were carrying my luggage, in my Chinese, to take us to the District Officer. We had to pass through the small roads of the town, upstairs, downstairs—continuously going up and down. We went through some city gates and through this and that, passing between houses. Finally, after about half an hour, we reached the courtyard of a large house that I presumed to be the house of the District Officer. However, a very friendly man from Chinese Turkistan, who looked like a real Turk, told us that we had just arrived in the Muslim School. The old schoolteacher was there as well, and a lot of curious young Chinese Muslim children. The Turk said that we were his brothers. He paid the carriers, as well as the two people who were going to take us both in palanquins to a Buddhist Monastery and to the District Officer. But we never got to the District Officer. We were sent from one office to another, and every time we had to show our Chinese passes. Finally we arrived at an office where the officer spoke English. He checked our passes and then asked us to go, with two soldiers as escort, to the Military Office and from there we would be brought to a monastery.

So, with the four carriers who were carrying our luggage, we continued our journey to the Military Office, and from there to the monastery. The monastery was entirely occupied by soldiers. The officer of these soldiers then telegraphed somebody, and finally we were told that we should go to a hotel. I told him that I was a monk and that I belonged to a monastery. Our carriers continued and we followed them in our palanquins.

Suddenly I heard someone calling behind me: "Now, how did you come here?" He was the Assistant Ambassador, the engineer Glaubitz, a very friendly and courteous man. He said that although he would like to, it would not be a good idea to accommodate us in the embassy, as this would lead the authorities to distrust us. The British had already many times aired their suspicions about him to the authorities, saying that he was working in the interest of the Germans. He recommended that we, accompanied by his servant, should proceed to the hotel where most Europeans usually stayed. The hotel turned out to be a miserable, dirty shack where, after a long negotiation, we were able to get a single room for two dollars instead of four.

After we had taken "*chow chow*" (pidgin English for "food"), we put up our two foldable beds and rested. That same evening the Ambassador came over and we talked for a long time. We were to meet with him and Dr Asmi the next day at one o'clock at the Medical Council to talk further–first about a monastery where we could stay, and then about a pass to southwest Yunnan, near the Burmese border.

Our carriers came the next day with two palanquins. The roads teem with palanquins in this part of the world. A European who is not used to these palanquins may get terrified when it goes up and down stairs, fearing an accident with porters carrying liquid human excrement. This noble dung, which is used as manure, is transported in two big buckets that are dangling from the ends of a bamboo pole carried over the shoulder by a porter.[116]

After many turns up and down the mountain, we finally reached the clinic where we were to meet the Ambassador and Dr Asmi. We were brought upstairs and treated with tea and biscuits. Glaubitz developed a strong interest in our case. He told me that his friend, the General, would help us and was ready, even against the orders from Hankow, to give us a pass so that we could go to Yunnan. As a guide we were given a very well-educated young Chinese who spoke German and English. He took us to a monastery in town. When we got there we were told that they didn't have any room available, we were given a monk to guide us to another monastery that was further up on the right side of the river on the top of a mountain.

After we had managed to successfully pass between rows of dung buckets and the Chinese who were squatting down to fill them, we hurried on in order to escape this horridly smelling city, where the so-called "flower beds" were filled to the brim with human excrement.

We took a boat up the river and, after about one and a half hours, we reached the foot of the mountain where the Hsiang Kuo Ssu monastery[117] was situated. Steep stairs led us up to the monastery where a young monk, who seemed to be the only inhabitant of this relatively large monastery, received us and assigned us two rooms. From my room I had a beautiful view over the river far below, the rice fields, and the mountains far away in the distance. What a difference this was compared to the noisy town, pervaded by the smell of excrement. The Ambassador sent us our luggage on the very same day.

On the following day a boat came from the Ambassador and took us to the Foreign Office. I went without Sobczak, but I took along his passport picture. At the Passport Office I met the same man who had been so quick to get rid of us the day before, but this time I was taken further inside through several wide courts until I came to the very innermost part. There I was offered an armchair. Soon after two officers came, one speaking English and the other German. Both were very polite, as was in fact the case almost all the time here. A third, somewhat overweight man also joined us. I was greeted in the European manner by shaking hands. I was told that the General would give us a pass. After about half an hour of informal conversation and the handing over of passport pictures, the higher officer stood up with his teacup in his hand. As this was the sign to show that the interview was finished, I also stood up, as courtesy demanded, and took my leave.

After this, I went by palanquin to meet the Ambassador, whom I met in the courtyard of his house. He welcomed me in a very hearty and friendly manner. He had been able to convince the General, after going back and forth there many times, to give me the pass. We had a very European meal with many different servings. Glaubitz made me his friend; he even gave me his photograph with his signature and also a number of Chinese photographs. He apparently had found in me someone to whom he could open his heart. I also gave him my newest picture. Then he had the Secretary of the Ambassador come, with whom he consulted about the four carriers needed to carry our luggage. For protection against the rain, the luggage would be wrapped up in oilcloth, which had to be bought together with two oil-coats.

The passes were going to be sent by the Foreign Office directly to the Embassy, supposedly the next day, or at least the day after. The Secretary was worried because in the Schwefu area, through which we had to pass, there were battles between the Yunnan and the Szechwan troops at that time. In China, similar to Germany in former times, often one small state was at war with the next. Here, however, we have to add that the province of Szechwan alone is about as big as the whole of Germany and that Chungking, the capital of Szechwan, had about six hundred thousand inhabitants.

I returned to the monastery, this time in the rowing boat of Dr Glaubitz. Soon after I arrived, a young officer came to visit me together with a translator and two heavily armed soldiers. I invited both to take tea with me on the veranda in front of my room. Both greeted me very respectfully. The translator told me that the officer was sent by the General in order to check through my luggage. I took out everything, including a general map of China with my intended travel route. I had drawn it myself in three parts with the help of all the different information that I had been able to collect. He asked permission to take the map along and gave me a receipt for it. He excused himself many times for giving me all this trouble. I responded to him that it was quite understandable that the General had to check me out if he was going to give me a pass and take responsibility. After having checked my luggage, both bowed down and going out they turned around from time to time in order to bow down again as Chinese custom requires.

The food in the monastery was rice with two or three types of vegetables cooked in water, with salt as the only seasoning, followed by the usual unsweetened tea. This tea, which is similar to the one taken in Japan, is apparently very healthy.

Another disappointment

The second of May gave us a new disappointment. A servant of the Ambassador, who spoke very good German, brought me a letter from Glaubitz informing me that the Foreign Office was not going to give us a pass for the time being because of the strife in Yunnan and Szechwan. He asked us to stay for the time being in the Three Ghosts Monastery. I was wondering again whether the British were behind this.[118] We decided to wait for some time and then I would try to contact the Dutch minister in Beijing through Glaubitz. The Dutch minister was representing German interests since the disruption of diplomatic relations between China and Germany. From that day on, there were two or three soldiers staying here for our protection (or maybe for our "surveillance"). When evening fell, the number of soldiers went up to six.

Sobczak found that some soldiers and the secret police had followed him on returning from Chungking, where he had gone to settle some financial matter. They had followed his palanquin to the boat landing place, then boarded the boat with him and came with him to the monastery. It was amazing to see how the British were able to have their way with China. We were only radiating loving kindness and goodwill, without making any kind of distinction, to all living beings whether small or great; yet we were thought of as spies and up to agitating the people or doing similar things. We were not doing the smallest harm, even to small animals. Nevertheless, one should not forget at this point that the British were not simply to be blamed, since in China only too often Germans themselves had made trouble in all possible ways.

On 4 May I met Glaubitz and Dr Asmi in Chungking. It was rather difficult to get there; we went first by boat, then walking, and then in a palanquin up and down through the dirty and smelly roads of the city. As on the previous evening the number of soldiers stationed at our monastery had risen to ten, I asked Mr Glaubitz to let the General know that there was no need to be so worried about our safety and that two soldiers would probably be enough. Soldiers are not really the kind of people one likes to have hanging around in a quiet and solitary monastery on the top of a mountain where, as a monk, one likes to meditate.

According to a letter that Glaubitz had received, there was heavy fighting in Chengdu, the capital of Szechwan, between the Yunnan troops of General Lo and the Szechwan troops of General Liu. In nearby Luchow, the place we would have to pass through on our journey to southwest Yunnan, there were large numbers of troops. Another German was also not allowed to travel to Luchow. Chengdu was still being attacked by Yunnan troops and the whole area was full of trenches.

Dr Asmi told me that the abbot of the other monastery that we had visited on our arrival was now willing to take us in. He originally had not allowed us to stay, not because he had no place, but because he was afraid of difficulties due to the fact that diplomatic relations between Germany and China had been interrupted. Now, he was told by the authorities that everyone should be very friendly and respectful to Germans.

We went into town again followed by two soldiers whom I made use of by having them carry some things. They actually turned out to be quite good servants and guides in this quite complicated and sprawling town. Dr Asmi told me that now even boats going upriver would only do so if they had a strong military company aboard. There were several gangs of armed robbers who had taken to capturing boats, and this was happening even up to Chungking. So, we really were given so many soldiers for the sake of our protection.

Every morning and evening at six o'clock, the monk with whom we were staying would do chanting. He would be fully dressed in his robes. Occasionally he would be dressed in a toga, similar to our yellow robe, which was held together by an iron buckle. During his litanies in front of the Buddha statue, he sometimes hit a kettle drum and sometimes rang a bell. Occasionally one would hear the kettle drum with a drum alone, and then there would be some quick hitting on the kettle drum that got faster and faster until it turned into a whirl. This was repeated day after day. When he was reciting, it seemed to me as if he was chanting not only some Sanskrit but even some Pali words, spoken with a somewhat Burmese type of pronunciation. I asked him to recite it in front of me, and I found out that I was able to recognize a few Pali words (such as *su-pañña*, pronounced as *pyiñña* in Burma, and *desito*.) As I did not have a translator at hand, I could not find out any more.

Every day, usually already in the morning, there was heavy rain. All day long we were enveloped in mist and clouds. I yearned for the fertile, warm South. I would rather have been "south of the clouds," that is in "Yunnan," than in the "cloudy" Szechwan. During my stay at the "Three Ghost Monastery" I was usually busy with my translation work from morning till late evening. It was here that I finished the draft of my translation of the six volumes of the *Aṅguttara Nikāya*. After my return from Hankow I typed it out with a typewriter that I borrowed from the embassy.

Return to Hankow

As we had no hope to be able to continue to Yunnan, we decided to return to Hankow. When I discussed this with the Ambassador, he strongly advised me not to take the next boat. That boat was quite good, but he nevertheless had a strong feeling that there could be an accident. As I do not like forebodings, I did not listen to him and, together with Sobczak, we started our return to Itchang the next day. In Itchang we changed boats and took one to Hankow. On arrival in Hankow, we were told that the very boat that had taken us up to Itchang, on the return journey to Chungking had sunk in the rapids with its whole load.

After the interruption of diplomatic relations between China and Germany, Clément had to leave his house in the French Concession and now only had a very small house. He put us up at the former German police quarters. Sobczak stayed in a garden hut, while I took residence in a corner room near the veranda overlooking the garden. After some time, Clément found us alternative accommodation in the German Technical College, which was a little bit out of town. We were given a large hall, intended for storing machines, though they had not yet arrived. Sobczak took the upper level, while I took the lower one. I put up my foldable bed and along one of the walls I put my luggage. I hung my robes on a string, which I had strung up from the other side.

One night, at about two o'clock in the morning, I was woken up from my sleep by a strange sound. I shouted, "Who's there?" without getting a response. I thought that it might be Sobczak, who was sleeping above me, turning around in his bed. Nevertheless I kept an eye on the string with my robes and stayed awake, while pretending to have fallen asleep again. After some minutes I had the impression that someone was indeed moving behind my robes. I felt a cold shiver running down my back as I realized that this was a burglar. I jumped out of bed and stormed towards the burglar, shouting with a loud voice and pretending to have a revolver in my hand. The burglar, fortunately, jumped out of the next window and disappeared. On the windowsill I found some burning tinder and a crowbar nearby, indicating that there had been at least two of them. If I had really tried to catch the first burglar, the other one would have certainly smashed in my skull.

Imprisonment in Hankow

I had only taught German at the Technical College for about one or two weeks when China declared war on Germany[119]. Soon after, the Chinese military police came with the order to take Sobczak and me away as prisoners. I told the soldiers to inform their boss that I would only come with them if they would force me to do so by putting me in chains. They disappeared but came back after one or two hours with a letter from former German police officer Grabe who asked me in a very kind way to follow the military police voluntarily, since otherwise I would get into much more difficulties later on—so I followed them voluntarily.

At the Foreign Office I made a formidable commotion because we were told that they had proof of us acting as German spies or agents. I heard this same accusation in the 1920s in Thailand, where I was imprisoned for months while afflicted with a terrible malarial fever. This is what is called the working of previous bad Kamma or Action. I can, by the way, affirm with certainty: whatever I had to suffer in this manner, I did (in this life) solely on account of the English.[120]

We were brought to the police prison and immediately accommodated in a kind of attic in the main building. For two days guards with bayonets affixed to their guns were stationed in front of our door. They would follow me even to the toilet! Finally we got a secluded corner with two rooms, a kitchen, and two toilets. As Sobczak stubbornly wanted to have the larger room with a view over a small park, I finally took the small and dark room. It only had a very small window under the roof from which it was not possible to see anything outside. Everyday we were given one Chinese dollar for food that was brought by a young Chinese boy. We were the only Europeans—a German and a Pole—who were in this prison. In spite of all the negotiations undertaken by the German Ambassador, we were not allowed out of prison.

In the winter of 1917–18 I suffered from the cold as both my ears froze and then burst open. In this small dark room I typed out my two-thousand-page draft of the German translation of the *Aṅguttara Nikāya* on the Embassy's typewriter.[121] The duplicate I made on yellow toilet paper.

I was often visited by three Germans, with whom I rehearsed songs for choirs of four voices. In this same place I also composed and rehearsed Goethe's *"Wanderer's Nachtlied"* for a choir of four voices. These compositions of mine, together with three songs from my time in Paris, were later published in Tōkyō. Even on the night before we were to be repatriated to Germany, we sang together a song called *"Es ist bestimmt in Gottes Rat,"*[122] while standing on the flat roof of our building. Our song could be heard all over the German settlement and made many extremely sad; especially those who had to leave their wives and children behind—only women married according to the European custom and legal children had been allowed to travel along.

Before the repatriation, I had an attack of smallpox and had to be taken to the hospital on a stretcher. I was accommodated there in an isolated building. My body was covered all over, front and back, with small black pox that looked like black pearls or small grapes. I could not close my hands anymore, as between the fingers there were too many of these pustules. I made a complete recovery after about fourteen days without having had any real suffering or having to take any kind of medicine. I was on very friendly terms with the military police who were guarding me and who spoke some German. When I went out for the first time unescorted, I felt nervous, as there was nobody following or watching over me; however, at that point the guard in front of the door turned his back towards me while saying very quietly: "Go, go, I not see!"

The owner of the hotel on the opposite side of the road, whose two sons I was teaching, invited me to live in his hotel. I went over there directly without the Chief of the Police ever knowing about it. I even took the bed belonging to the police over to the hotel and gave it to my young Chinese servant to sleep on. His only job now was to clean my room. Henceforth I was able to visit the Chinese theatre and bathe in the public bath. I also sent a letter from Hankow to Prince Damrong[123] in Thailand, the most important of the Thai ministers, asking him to allow me to come to Thailand.

Chapter 12: In Germany Again, 1919–1920

In the autumn of 1918 the cease-fire agreement with Germany was put in effect, followed by the Peace Treaty of Versailles, which eventually led to the even worse World War II. In February or March 1919 all Germans living in China were robbed of their possessions and forcefully transported back to Germany. I don't remember anything of the journey besides the mutiny that nearly broke out on our ship in the harbour of Singapore. The prisoners wanted to force the captain to continue because there was an unbelievable heat aboard the ship. There was not the slightest breeze of wind. The intelligent English captain, however, gave a speech and said in a friendly way that he would do anything that was within his power.

It was 49°C in the narrow dining hall and some Germans succumbed to heatstroke. The other passengers, who were almost naked during our eight-day stop, endured the heat by putting moist towels on the head even during meals. Big kettles with tea were prepared, and although I normally don't drink tea, I then drank about twenty big cups a day to protect myself against the heat.

I met an interesting personality aboard. He was an elderly gentleman with a mighty beard–Reichsgraf von Pappenheim,[124] who was suspected of being complicit in the murder of King Ludwig II of Bayern. He had been banished from Germany, but now finally had the opportunity to return. Both of us had made our beds under the loading cranes.

In Europe we stopped over in Gibraltar and Dover, where we stayed outside the harbour, and continued the next morning to our destination, Rotterdam. After arrival in Rotterdam, we were brought to a large warehouse, where we were treated with bean soup and other foods. I was almost moved to tears by the very warm reception and the generosity of the Dutch government as well as the people, who gave us chocolate, cigarettes, etc. They gave us pamphlets that stated that we, the Germans who had returned from afar, were welcome and were wished a happy journey to our troubled home country.

Until the German boarder station Wesel, we were greeted at every station with speeches and were again and again treated with chocolates and cigarettes, etc. In Wesel we were housed in the lodging for repatriates. As I suspected that my mother was no longer alive, I sent my brother a letter to Hamburg, without further address, with the request to inform me how our mother was doing. Since I did not get a reply from Hamburg, I decided not to wait any longer and went to Hamburg by way of Bremen. In Hamburg I stayed for some days in the lodging for repatriates, from where I searched for my brother. Finally, I learnt in a police office that my brother, the lawyer, was registered to live at a certain address. I immediately went there, but found a strange name on the address board. Nevertheless, I rang and asked the young man who opened the door whether the lawyer Gueth was living here. He said yes, but immediately continued by saying that he was out. When I said that I would wait for him here, he said that he was not sure when he would come back. However, when I said that I was his brother who had returned, he quickly explained the whole situation.

My brother had shirked military service. He had taken, against payment of course, the address of the house of an acquainted waiter working at a café near the railway station as a cover address. His real address, however, was in the nearby area of Blankenese, which belonged to Prussia. In the Free State of Hamburg it was quite easy for him to remain undiscovered. While the waiter was bringing me to the tram station for Blankenese I found out from him that my beloved mother had died in 1918. This touched me deeply, though I was able to control myself.

At first, when I entered my brother's beautiful villa in the Goethestrasse, I did not know the lady who welcomed me, but soon after I found out she was my brother's wife. That very day my brother was on business in Helgoland. He was working as a salesman for an insurance company and often had to undertake short or long journeys. I stayed with him for about one month. As I was receiving unemployment benefits, I had to go to Hamburg nearly every day to report in (to the unemployment agency). Because of the Communist uprising it was sometimes quite dangerous to be out on the road. At times bullets were whistling past my ears, and I had to flee into the houses in order to avoid being hit. One day, even the city of Hamburg fell into the hands of the Communists.[125]

Dr Grimm sent me all the books written by him, trying to win me over to his pseudo-Buddhism.[126] He invited me to stay at his villa in the forest at Neubiberg, near Munich, but all his efforts were in vain. However, I also received an invitation by the wealthy Else Buchholz[127] to stay in her beautiful forest hut on the Bergstrasse near Oberhambach, opposite the famous Free-German School founded by the Dr Geheeb.[128] As I had a repatriation pass which allowed me free railway travel, food and accommodation throughout Germany, I immediately accepted the invitation and went down to Oberhambach. On the way in Frankfurt I visited a friend from former times, Captain Viktor Henn, whom I had not seen for about twenty years. In the past I had sent him many letters, in which I always spoke about morality. He had kept them all.

The next day I continued my journey to Oberhambach. Although the city population suffered hunger after the war, here in the countryside it was possible to get milk, butter, cheese, bread, and oat porridge every day. In the forest close to the forest hut, with Vappo who had come to join me, I found many raspberries, mushrooms, and so on. We owed all this to the friendliness and support of Else Buchholz, who later became the nun Uppalavaṇṇā. Also, my later stay near the Harz, my one month's stay in Berlin, and my stay in the Black Forest were all due to the kindness of Miss Buchholz. Without her help, we would have had a very difficult time in Germany.

During my time in Berlin I visited my brother, who was doing some business there. When we were near the Anhalter railway station, we saw about twenty-five thousand Communists going through the town with banners approaching the seat of the government, the Reichstag. This was not a good sign as we had to go past the Reichstag to get to the station of Lehrter Bahnhof. From a distance we could see masses of people, so we decided to take another road in order to avoid any risk. Soon afterwards, thousands of people came running towards us from behind, shouting loudly in fear. We could hear the sound of shooting and exploding hand-grenades following them. Even now I can remember quite vividly how my brother, all white with fear of death and holding his small suitcase under his arm, ran as fast as he could. In the end, there were about one hundred and fourteen deaths on that day and many people were caught up in barbed wire.[129]

In Berlin my publisher gave me two boxes with copies of the first volume of my translation of the *Milindapañhā* (*The Questions of King Milinda*). In the city library I worked almost every day from morning till evening on the second volume of my translation of the *Milindapañhā*. I had at my disposal the Sanskrit dictionary by Böthling and Roth in seven volumes, as well as the Sinhalese translation by Hīnatikumbara Sumaṅgala. With the help of the library catalogue, I found out that all of my writings, even the smallest one, were present in the government library. After a month, we returned south. From Frankfurt I went to Wiesbaden to see my sister, and then I followed Uppalavaṇṇā to Oberhambach. That was in January 1920.

In Wiesbaden I was visited by my friend, Oskar Schloss, the publisher from Munich.[130] He invited me to stay for some days with him in Neubiberg before undertaking the journey to India that we had planned together with Uppalavaṇṇā. Neubiberg is in the Black Forest region. We arrived in Munich at midnight, while everything was in deep snow. At the railway station, I was picked up by the actor Zichtig and his wife and brought to the Hotel Fürstenhof. By mistake I was given a very small room with a toilet only. Next day, Schloss came and we went to his beautiful villa situated in a forest park at the Schopenhauerstrasse in Neubiberg. The opposite villa belonged to the famous indologist Dr Geiger.[131] The next villa was Dr Grimm's but, due to certain reasons, the connecting door between the gardens of Dr Grimm and Schloss had been blocked by Schloss.

After about fifteen days, Vappo and Uppalavaṇṇā arrived. Everything was ready for departure now.

Chapter 13: To Japan, 1920

We travelled by train to Trieste in order to board a ship bound for Singapore, taking only our smaller luggage. Going by fourth class without a bed until Singapore, would cost us twenty-eight thousand German marks. This was because of the shortage of ships and the devaluation of the mark. Later on, the German mark was devalued to such an extent that a piece of bread would cost forty-five million marks! This devaluation made an end to Uppalavaṇṇā's wealth.

From Singapore we planned to go to Java, where we intended to stay in case we were not allowed to proceed to Ceylon. Due to the recent war conditions almost the entire railway system had been suspended and the rest had gone haywire. On the first day we only reached Salzburg, the place where Mozart was born, and there we stayed in a hotel on the bank of the Inn River. The following day we managed to get to

Villach, the birthplace of the great Dr Paracelsus, where we stayed in a hotel close to a statue of him standing in the middle of the street.

The following day, at the railway station, a fight broke out between German passengers and Italian officials who were unfriendly and hostile towards Germans and Austrians. I dropped the word *idioti* and was almost beaten up by furious policemen.

On arrival in Trieste, as the ship was about eight days late, we lived in a simple guesthouse with a German-speaking host. When we had boarded the ship and looked around in steerage we noticed far down below a seemingly poor, but actually very rich, little old lady sitting on her suitcase. It was Mrs Grauert, who was returning to Japan, where she had many possessions, which the Japanese government had apparently confiscated.

On board the ship there was no order and obedience because the crew were communists. They even refused to give us plates, spoons or forks. I took it upon myself to complain in the name of the German passengers at the office of the shipping company and was promised that they would try their best to make the crew obey orders.

On arrival in Colombo, I was given a letter by Dr Cassius Pereira (the later Bhikkhu Kassapa). He wrote saying that he had not been able to convince the British Governor, W.H. Mannis,[132] to give us permission to land. That was on Vesak 1920, the birthday of Lord Buddha. Then our friend Arthur de Soysa came, the brother of my supporter Roberto de Soysa from Balapitiya, who was to later become a member of parliament. I gave him twenty-five copies of the first volume of my translation of the *Milindapañhā*, to be distributed to all those who had financed its printing, like F. R. Senanayake (brother of the later Prime Minister), Minister for Health A. E. de Silva, Dr Hewavitarne, and others. As soon as he left, my dear student Ñāṇāloka came to visit. It was he, as a boy of fourteen, who had come with me to Sikkim in the Himalaya and had become a novice on my return to Ceylon. I could still not mention anything about his caste for the time being.

Upon our arrival in Singapore we were not allowed to disembark, even though we had paid a hundred German marks for a transit visa. We were not even allowed to go by boat directly, without going on land, to a Dutch ship bound for Java. I appealed to the Head of the Police and to the American Ambassador, who was representing German interests, but it was all in vain. So we decided, like it or not, to continue our journey to Shanghai and from there, after having obtained a visa, to continue on to Yokohama in Japan.

Japan, 1920–1921

In the end it turned out to be a great piece of fortune for us that everything went this way. All this time I had had a presentiment that we should go to Japan. For years I had thought and dreamt of teaching at a university in Japan. From a Japanese priest in Honolulu in December 1916, I had already received the address of the famous Japanese monk, Professor Watanabe,[133] who had studied in Strassburg under the indologist Professor Leuman.[134] I had wanted to go to Japan in 1916 and stay there during the war, but at the time had not been permitted to do so.

The address was for a Gymnasium high school near Shiba Park in Tōkyō. There we met Dr Watanabe. He greeted us stuttering in German and was highly interested in our case. He generously offered to pay for all our hotel expenses because, due to the inflation of the German Mark, our money was insufficient. He also invited us to stay at his Temple until he could find suitable teaching employment for all three of us.

In this way Uppalavaṇṇā was the first to find employment as an English teacher in a girls' school in Denzuin in the centre of Tōkyō. Vappo had to teach conversational German in a nationalist school outside of Tōkyō, and for me the position of lecturer in Pali at Taisho University had been organised. At first our income was rather nominal, but as I had free food and lodging and was paid for Buddhist lectures at Keio University, at the Imperial University, at Nichiren College, as well as other places, I could get by for some months. I also found some private students for English and German tutoring. During the first six months of my stay in Japan I lived completely amongst the Japanese and almost never saw other Europeans. I was invited to school festivals and other occasions and therefore had a wonderful opportunity to come to know the best side of the Japanese people.

At the beginning of winter in 1920–it was already beginning to get fairly cold and deep snow was covering the roads of Tōkyō–I made my first attempt to get permission to enter Siam (present-day Thailand). I visited the Siamese Ambassador and also the recently arrived German Ambassador, Dr Solf,[135] who was the former governor of Samoa and later the secretary of state. Solf had refused to sign the shameful peace treaty in Versailles. Through this first contact we became friends and he often invited me over to lunch. He also invited me to give a lecture on Buddhism at the German Asiatic Society.[136]

I would have really loved to have stayed in a Japanese monastery, but this was impossible for any long period of time. The food given in the monasteries there is also rather insufficient, often only polished rice without any vitamins and two small pieces of pickled radish. In addition, almost all the monks of the about fifty-two sects of the Mahayana tradition in Japan are married. All of them openly drink rice-wine and do not see anything bad in killing animals, etc. In brief, their lifestyle has nothing in common with original teachings of the Buddha, either theoretically or practically, because in the Buddha's original teachings, morality is the very foundation. Here, I do have to say, though, that the Japanese, in spite of all this, are unsurpassed by any other people in their many noble human and social characteristics and virtues.

Both Dr Solf and the Siamese Ambassador gave me a pass and visa, respectively and free of charge, to visit Siam. When I asked the latter whether there would be any problem in going to Siam, he told me not to worry at all as no one would create any kind of difficulty for a Buddhist monk who wanted to enter the country. On the day of our departure, Vappo and I were accompanied to the railway station by Dr Watanabe and his student Sato.[137] They came along until the port of Kobe where we were to board the ship. At the railway station there were also the students and professors from the Taisho and Kumazawa universities, with Professor Yamakami leading them. As the train was about to depart, three times they shouted, *"Banzai, Banzai Ñāṇatiloka!"* Moved to tears, I left the enthusiastic crowd behind me.

After travelling for about 12 hours, we reached Kyōto station in the early morning. First, we went to the main monastery of the Jōdo Sect, where Dr Watanabe introduced us to the Patriarch of the sect, and on our departure, we were both given souvenirs and presents. We went on to a girls' high school, which was under the guidance of a Jōdo monk, where I gave a talk to the students, which was translated into Japanese by Dr Watanabe. From there we went by train via Osaka to Kobe, where after much searching, we finally found our luggage, which had been sent ahead from Tōkyō.

Chapter 14: To Bangkok via Java, 1921

We had a third class ticket for a ship to Batavia (the capital of the Dutch East Indies, now called Jakarta), from where we planned to continue with another ship to Bangkok. Our journey took us via Formosa (now Taiwan) and Manila, in the Philippines, but we were not allowed to leave the ship. As Germans, we were not allowed to enter Formosa for political reasons, whereas in Manila we were not allowed to disembark because there was cholera. Until Formosa, we were the only two people in steerage, while the first and second class passengers had little room and they started to envy us. After Formosa, however, steerage was almost filled with Chinese families who were going to Java; all of them busy learning the Malayan language.

The New Year celebrations of 1921 began before we landed in Java, so that almost all the Japanese, the crew and passengers were drunk from drinking the Japanese rice wine called sake. The crew was playing with the officers who were also drunk; they threw them up into the air and caught them again. They tried to get us to participate in such doubtful enjoyment, but fortunately we were able to avoid that.

On landing in the port of Batavia[138], we did not have to hand over a deposit of twenty-five guilders, as was usually required by those entering the country, because we were going to leave Java within a fortnight. The ship for Bangkok was already in harbour, but the passengers were only allowed to board it in Surabaya in fourteen days time—and then only the first class passengers. Because of our yellow robes, it was extremely difficult to find a hotel in Batavia that would accept us.

In the evening of the first day, a young Sinhalese by the name of Silva spoke with us and under his guidance we visited the Theosophical Lodge. There I was told that they had a Sanskrit scholar, Professor Labberton, who would have been very happy to meet me, however at that time he was not in Batavia. (I was to meet him later on in Tōkyō.) At the Theosophical Lodge, I was given the address of Dr Fitz, whom I had accepted in 1913 under the name of Bhikkhu Soṇo. He was now working as a librarian and living in Samarang (town). As we had to go via Samarang anyway, I decided to visit him and stayed two or three days with him.

As far as language was concerned, we Germans had no difficulty at all. We just spoke German and were given answers in Dutch. So we left Batavia at six in the morning on the third day after our arrival. On the train, we met a very friendly eighteen-year-old Javanese, who was going to be married that day. He offered us completely unknown, but excellent, fruits.

In the evening, we arrived in Samarang. At the railway station we met a compassionate Dutchman who was kind enough to take us, with our entire luggage, in his nice horse-cart to the house of Dr Fitz, which was rather far off. When Dr Fitz, who must have gotten a telegram from Batavia, saw us from his bungalow, he came running down the road and made a very respectful salutation, by kneeling down in the traditional Buddhist way. After a short stay, Dr Fitz took us to a Chinese hotel, which unfortunately did not appear very inviting. This impression worsened when we saw somebody lying down sick with malaria beside the stairs leading to our miserable little room filled with mosquitoes. Dr Fitz also took us to a Chinese restaurant where we could eat our fill.

It must have been on the second or third day towards evening that Dr Fitz took us with his car to friends of his who were staying in a bungalow on a mountain outside of town. There we were given the address of a Theosophical family, who had been given notice by telegram of our pending arrival in Surabaya. On the day of our departure to Surabaya, at about 5.30 in the morning, a lady from the bungalow took us, driving in her own car, to the railway station. On arrival in Surabaya in the evening, we were greeted by a teacher who took us with his small horse carriage to his house and received us in a very friendly manner. We stayed with him until our departure for Bangkok.

When we finally boarded the ship, we were the only passengers. As we were first class passengers, we took our meals with the officers and the captain. On arrival in Singapore, a high-ranking police officer and detective introduced himself to us. He had been given the duty of observing us, but at the same time he talked rather negatively about the British. He told me that he regretted that all other ships could proudly carry the flag of their own country, but India was still not allowed to do that.

Both Vappo and I were feeling somewhat depressed as we were uncertain about our future, and we were also having frequent minor fever attacks, which was not a good sign for us.

Bangkok, February 1921

On the evening of the third or fourth day, we arrived in Bangkok. For the time being we left our luggage on board and went to a small temple, where we slept on the polished teak wood in front of the Buddha statue. The next morning, we went to the house of the prince and former minister, Prisdang Jumsai.[139] On our way we passed a Jesuit College where we met a Jesuit priest who gave us the exact address of the Prince. On this occasion I also met the ministerial instructor, Mr Gilles from England, who had taken the Siamese name of Indra Montri. In 1926 and 1927 he interceded on my behalf with the King so that I was given the entire Pali Tipiṭaka in Siamese script. Even when he was eighty years old and was almost completely blind, he still wanted to become a monk and learn Pali under my guidance.

While we were talking with Prince Prisdang, with whom I had lived in 1906 in Ceylon on the small island of Culla-Laṅkā near Mātara, some high police officers entered and volunteered to accompany us to the local government office in order to check our identity. (I should mention here that during the First World War, Prince Prisdang had been arrested and his possessions had been confiscated because he had published an anti-government newspaper called The Truth.) So we went to the police station, where we had to wait for some time and could look at the cages containing tied up prisoners that had been put there. Then, on our way to the local government office we came across a rather large monastery where we asked for permission to stay but were not allowed to do so—obviously out of fear for the government and the malevolent monk, Vajirañāṇa, who was hitting monks with a stick.[140] He was the brother of King Chulalongkorn and the so-called "Ruler of the Saṅgha" (*saṅgharāja*) and the "Great Ascetic" (*mahāsamaṇa*).

We continued by car to the local government office where, I must admit with shame, we were treated like two spies. I protested strongly against this accusation and explained it as vile slander and lies. In spite of our passes, which had been given to us by both the German and the Siamese embassies, we were arrested and put into a small bungalow used as a prison at the police training school. In one room of the bungalow an officer was keeping a record of everything we were doing day and night, whether it was eating, drinking, bathing, what time we went to sleep, or the times we used the toilet.

A young "one year" military doctor[141] secretly translated some pages of these notes for us. He was making fun of it all and told us many stories about his unjust and mad king.[142]

In the evening of this unfortunate and extraordinarily hot day, Vappo and I felt exhausted and we were afflicted by fever. Our pulse was heavy and fast and the veins at the side of my head were very swollen. Without delay, we informed the young military doctor who determined that we had malaria.

We must have caught this on an evening in the garden at the bungalow in Surabaya where I had seen big swarms of mosquitoes. The next day an American doctor who was working at the hospital came and gave immediate orders to bring us to the hospital. The young Siamese doctor agreed but on the following day he changed his mind and agreed with our wish to stay at the prison, because the hospital was particularly dirty and was situated in the middle of the dirty, noisy town.

I appealed to the Dutch envoy,[143] who represented the German interests, but he gave me a rather impudent answer. With the help of the Minister of Forestry ("*araññarakkhu*") who was of Burmese descent and was friendly and well disposed to us, I wrote a request to the King to be freed from prison. I also wrote to the so-called "Patriarch," the aforementioned brother of the former King Chulalongkorn, but he sent me a very venomous reply, something that did not really seem to be proper for a Buddhist, especially for a Mahāthera. He showed little compassion for our suffering.

The Chief of Police was very different, however; he offered us an excellent meal and would kneel on the floor while having a conversation with me. The Burmese Forestry Minister was also very respectful, but soon after he was no longer allowed to come and visit me. Our condition was getting worse by the day—Vappo was having high fevers, while I had strong shivering attacks which made me toss about the entire night, alternating with bouts of vomiting. We were fortunate in that we had tertian malaria fever (that is, occurring every other day), which one of us had one day, and the other the next; thereby one of us could look after the other one. My fever reached its peak on 18 February, and I expected that my forty-third birthday, on 19 February, would also be the day of my death.

In March we were deported with an armed escort. We were taken to a boat, which was to take us to the nearest Chinese port called Swatow. There, we were to be left to our own fate. Until the last Siamese port, we were guarded by about ten men, day and night. On the day of our departure, the officers and the crew assembled at the front of the door of our cabin and all of them went down on their knees and made a Buddhist prostration.

After arriving in the Chinese port of Swatow, I left the sick Vappo with the luggage on board and went to the Japanese Ambassador in order to get visas. After a short while at the office of the Japanese Embassy, I had another strong attack of the shivers and had to ask the Ambassador for some vinegar or lemon water and a place to lie down. After about half an hour, I departed with the visa and took the sick Vappo, together with our luggage, off the ship.

We went to the ship office in order to obtain tickets for Shanghai but were coolly refused by an Englishman who told us that we, as Germans, were not allowed to buy tickets. All appeals I made were of no avail. After that a very sympathetic Chinese clerk approached us and told us that he would try to help us to get tickets to Shanghai, and in fact he managed to do so. Our saviour was a very devout Mahāyāna Buddhist who, if I remember rightly, also arranged a lunch for us at the office. There, Vappo had a strong attack of the shivers that forced him to lie down on an improvised bed on the floor. After we rested for about an hour, we left the office and went with our luggage to the ship where we were told to go to the hold where we had to find a place among the badly smelling coolies. It was fortunate that we still had our foldable beds, so that we did not come into direct contact with them. Here, too, we continued to have regular attacks of the shivers. The next day the English captain, who must have heard about our misery, came to the hatch and looked down into the deep hold. He was moved by compassion, called us to come up the ladder, and then provided us with a cabin in first class.

After our arrival in Shanghai, the German Ambassador had us taken to a refugee house, as we still had not recovered from the malaria and the attacks of the shivers. Before our return to Japan, the German Ambassador in Shanghai gave me a huge document in a giant envelope, which I was to keep hidden deep in my suitcase. This was the new trade agreement between China and Germany, which had not been made public yet. I was requested to give it to the German envoy in Japan, Dr Solf.

Chapter 15: Back in Japan, 1921–1923

On our arrival in Japan, we were welcomed by Miss Buchholz and by Sato, the student of Dr Watanabe. At the medical checkpoint I had another attack of the shivers and I feared that the doctor would not allow me to disembark. When he questioned me, I told him that this was only a small recurrence of the malaria I had earlier, even though I was shivering over my whole body. That was in April or May of 1921.

Dr Watanabe supported us again in a really selfless manner. He paid for us to go to Iisaka, accompanied by Sato, where we could get a radium water cure to completely recover from our ailments, for Vappo and I looked like real skeletons. We were also helped by Professor Ekai Kawaguchi, who had become famous due to his interesting book, *Three Years in Tibet*.[144] He was working at Taisho University in Sugamo. He further helped to get us a special iron tonic from the Imperial University. It was made by the electronic breakdown of iron and was not yet available to the public. With Prof. Kawaguchi, who looked very dignified with his long beard, Vappo and I had visited the only two Japanese Theravādan monks in their small monasteries during our first stay in Japan. At that time I had been able to converse in Pali with both of them without any problem. They had received their acceptance at the Simbili Āvāsa near Galle in Ceylon. Their main supporter was the Pali scholar Mudaliyar Edmund Gunaratana, to whom one of the Japanese monks owed his name, and who was also a friend of mine. We would have loved to stay in one of these two small Theravāda monasteries, but unfortunately this was not possible.

From April 1921 until May 1926, during my second stay in Tōkyō, I taught Pali and German again at Taisho University. At Meiji College and the Medical College in Shiba, I taught German and Latin, and, above all, I taught Pali at Kumazawa University. In addition, I taught at the Military Academy and had a position as stand-in at the Government College for Foreign Languages. At the Military Academy, Prince Yamashina[145] was among my students. He had his villa in the park of the academy. My income was rather poor in the beginning, but due to these jobs it went up to twelve hundred gold marks per month. However, even if it had been hundreds of thousands, I would have given it all away there and then if I had been allowed to live in Laṅkā[146] again.

Besides my teaching work, I used every free hour for my real Buddhist task. At this time I worked on the Pali anthology with an accompanying dictionary, and I also finished the second volume of the *Milindapañhā,* as well as the last books of the *Aṅguttara Nikāya.*

I also took on a small job for the Manchurian Railway Company. I did an English translation of a German technical scientific work on the utilization of slate for which I received about eight hundred gold marks.

Again and again I tried to get permission to return to Ceylon. Dr Solf was also trying his best to help, together with his friend Eliot,[147] the British Ambassador, who again and again sent telegrams to the Governor of Ceylon. But only after some years would I be allowed to see my beloved Laṅkā again. I felt that nowhere else in the world would I want to be at home for a longer time. During my last stay in Germany, I felt homesick for Laṅkā all the time. At a moment's notice I would have been ready to leave Japan and immediately return to Laṅkā. I felt that I didn't belong in Japan. To my students I often indicated that, although I had to play the teacher here, in my innermost being I was aspiring for quite different ideals.

Among the many Japanese and Europeans who became my closer friends during that time, I would like to mention Professor Watanabe and his student Sato; Professor Tachibana,[148] the later Director of Kumazawa University; Petzold,[149] of the Royal High School, and his wife, a famous singer and piano-player in Japan; Schneider from Fiji; Prof. Saito of the Medical College in Seoul; Prof. Entai Tomomatou and Dr Matsumoto,[150] my former Pali student in Japan and Ceylon; Prof. Okubo Koji of the Kumazawa University; Prof. Heiss of the Nobles' College; Prof. Jiriyo Masuda; Prof. Ekai Kawaguchi; Professor Takakusu,[151] the above mentioned Tibet scholar; Major Prof. Tomita, my former student at the Foreign Languages College; Prof. Dr. M.D. Suguhara of the Imperial University, my former student and boarder; etc., etc.

At the house of the Solfs, I met Mrs Shimitsu, the famous violinist and student of Professor Joachim, and also the philosopher Professor Driesch[152] and his wife, and also the law philosopher, Professor Sternberg from the Imperial University. I further became acquainted with Rasbihar Bose,[153] the liberation fighter who had tried an attempt on the life of the Governor of Bengal and who during the Second World War would play a political role in Burma. In addition, I met the somewhat visionary love and peace apostle Raja Mahendra Pratap[154]. During the First World War, he supposedly conducted negotiations with Khemal Pasha and the German Emperor.

I might also mention that I was invited to a garden party by the Japanese Empress, but as a monk I did not accept the invitation. My best friend was Kenkichi Okiyama, who was my translator and who followed me wherever I went. I took care of his education and later on he followed me to Ceylon.

The houses I inhabited in Tōkyō were the following: a small Japanese villa near Kumazawa University, a two-storey stone villa in Sugamo, a knight's mansion on Heavenly Mountain near Omori, and a two-storey villa with a vegetable and flower garden.

In 1922, Vappo returned to Germany in order to get thoroughly cured of his malaria. I invited him, when he felt better, to rejoin me in Japan. At this time I was staying in a manor house with a tea plantation and a bamboo grove on Heavenly Mountain near Omori. I had been allowed to stay there for free, the reason being that astrologers had made a prophecy to the owner of the house, who also owned another forty buildings in Tōkyō. The prophecy was that if he were to live in this house, the entire family would suffer illness, despair and destruction. However, I immediately accepted the offer to stay in the knight's manor house. In the end, events turned out to be quite different than predicted, because this very house was the only one of the owner's forty-one houses that escaped the devastation of the (coming) earthquake.

Vappo returned to join me in 1923. I went to pick him up in Yokohama during heavy snow fall. However, the nice life in the manor house was to last only six months. Then the earthquake took place—the most terrible earthquake known in history.[155] In a single day thousands of people died in the most terrible manner.

The Great Earthquake, September 1923

The earthquakes began on 1 September 1923. Two minutes before twelve midday, just as Vappo and I were swallowing the last of our lunch, the most terrifying thing started to take place—accompanied by a mighty roaring noise, the earth started to shake under our feet. It was as if we were rolling in a small boat out on a stormy sea, being thrown forwards and backwards, up and down, again and again. Vappo was excitedly running back and forth with some tofu still on his plate, so I shouted to him to sit down quietly on the ground and to be prepared for the worst. I started to recite in Pali the well-known passage:

> "Whatever there is in this world: body, feelings, perceptions, formations, consciousness, past, present, future, internal or external, gross or fine, inferior or superior, far or near, of all these things, the monk of right understanding knows: 'It is not mine, it is not me, it is not myself.'
>
> "All formations are impermanent, all formations are suffering. Everything is empty, without a soul, impersonal, without essence, etc."

Every second I expected the earth to simply open up and swallow us—something that indeed did happen in many parts of the province. If I am not mistaken, on that first afternoon there were about hundred and fifty long and short earthquakes. "Vappo," I said, "Now, Tōkyō is done for!"—and that is how it was within a few hours. It was as if we were in the midst of a world war, or as if a huge volcano had opened up in the centre of Tōkyō. At any moment we expected our house to collapse, as happened with all the other houses in the villages and cities around, but our house braved all the assaults of the earthquakes. That was because it had been built on a solid rock bottom.

The earth thundered and boomed throughout with continuous crashing of inhabited houses. It shook mightily, accompanied by explosions of oil tanks, gunpowder factories, ammunition depots, and the like. This continued on and on until late that night. In between each earthquake, we went inside very quickly to get chairs, tables, mattresses, blankets and books. We brought these things out into the open, where we made ourselves at home between two trees; Vappo under one tree and I and my friend under another. Suddenly, there was a sound like loud thunder coming from the entrance door. The door, over three meters in breadth and completely covered with copper plate, was hurled onto the ground despite its one-foot-high hinges. We had never opened it throughout the whole year because we were using the smaller entrance called the "eye of the needle."

At about nine o'clock in the evening, we came out of the garden. The sight we had from our Heavenly Mountain was overwhelming: the night was brightly illuminated and the sky was blood-red! We could see terrible fires spreading ashes all over the entire province, including Tōkyō, a city with six million inhabitants, with all its palaces and modern buildings. The light from these fires could be seen throughout Japan, even in the North.

Earth tremors continued throughout the whole night and for several days afterwards.[156]

The next day volunteer police had already been organized everywhere; they patrolled all the gardens and inhabited places three times a night. They were armed with lanterns and swords or whatever they could still find as a weapon. We were asked to participate, but we refused. We were also told that no food was to be sold. Food and also candles and clothes were to be given out by the government free of charge; the Emperor and the Prince would get exactly the same as anyone else.

During 2 September, the second day of the earthquakes, we suddenly heard trumpets and gongs. We looked down into the valley and saw a group of men with their belongings and with swords in their hands, and also bamboo spears and other weapons. They were going very fast in the direction of Tōkyō. Immediately, we hastened down the mountain and joined these people, as we thought that everyone was going to be delivered from the earthquake zone. Then, suddenly, a thunder crashed, which made the whole earth shake, obviously caused by one of the many explosions. Only then did we learn what was going on: these people wanted to escape from several thousand Koreans who were supposedly plundering all the houses in Ikegami, burning them, and raping the Japanese women. I considered this to be mass hysteria and wanted to turn back immediately. At this moment a German came hurrying towards me out of a solidly built little house and offered me a gun for my own protection. However, I resolutely refused it. In front of the entrance to our garden there were about thirty Japanese from Ikegami, whom, upon their begging, I allowed to stay overnight in the bamboo grove.

Towards the evening, we lay down on our improvised sleeping places under the two trees. Vappo and my friend soon fell asleep, but I stayed awake. I had asked the other two to be ready to run out of the mango grove in the dark of the night and hide downhill if I gave them a sign. Already, at the beginning of the night, I had heard some shots behind and in front of the garden. After some time, however, there were shrill gong and trumpet signals followed by shrill shouting and the wild screams of agony of half-mad people turning against each other with spears. This continued throughout the night and until the early morning, alternating with crying, trumpet blasts, and rapid gunfire. I cannot recall anymore the number of people who died.

It must have been on the third day of the earthquake when, possibly together with Vappo, I went partly on foot and partly in a very primitive hired car to the centre of Tōkyō. How different it looked compared to before! One could not imagine traffic with steam and electric trains, or trams. Everything was completely destroyed between Tōkyō and Yokohama, even the electric lights and the water supply system. Of the many railway stations, there was only one left intact: the huge Central Station of Tōkyō. All its rail lines, waiting rooms, corridors, and platforms were filled with the victims of the earthquake. Everywhere, above and across, clotheslines were hanging, laden with washed clothing, and on the railway lines, people were cooking food. They were sleeping here and there, with and without mats, as it was the hot season in Japan. Going towards Yokohama, one could see thousands and thousands of burnt-out skeletons of railway carriages. Some of them were still standing; some of them had rolled off the rails. As far as one could see, all the beautiful buildings, the palaces, the banks and the Royal Theatre, and so on, were not to be seen anymore. Where was Tōkyō? Tōkyō had vanished and only a wasteland of ashes and debris were left.

It must have been about the eighth day of the earthquake that I was able to go, with many interruptions, and partly by walking, to Yokohama. Here and there, the city was still burning. That everything had caught fire so quickly becomes clear when one considers the fact the earthquake had started at the hour when people were cooking their food on their coal ovens. While most of the houses in Tōkyō were mainly destroyed through the fire, the houses in Yokohama were destroyed after the first earthquake and the fire had then finished them off completely. The reason for this was that the centre of the earthquake was the volcanic island of Oshima, close to Yokohama. With the exception of just two houses what had been Yokohama everything had been completely annihilated. The earthquake had been so sudden that several hundred people, trying to run out of a bank, died miserably when the huge staircase collapsed. Others had fallen into fissures in the earth that had opened up in front of their feet.

It would be going too far to relate here all of the details of the mad, atrocious and gruesome acts of felony which were partly carried out even by policemen in the name of misguided patriotism, and partly by many of the robbers, murderers, and sadists that had joined the so-called police-troops.

I can retell many more terrible and touching episodes in connection with this earthquake. One of the most gruesome events might well be the death by fire of thirty-five thousand people, of which a secretly made picture had been sent by me from the Buddhist journal *Der Pfad* with the caption "*ecce vita*" ("behold life").[157] It happened not too far away from the left shore of the Sumida River on an open field that seemed to be the safest place to escape from the fire. On being advised by the Police Prefect of the district, about thirty-five thousand people went there with their belongings. However, the radiant heat of the sea of flames surrounding these people became more and more unbearable and there was no way out, so all these pitiful people, lying across each other, came to a dreadful end.[158] After some days I visited the square where the thirty-five thousand people were now stacked in the form of twelve mountains of bones. No 'I,' no 'you,' 'no man,' 'no being' was there, only bare bones. I don't know whether the plan to create a giant Buddha image out of these bones has ever been realized.

Another, no less tragic, mass death happened in the public pleasure park in Asakusa where almost all the theatres, cinemas, and the like were situated. In the centre of this park a beautiful big pond had been created. Because of the constantly increasing intense heat caused by the burning entertainment palaces all around them, many people hurried to the pond in order to save their lives from the flames and to cool off. Nevertheless, as the radiant heat became more and more intense, all the people died a terrible death in the eventually boiling water.

The Sumida River flows right through Tōkyō. At other times it was a mighty river busy with ships and boats and spanned by many bridges. Now, however, due to the frequent explosions of petrol and gasoline tanks, the river was in flames together with all the boats and ships. Many people tried to use the burnt-out bridges to cross the river by making their way along the iron skeletons of these bridges with their hands, but all of them became too tired and exhausted due to the heat, and one after another they fell down into the burning river.

A certain port town, the name of which I do not remember, had been struck by a tsunami.[159] The entire land in and around the town was flooded and small ships had been carried by the waves into the centre of the flooded town. In some places along the coast the shore had sunk below sea level, while at other places the earth below the ocean had risen above sea level.

All the parks, even the Emperor's Park in front of the Emperor's Palace, were full of hapless people many of whom had lost everything they possessed, even their spouses and children, and were living in utmost misery. They were living in little huts, most of them as big as a dog kennel, which they had constructed out of old corrugated iron sheets lying around everywhere, using chunks of the destroyed water pipes as weight to keep the pieces of corrugated iron in place.

Everything was happening in the open air now. Even the Prince, who was in charge of the government in place of his mentally disturbed father, held a conference with his ministers in the open air. Also, an emergency newspaper, consisting of one page only, was more or less printed out in the open air. There were simply no buildings anymore.

In spite of all the terrible suffering caused by the earthquake, many people reacted to the conspicuous misery by doing good in a very selfless manner and were trying their best to help each other. Many times it happened that Koreans, who were otherwise the most bitter enemies of the Japanese, took small Japanese babies or children which they had found on the road and looked after them as if they were their own children, full of love and compassion. Even America, which just prior to the disaster had shown little compassion to Japan, was touched by the terrible conditions and sent many ships with food and clothing for the Japanese government to distribute among the needy.

Chapter 17: Last years in Japan, 1923–1926

It is astonishing to see the utmost self-control with which the Japanese person bears up with such strokes of destiny and is still able to smile. Even though the well-educated Japanese may reject all kinds of religion, it is a fact that his composure is due to the dormant Buddhism in him. It is also astonishing to see with how much energy and perseverance the Japanese rebuilt their cities. After only two months, teaching in universities, colleges, high schools and other schools resumed, though still partly out in the open and otherwise in the barracks.

It was fascinating for me to see the extreme interest the Japanese people showed for music—not only for their own, but also for Western music. Japan had readily produced a series of virtuoso musicians, also composers, even symphony composers like Kosaku and others. Once in the concert hall of the Music Academy, I heard a real Japanese harp orchestra. Another time, Beethoven's Ninth Symphony was played with a big orchestra and chorus, and I have to admit that it was nothing less than a first-class performance. I also met the music critic and actor I Ba Ko, who had brought Faust to Japan and had performed it himself. He recommended four of my compositions to the printer in Meguro for publishing.

As I had returned the manor house to its owner—it being the only one of his forty-one houses to survive the earthquake—I had to put up with a student apartment at Taisho University. From there I went with a friend[160] on a tour to the south sea island of Haha-shima (the "Mother Island"), one of the Ogasawara islands.[161] (In Chinese: "Bo-nin": "Islands devoid of people.") My friend had spent his childhood there and his brothers and other relatives, with whom we wished to stay for some time, were still living there. On the journey to and fro, the ship stopped at several other small islands. First we stayed overnight on Oshima Island, then we went on to Chichishima, the "Father Island," which was already part of the Ogasawara islands and had been a military stronghold for many years. Everywhere we encountered warning signs so that only a few places were accessible for us. On the main street of the town, I was addressed by a man walking barefoot who looked like a European beggar. He told me that he was the grandson of the American explorer Pearce, who had rediscovered these islands.

After about five days we reached Hahashima, the "Mother Island." My friend pointed out his brothers in one of the fishing boats that were swarming around our ship. Because of the high sea, it was very difficult and dangerous to jump down from the portholes on the side of the ship into their boats, which were bobbing up and down and being thrown against the ship again and again.

Both of us lived together with the whole family in a house consisting of a single large room. The next morning we visited a graveyard which was halfway up the mountain and decorated the grave of my friend's father, before hiking up a lonely forest path to the summit of the mountain. From the top of the grass-covered mountain which sloped steep down to the sea, we had an overwhelming view of the wide, blue sea.

The next day was New Year's Day, a day also celebrated by the Japanese, and we saw merry young women and men on the lawn of the village performing National Games. The male inhabitants of the island wear only one single piece of cloth, a sort of European shirt going down to the knees. Everyone goes barefoot, something that in the rest of Japan never happens. On the island, there were tropical plants such as bananas and custard apples. One can infer from such names as Tea Beach, Coffee Beach, and Cocoa Beach, that under the Americans there also must have been tea, coffee, and coconut plantations. Today the island is mainly covered with sugar plantations.

With an aching heart I have to confess that it is difficult for me to forget the terrible robber attack which almost cost Vappo his life during his stay in Kyoto. Vappo, after having climbed the holy mountain Hiye-San, came down very early in the morning. He was followed by a man who, on his way up through a narrow tunnel path, suddenly thrust a sword into Vappo's back in the direction of the heart. It made a twelve-centimeter deep wound. If Vappo had not suddenly looked around, the sword would have gone straight through his heart. Overcome by panic Vappo raced down the mountain. People finally saw him and took him by a police car to the hospital. Everybody treated and served him in a most loving and kind way. Everywhere prayers were being read for him. On the same night, I was visited by journalists who wanted me to give them details of his life, since they thought Vappo had been murdered. After some time they telephoned and revoked the report of Vappo's death. The next day, I went together with my friend to Kyoto to visit Vappo and I was allowed to be present during his operation.

My last stay was in a house provided to me by my friend, Professor Miyamori. It was in the secluded small suburban town, Okayama, where he was also living. The house could be reached from Meguro by tram and was a two-storey villa, partly built in the Japanese style and partly in the European style, having a vegetable and flower garden. I had to pay a hundred and thirty gold marks per month for it.

Towards the end of 1925 I was told by the British Ambassador, Sir Charles Elliot, that the new British Governor[162] of Ceylon had given permission for me to come back to Ceylon. I, however, stayed on in Japan until April 1926, as I did not want to break the contract I had with the Military Academy. I obtained a travel pass with visa for Ceylon and was now looking forward to finally returning to my beloved Laṅkā.

Though I had come to Japan as a stranded person, without means, and not known personally by anyone, I had soon made so many friends that my departure was celebrated by about fifteen departure meals given by professors and students of the different colleges and universities, and by the General and Director of the Military Academy, and so on. The most important meal for me was the vegetarian and non-alcoholic departure meal given by my real friend and helper, Professor Dr Watanabe. At that meal, there were Chinese, Mongolian, Korean, and Japanese monks, as well as my friend, Rasbihar Bose, the Indian freedom fighter. The departure meal for Vappo and myself in Kyōto, at which all the so-called monks and nuns drank rice wine, made me feel quite sad.

My friend Sato, the student of Dr Watanabe, went with me all the way to Osaka as the representative of his teacher. Just before my departure I realized that my friend, who was standing on the pier, was suddenly overcome with deep sorrow at my departure. My former student Sugihara—now a famous doctor and professor at the Imperial University who has his own research institute—came by train all the way to the last Japanese port with his bride, in order to be able to say goodbye. So I took my departure from the Japan that had become so dear to me, and finally returned to my real home, Laṅkā.

Chapter 18: Return to Ceylon, 1926

When our ship arrived in Singapore, the first one to come on board was the Chief of Police. He told me that I was not allowed to go on land, and if I were to be found on land, I would be punished by being put into prison. I told him that I had not the least interest in Singapore. It was enough for me that the Governor of Ceylon had given me permission to settle permanently in Laṅkā. Nevertheless, I told him that I was curious to know why I was not allowed to leave the ship. The official then told me that I was known to him due to an incident I caused in earlier times. This obviously referred to my past protests against the landing prohibition, in particular the transfer prohibition for all Germans travelling to Java, although we all had visas issued in England.

The ship had hardly left Singapore when Mr Gilles (Indra Montri) appeared. He was now half blind and was led around by his Siamese servant. It was due to his help that later on the King of Siam presented me with the thirty volumes of the Tipiṭaka. This is the same Mr Gilles who, when he was eighty years old, was resolved to study Pali and Buddhism under me.

It must have been the last day before our arrival in Laṅkā that Coroner W. Wijesekera, my supporter from the Island Hermitage, sent a radio telegram welcoming me to Laṅkā. However, after all the earlier disappointments, I was still somewhat unconvinced whether we would really be allowed to disembark. After the ship had been anchored and all the passengers were called to the saloon to show their passes, I was the very first to hurry towards the passport officer and ask if we were really allowed to land. He replied: "If you have a visa, sure!" I then replied, "Here is the entry permit from the governor and here the passport with the visa." Soon after, a boat came from Robert de Soysa, my supporter and a relative of Coroner W. Wijesekera. In the boat was Alton Wijesekera, the son of the Coroner (who at the beginning of the war in 1914 had been a small schoolboy), together with some of his relatives. We were taken by car to Soysa's bungalow on Slave Island, where all the relatives greeted me and invited me for a meal. After that, we were driven the 100 kilometres to Dodanduva.

Finally, I left behind the twelve years of exile and imprisonment caused by the war. These had been twelve years of suffering: that is I had been in prison in Diyatalāva from 1914 to 1915, then in Australia from 1915 to 1916; in December 1916 I left for Honolulu and was in China from 1917–1919 where I was in prison and contracted smallpox; next I stayed in Germany (1919–1920), and then from 1920–1926 in Japan and in Siam, where I became ill with malaria. All this happened between my thirty-fourth and my forty-eighth year.

* * *

Editor's note: *Ñāṇatiloka's autobiography ends here. What follows is a sketch of his remaining years mostly based on information found in Hellmuth Hecker's* Der Erste Deutsche Bhikkhu *and the* Ñāṇatiloka Centenary Volume.[163] *Because Ñāṇatiloka's life is less eventful than before and because there is only information available about this period from the accounts of his disciples and visitors to the Island Hermitage, the focus in this section is often more on his disciples than on Ñāṇatiloka.*

Yangtze River, China

Foreign enclave, Hankow, early 20th c.

China, early 20th c.

Temple in Chunking, early 20th c.

Vappo, Japan, 1920s

35000 victims of the inferno following the Great Kanto Earthquake

Ashes remaining after cremation of the victims

The great fire

Island Hermitage (IH), 1928

Ñāṇāloka and Vappo, IH, 1928

Monks eating, IH, 1928

Boatlanding Place, IH, 1936 or 37

Maetiduva Island, IH, 1936 or 37

Kuti, IH, 1911, drawn by Bhaddiyo

Novice Ordination of Nyanaponika & Gauribala, IH, June 4, 1936

Ñāṇamālita, Ñāṇatiloka, Ñāṇaponika, 19.2.1937

Ñāṇatiloka in his cottage, 1936

Ñāṇatiloka, 1938

Boat going to IH for ordination, June 4, 1936

Boat going for ordination of Vipulañāṇa, 1930s

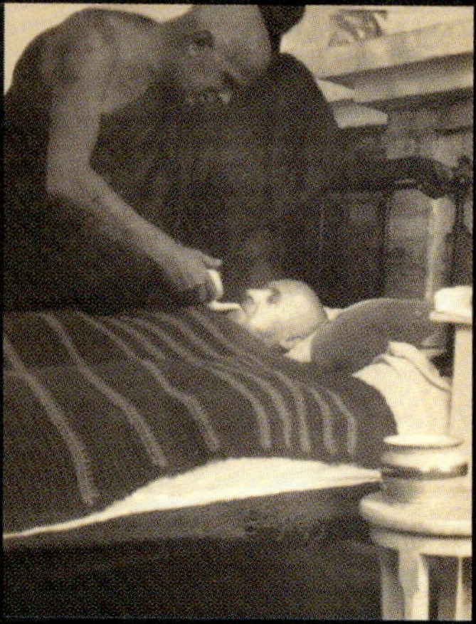

Deathbed & cremation of Ñāṇādhāra in Mogok, Burma, May

Upalavaṇṇā: 1938,
1976

L to R: Maung Maung Hwin, Kyaw Hla, Govinda, Ñāṇatiloka, Adinavaysa. April 1929, Mandalay, Burma

Paul Debes

Front: Ñāṇakhet
Ñāṇasisi, ?, Back
Ñāṇapiya, Ñāṇal
Ñāṇaloka, Ñāṇa-
ponika. April 193

PART III

BIOGRAPHICAL POSTSCRIPT

CHAPTER 19: CEYLON, 1926–1931

Return to the Island Hermitage

On returning to the Island Hermitage, Ñāṇatiloka and Vappo found most of the huts had fallen down due to decay and vandalism. The paths were overgrown by the jungle and the place had become a paradise for animals such as wild dogs and snakes. Besides this material drawback, there was also a legal one. The British colonial government had confiscated the island in 1914 as enemy property and then sold it very cheaply to the first interested Sinhalese. The present owner was expecting something for it and the property was legally his. However, with the help of his supporters, Ñāṇatiloka was able to get the island back from its new owner against the price at which he had bought it from the British. After a lot of work, the Island Hermitage was again made to accommodate the monks. Once a week, Ñāṇatiloka would go to Dodanduva to beg alms for himself and the other monks, on the other days the other monks would do the same in turn.

Govinda and other visitors

The visitor's book of the Island Hermitage shows that not only scholars—especially Japanese ones—spiritual seekers and adventurers but also diplomats and other high ranking figures such as the King of Sachsen came during these years to visit the Island Hermitage and learn from Ñāṇatiloka. In 1928 the German student of Buddhism, Ernst Lothar Hoffmann,[164] came to stay at the Island Hermitage. He intended to become a bhikkhu later on and was given the Pali name Govinda by Ñāṇatiloka. Mahānāmo (Victor Stomps) had returned from Germany to the Island Hermitage in the same year, and Vappo left the Island Hermitage to stay in a solitary hut in the area of Bogavantalāva.

Else Buchholz, who had left Japan and returned to Germany due to health reasons, also came to Ceylon in 1928. In Anurādhapura she became a ten-precept nun (*dasa-sīla-mātā*), dressed in ochre robes, by the name of Uppalavaṇṇā. She stayed for the rest of her life in Ceylon, living as a hermit in the Variyagoda Hermitage near Gampola and then in the Manāpadassana Cave in Dulvala near Kandy.

Besides teaching new pupils, Ñāṇatiloka continued his literary work and the propagation of Dhamma. Govinda, who gave himself the title *brahmacāri* ("a celibate"), convinced Ñāṇatiloka to found the International Buddhist Union (IBU) in 1929 and to become its president. The main aim of the IBU was to unite all Buddhists worldwide and to promote Buddhism through the virtuous and exemplary conduct of practising Buddhists.

In March 1929, Govinda, as secretary of the IBU, travelled to Burma to raise support for the new organization. Ñāṇatiloka followed him shortly after because his preceptor, U Kumara Mahāthera, had passed away. They travelled to Mandalay and the Shan state promoting the IBU. Many Burmese became members of the union.

Govinda had been convinced by Anāgārika Dhammapāla to give up his plans to become a bhikkhu if he wanted to continue his work for the IBU because the bhikkhu rules would be a hindrance for his work. Thus he took instead the yellow robe of the Anāgārika, a "homeless one," and now was called Anāgārika Govinda.

After visiting Europe for the IBU, Govinda returned to Ceylon with his adoptive mother from Italy who temporarily stayed at the Mätiduva Island next to Polgasduva. At the Island Hermitage new huts were being built and also a library to accommodate the large amount of Tipiṭaka books that Ñāṇatiloka had brought back from Burma. In 1930 Govinda founded the Variyagoda Hermitage near Gampola. It was in the scenic and cool upcountry on a mountain tea estate belonging to Baron Rothschild. In the 1930s Ñāṇatiloka, Vappo, and other monks from the Island Hermitage would often stay there to escape the sweltering heat of the low-country.

Govinda only lived for one year there with his stepmother. In 1931 he received an invitation to participate in the All-India Buddhist Conference in Darjeeling, which he accepted with the intention of propagating the "pure Buddhist teaching as preserved in Ceylon, in a country where it had degenerated into a system of demon worship and fantastic forms of belief." However, while staying in the Tibetan Yi-Gah Tschö-Ling monastery of the Gelugpa sect in Darjeeling, he met the impressive Tibetan meditation master Tomo Geshe Rimpoche[165] and then became a zealous follower of Mahāyāna and especially of Vajrayāna. Govinda stayed on in India and lost interest in the IBU, which caused the organization to collapse. For a few months each year he came back to Variyagoda where Sister Uppalavaṇṇā and Vappo were then living.

Paul Debes

A half year after Govinda had departed, Paul Debes[166] arrived at the Island Hermitage. Like Govinda he had learnt about Buddhism years earlier and was also determined to spend the rest of his life as a monk in Ceylon. His account is of particular interest because it is the only one that describes his internal, meditation experiences rather than the external life at the hermitage.

Debes, who later became a popular Buddhist teacher in Germany, had encountered Buddhism through reading a book and because of their clarity was particularly impressed by the discourses of the Buddha. He had found what he was searching for—the truth about existence. The Dhamma made such an impression on him that he did not see any other goal in life than to become a monk. Because it was only possible to do so in Asia, he wanted to go on foot to India. After being discouraged from doing this by a German Buddhist publisher, and after he had received permission from Ñāṇatiloka, he went by ship to Ceylon. His brother, who had also become a Buddhist, accompanied him. In September 1931, on Paul Debes' twenty-fifth birthday, the brothers arrived at the Island Hermitage. Ñāṇatiloka accepted them as *upāsakas* in earth-coloured clothes. Although it was not necessary at this stage, they immediately took on the ten novice precepts. They also wanted to throw their lay-clothes in the lagoon, but Ñāṇatiloka wisely discouraged them from doing so. They were given huts on the island and were taught Pali by Ñāṇatiloka, so that they could read the teachings of the Buddha in their original language.

Paul Debes started off with the severe meditation of contemplation of the body (*kāyānupassanā*). He forsook the rice-soup that was given as breakfast and ate only lunch. He quickly lost weight, until one day, after he had eaten a large quantity of food, his conscience was so stricken he almost began to have doubts about his "renunciation." Then he let go of all tension. Sitting at the edge of the well, he transcended the five hindrances and experienced a meditative absorption of indescribable beatitude. He wrote the following about his meditation experiences:

"During the many periods free from rain I would do my contemplations in the open. I would sit mostly in front of a dense row of bushes with small, dark leaves, which would not offer anything distracting for my eyes. Here I would daily sit for several hours and cultivate the silent, ever more clear contemplation of the change of the body from the time of death through all stages of decay (as is described in the tenth discourse of the Majjhima Nikāya) until the bones had finally decayed and just fine powdered dust remained, which would be blown away by the wind or washed away by the rain.

This transcendence through the vanishing of corporeality as far as the full release from the "I am" conceit brought me every time, for several hours, an indescribable invulnerability, lightness and freedom, which in a different way was more wholesome than each incidentally experienced beatific absorption. Within the absorption, all five senses are silent, so that neither the world nor "I" is experienced, because all that has disappeared. However, the contemplation of the body taken to this degree gives the completely positive feeling that this world together with one's own body is something really, really negligible, and that the fully victorious awareness cannot be affected by anything at all in the whole world. In this state none of the sudden transcendent experiences can scare one, on the contrary, unaffected one observes whatever one might see, and knows it.

This is what happened to me one time. Towards the end of such a contemplation the row of bushes in front of my eyes appeared to dissolve or transform, then I saw a group of women fleeing in panic coming into my field of vision from the right, they hurried past in front of me—anxiety and consternation showing in their faces, and their long hair standing almost upright—and then disappeared to the left. One of these hounded women looked at me when she came by and I recognized a close relative.

Under normal circumstances I would have interrupted such a vision with great fear, however, now there was not the least astonishment or shock. I saw, and knew, 'This is a scene from one plane of saṃsāra. We all have been everything in our beginningless wandering in saṃsāra, and will be again so until we understand the exit—and go on the way to the exit.'

Both these experiences—the free state of consciousness through absorption, and any other state of consciousness through the experience of the other dimension—eventually conduced to a different relationship to the normal world-experience for me, and changed me."

Later Paul Debes desired greater solitude and Ñāṇatiloka brought him to an area with big granite boulders south of Dodanduva, towards Galle, where hermits had meditated before. There Paul Debes practised even more intensively: however he returned to the Island Hermitage after some time where his brother had stayed on. He had realized that it was not possible to meditate with such an extraordinary intensity any longer; as a Chinese proverb states, "One can't go walking for fourteen days on the tips of one's toes." Later he wrote the following about this period:

"Many Buddhist teachers recommend certain exercises to beginners who train in (them) without the right orientation towards their own existence, which determines the significance of the exercises. In Ceylon I too received instructions for exercises which the Buddha taught as the last steps towards Nibbāna. Much less was said about the exercises belonging to the beginning of the entire, well-structured teaching of the Buddha."

And thus the "Debes brothers," as Ñāṇatiloka called them, left the Island Hermitage in the spring of 1932. Ñāṇatiloka regretted this as he had seldom seen such serious and intensively striving candidates.

More than thirty years later, in 1963, Paul Debes returned for one year to the Island Hermitage to meditate. He was often contemplating his first experiences at the Island Hermitage and penetrated their meaning further, finally losing his fear of Nibbāna:

"As much as I love the jhānas, appreciate their tremendous value, and therefore strive for them systematically, I would not appreciate the day I first entered such an experience here at Polgasduva as highly as any recent day. Because of my own experiences and insights I value more and more the security against downfall and decline rather than the un-assured, sporadic, and incidental ascents. The latter are like high jumps after which one finds oneself again on the same old level. How helpful these "high jumps" are I have known for thirty years, after having had such experiences here. The awareness of this experience—an experience of incomparable transcendental beatitude and an experience of transcendental vision—was for me the only light in the thirty years of darkness. I saw the congruity of the Discourses (of the Buddha) from the experiences. I realized that something like that light exists, must exist, and that we, affected by craving, are enveloped by darkness.

My faith (*saddhā*) was unshakeable, but equally absolute evidence was coming out of my own experiences. However, the light from the two experiences was, all along, both helpful as well as painful. It summoned me and did not leave me any rest in the world. It protected me and finally led me here, but it had shone from a tremendous remoteness and always reminded me of the remoteness. And I was remote from it even in the days that I experienced it. At that time I was not mature enough for the transcendental level of these experiences, but not knowing about the right development and sequence of ascetic exercises, I had grasped one of the highest ascetic exercises and had done it with a steely perseverance for many hours. Out of the accumulated power of these exercises, which expel one far from the sense-world, I was then catapulted twice as high in my mind. But because I had not ascended from a secure foundation, and was not mature enough for it, because the (five) shackles that drag down were not disposed of in any way, I fell down again.

Lastly, I owe to these experiences and the painful impression of their great, great remoteness that I thoroughly and comprehensively sought for the laws of spiritual maturity, for the effects of the only exercises needed for this impassable state of maturity, until, today, I have become certain through uninterrupted comparison of my practical experiences of the central declaration of the Buddha in the Majjhima Nikāya."

Chapter 20: Flowering Period, 1932–1939

Ñāṇādhāra

The period from 1932 to 1939 was the Island Hermitage's best period, during which several bhikkhus and novices, mostly German, were admitted, and many important visitors came to visit the island.

Conrad Nell, the son of an important evangelical priest, came to Ceylon in 1931 to become a Buddhist monk. He was accepted as a novice by Ñāṇatiloka in 1932 and given the name Ñāṇādhāra[167]. Soon, however, Ñāṇādhāra developed a liver disease and, on the advice of Ñāṇatiloka, went back to Germany to recover. Within a few months he returned. His seriousness and religious zeal were such that Ñāṇatiloka considered him his best pupil. Nevertheless, in 1933 he let Ñāṇādhāra go to Burma where the climate seemed more suitable for his pupil's weak health. Ñāṇādhāra was accepted as a bhikkhu in Rangoon in November 1933. His health deteriorated towards the end of 1934 and Ñāṇatiloka came to Upper Burma to take care of his ill pupil personally. Again, he encouraged his pupil to go back to Germany as soon as he could in order to get cured. Ñāṇādhāra, however, was never able to do so—in spite of the care and the more suitable climate, Ñāṇādhāra got malaria and died of tuberculosis of the blood on the 17 May 1935.[168]

Ñāṇaponika and Ñāṇakhetta

On 4 February 1936 two friends, Sigmund Feniger and Peter Schönfeldt[169], arrived at the port of Colombo and were welcomed by Ñāṇatiloka personally and taken to the Island Hermitage.

Feniger and Schönfeldt, were both from Jewish backgrounds[170] and were both involved in the book trade—Schönfeldt as bookbinder at a small press and the Feniger as bookseller at a bookshop. They had met each other at the Buddhistische Haus in Frohnau near Berlin where the Buddhist teachers Paul Dahlke and Martin Steinke were active. The friends decided to become Buddhist monks in Ceylon after having read the enthusiastic letters of their Buddhist friend Conrad Nell who had become Bhikkhu Ñāṇādhāra.

In 1935, Feniger had moved with his mother to Vienna, to avoid the increasing persecution of Jews by the Nazis. Having received permission from Ñāṇatiloka to stay at the Island Hermitage and arranging for his mother to stay with relatives, Feniger and Schönfeldt both left by ship from Marseille to Colombo.

When people from abroad would write to Ñāṇatiloka to apply for acceptance into the Saṅgha at the Island Hermitage, they would get a reply such as this:

> If you are willing to be content with the food given, with the clothes to be worn here, with the lodging assigned to you, with the arrangements for your study; if you want to study Pali and follow my instruction in the so important teaching of Anattā, you may prepare yourself to come with a valid passport, a return ticket and some money needed to buy the special clothes for candidates and any other things before you become a monk. Once accepted, the Buddhist community will look after your needs and money is not required.

At first, Feniger and Schönfeldt were living as upāsakas (lay followers) wearing white clothes and observing the eight precepts. They stayed in the house at Mätiduva, the island which adjoins Parappaduva and was not yet part of the Island Hermitage. Every day they would row to the Island Hermitage to get instruction from Ñāṇatiloka. Like all the pupils of Ñāṇatiloka they had to learn Pali under him and would be able to read the discourses of the Buddha and continue studying by themselves after about six to nine months of intensive study. Ñāṇatiloka wanted his pupils to know at least enough Pali to be able to read texts without needing the translations, which were often faulty.

With newcomers Ñāṇatiloka would first read from the first discourse of the *Majjhima Nikāya*, the *Mūlapariyāya Sutta*, pointing out the inadequate translations by the first English and German translators. He then would give the correct interpretation of the Buddhist doctrine of not-self, *anattā*. Based on this text, that is, a bhikkhu who understands the Dhamma does not consider the five *khandhas* (aggregates) as self, or belonging to a self, or within a self, nor does he consider a self beyond them. He views all elements of any possible experience as not self. After this he would start to teach Pali to the pupil, either individually or within a group. Ñāṇatiloka placed great importance on a proper understanding of the doctrine of not-self, which he stressed as being the most crucial and fundamental part of the Buddha's teaching.

With his German pupils Ñāṇatiloka would go through his Pali Anthology which contained texts mostly related to kamma, rebirth and the doctrine of not-self, but also some texts related to the novice-acceptance and training.[171] He would first go through a few easy texts from the *Jātaka* commentary and passages from the *Milindapañhā*, then two passages were studied from the *Khuddakapāṭha* relevant to the novice acceptance, followed by some important verses from the *Dhammapada* and parts of suttas from the *Suttanipāta*. After that, important texts would be studied from the *Aṅguttara, Saṃyutta,* and *Majjhima Nikāya*, such as the *Dasadhamma Sutta*, the *Girimānanda Sutta* and the *Anattalakkhaṇa Sutta*, the *Saccavibhaṅga Sutta* and the *Satipaṭṭhāna Sutta*. The *Satipaṭṭhāna Sutta* would be considered in great detail with the help of Ñāṇatiloka's interlinear translation of it. Finally, a passage from the *Manorathapurāṇī* would be examined, the commentary on the *Aṅguttara Nikāya*, on the Abhidhamma view of the person (*puggala*) from the viewpoint of the "ultimate truth" (*paramatthasacca*) and a passage from the *Visuddhimagga* on loving-kindness meditation. The texts would be explained grammatically by Ñāṇatiloka, who was an accomplished Pali scholar.

Ñāṇatiloka knew several other languages besides German and Pali. In high school he had learnt Greek and Latin and had also mastered French, Italian, and English early in life. He spoke Sinhala fluently and he also had a fair knowledge of Burmese and Sanskrit. While in Algeria, he had learnt some Arabic and, while in China and Japan, some Chinese and Japanese. He impressed his students with his ability to show the relation between words of different languages; indeed he could have been a successful linguist or lexicographer.

Feniger and Schönfeldt were admitted as novices by Ñāṇatiloka on 6 June 1936 and were given the names Ñāṇaponika and Ñāṇakhetta. The two other German novices who were admitted in the Saṅgha together with them were Otto Krauskopf[172] and Joseph Pistor[173] who were given the names Ñāṇasīsi and Ñāṇapiya. Thousands of people from all over Ceylon flocked to the Island Hermitage to witness the event. A year later, in 1937, the four and Ñāṇabrūhana[174] were given full admission into the Saṅgha.[175] About the same time Ñāṇakhetta's ten-year younger brother[176], who had come to Ceylon in 1937, became novice and was given the name Ñāṇamālita.

Ñāṇasatta, a Czech, came to the Island Hermitage in 1938 and was accepted as a bhikkhu under Ñāṇatiloka ten days before the war started in 1939.[177] He related the following two anecdotes about his time there with Ñāṇatiloka:

"A supporter used to regularly send a tin of condensed milk from Colombo, fresh butter and good bread for the ageing Ñāṇatiloka. However, instead of using these extras all by himself, he shared everything with his pupils. The milk tin was cut open in the morning and placed in a niche in the dining hall about six feet high from the ground. It would be used for making milk tea. One day however the monks had plain tea with their meal, as the cat had jumped up, brought the tin down and drunk all of it. Without grumbling, Ñāṇatiloka pointed to the empty niche and asked his pupils to explain in Abhidhamma terms the relation between the milk and the cat who drank it. Some of the monks suggested that it was the object-condition (*ārammaṇa-paccaya*), others said that it was a presence-condition (*paccuppanna-paccaya*), and still others took it to be the root-condition (*hetu-paccaya*). But Ñāṇatiloka said, 'All these conditions were not strong enough. It was a strong inducement-condition (*upanissaya-paccaya*) that made the cat jump so high to get the milk down.'

It once happened that the boat bringing our midday meal from the village capsized in the lagoon in monsoon rains with strong winds and high waves. All food was lost and the men rowing the boat had difficulty saving their lives. They brought back an empty boat and some of the empty containers that floated on the surface of the lake. Ñāṇatiloka had seen what had happened from the high elevation of his hut and promptly sent a boy up one of the coconut trees growing on the island to pluck a big cluster of the nuts. Each monk got one coconut at meal time, cut open with a big knife by the boy, and they ate the soft fleshy kernel and drank the sweet water. Ñāṇatiloka reminded everyone that a monk must be content with any food he receives.

If there was no sugar, he drank his tea in the Tibetan fashion with a little ghee, if there was any. When he went on a journey, he would go by bus or by train in third class. He would not ask supporters for food parcels when going on a journey but was satisfied with some bread and a few bananas. When arrangements for the midday meal failed, he and another senior monk would go by boat to the village in the forenoon and would go on alms-round, without suggesting to junior monks that they should go for him and without expecting too much from the villagers.

Ñāṇaponika related that his teacher used to say about people: "There are no bad people, only bad qualities"—implying that any qualities of human beings are of an impermanent nature and can be changed.

At the end of 1938 Ñāṇaponika moved from the hot and sticky climate of the Island Hermitage to the cooler climate of the upcountry near Gampola where he lived happily for a year as a hermit in an abandoned brick kiln in a rice field. Here he started working on his translation of the Saṃyutta Nikāya. A year later, after the annexation of Austria by Germany, he arranged for his mother and relatives to come and take refuge in Ceylon. Until she died in 1956 at the age of 89 his mother lived in

Colombo with a family who were supporters of Ñāṇaponika. She also became a Buddhist. At this time he was living with the Sinhalese monks Soma and Kheminda, first in a new hermitage near Gampola and then in an abandoned tea factory in Bandaravella. He had started working on the German translation of the Satipaṭṭhāna Sutta and commentary. This sutta formed the basis of most of his later literary work.

After Ñāṇakhetta had returned from India where he visited the Buddhist holy sites, Ñāṇakhetta lived as a hermit in the jungles of Ceylon, often not speaking to anyone for months. He was practising the *satipaṭṭhāna* meditation exercises in order to reach the state he called "ocean-like tranquillity of mind." He took the practice to such an extreme that he later said about this last period of practice, "I had driven the diagnosing and dissection of every stirring of emotion and feeling that arose to such an extent that I constantly felt I was sitting under a bright lamp burning day and night and illumining me completely. Under this ice-cold, supervising control of the mind nothing could hide." He however was not sure whether he was going mad or was about to reach his goal. In any case, both options were taken away from him forcefully because one day in September 1939 a Sinhalese policeman appeared, went into his hut, bowed to him, and told him with tears in his eyes that there was a war going on and that he had to arrest him.

Paul Wirz

Life on the Island Hermitage, although appearing to be idyllic at first, was not all that easy for many newcomers. Dr Paul Wirz,[178] an anthropologist had a house on the neighbouring island Parappaduva during this period and used to visit the Island Hermitage regularly. He writes about the disillusions many European newcomers faced.

The following is a translation from parts of Wirz' book *Einsiedler auf Taprobane: Geschichte Dreier Inseln* ("Hermits on Taprobane: Stories of Three Islands").[179] Wirz' descriptions show aspects of the life at the Island Hermitage and descriptions of Ñāṇatiloka and other monks that are not found elsewhere. Eventually, after WW II, Wirz gave the Parappaduva Island to the monks of the Island Hermitage. The barren and quite narrow island was made little use of until 1984, when the German born Theravāda nun Ayyā Khemā established the Parappaduva Nuns Hermitage—which only lasted for about five years. Wirz refers to Ñāṇatiloka as "Pandita" ("learned man").

"Parappaduva is not the only island in the lagoon. Two more were in the vicinity, which until recently were separated by a small channel. They appear splendidly green and shady, and the smaller one of the two is dominated by slender palm trees. In comparison Parappaduva is barren and bleak, only surrounded by a green belt of mangroves. Polgasduva, the "Cocos Island," is the bigger of the two, but was not rightfully named so, because only recently were some palms planted.

Well swept paths, bordered by flowering Hibiscuses and Croton shrubs with variegated leaves, meander through the jungle thickets from cottage to cottage. In the cottages live pious bhikkhus and sāmaṇeras dressed in saffron-yellow and brick-red robes. At a first sight their white skin-colour betrays that, not only natives, but mostly Europeans have chosen this Island Hermitage as their residence. In fact, this little island has had a moving history. ...

In 1926 it was possible [for the Pandita] to return to Ceylon again. The monastery had been sold by the government for a small price to a Sinhalese, but through the mediation of a benefactor the Pandita managed to get it back into his possession. The buildings that had been destroyed through time and vandalism were rebuilt. The Pandita started to do scholarly work again with unabated energy. Various scholarly works, small and large dissertations, and translations from the Pali were the fruits of his efforts. They contributed to the prominent position that the Pandita started to have among Buddhists and Pali scholars. Polgasduva had started to flourish again.

Friends of Buddhism from all countries came and went, many without seriously considering what would await them on Polgasduva. Therefore it is no surprise that many, coming with great expectations, became quite disillusioned. The monotone life, the oppressive solitude, the sudden abandonment of all that they were used to, and last but not least, the very monotonous, meagre food put into their begging bowls by well wishing Sinhalese during the begging round in the village in the morning—this all meant great sacrifice and asceticism for the mostly young, white Buddhists. For this they were physically and mentally not prepared. No wonder most of them were waiting for the time when they were ordained and could put on the saffron coloured robe so they could then quickly leave to upcountry or India or Burma and thus escape the oppressive solitude.

Few, very few stayed on the path they initially took;[180] the others would go their own way sooner or later. But how could most of them who came fresh and full of enthusiasm from Europe have known about the reality of practical Buddhism, and how could they have known what would really await them on Polgasduva? Full of inspiration and enthusiasm, they had turned their backs on Europe. However, they couldn't have expected what they would meet there, once the ship took them to the Promised Land—only to find upon arrival that everything was different than they had expected.

After arriving they were charmed by the beautiful nature and, in winter, the not too hot temperature. The first days and weeks were filled with the new and unfamiliar things that life offered there, and with learning and observing the surroundings. But soon everything would begin to lose its glitter, and when the new and unfamiliar became ordinary, so too the inspiration had gone and only naked and hard reality remained.

I could write a whole book about all the people who, with one intention or the other, mostly hopeful and full of all kinds of illusions, had turned their back on Europe to find here on Polgasduva a new home. If one would let the natives of the nearby villages report, then one would get to hear a mixture of amusing stories flavoured with their own dry humour. One can imagine what stories have accumulated over time. As in all cases like this, there is no lack of evil tongues, and although the Pandita himself was very respected and treasured by the Sinhalese, this was not the case for all of the white monks who followed him.

After all the negative experiences, the Pandita must have realised that in fact only very few people were fit for the life at Polgasduva and that caution would be needed before encouraging someone to come and follow the footsteps of the

Great Master. Isn't it a risky undertaking to immediately transplant a person who has never been to the tropics to Polgasduva, where he'll have to take on and fulfil the life of homelessness in sweltering heat and solitude? Ñāṇatiloka could have spared himself a lot of troubles if he hadn't been so accommodating to those who were overly enthusiastic and optimistic and had requested with great sincerity to stay at Polgasduva, without knowing what to expect when they left Europe. Then there were people, young and old, who did not always display the peaceful characteristics of the bhikkhu. There were also those who, as soon as they had established themselves on Polgasduva, would explain the Teaching of the Great Master in their own way. Thus, more than once, the peace on the island was disturbed. Usually these problems ended however, because those who disturbed the peace departed quickly of their own accord, realising they were not suited for the life on Polgasduva.

All kinds of people came to the Island Hermitage in the course of time: English, French, Italians, Poles, Czechs, above all Germans, and even the occasional Japanese, Burmese, and Indian. They came for different reasons and were driven by various motives, but all were inspired by the thought of the Great Master, the Buddha, who taught the irrefutable truth to humanity—the truth of suffering and the Eightfold Path that leads to the cessation of suffering. A psychologist could definitely have made interesting studies here. One could, as it were, see everyone's underlying motivations for coming. Even if someone was very silent and closed, after a short or long time he would have to open his heart.

There was a young German, an ex-Catholic priest,[181] full of enthusiasm and diligence for the newly chosen religion. Full of indignation he would vent his wrath about Catholicism and the Pope whom he had obeyed until recently. Now however he was a convinced Buddhist, sitting the whole day behind books until his head was fuming, writing fiery articles[182], in which he justified his conduct and in every manner praised the teaching of Gotama as the only way to salvation.

He also used every opportunity available to engage in discussions with people who came to the Island Hermitage. During these discussions he would eagerly offend and scold the heathens. He had his own, often really strange, ideas; and with regards to Buddhism, which he also felt needed urgent reform. He believed himself called to play the role of a trailblazer of the "Modern Trend" and that "there had to be more life in the business" and "the bosses are an appallingly lazy and morally degenerate company."

Why the many rules, the solitude, asceticism, fasting, the relinquishment of everything? And why, above all, this anxiety for and hiding from the opposite sex? Why the study of Pali when so much had been translated into German? He felt that everything had to change. He wrote article after article and gave spirited lectures, which lacked nothing in power of conviction and genius, but found little approval with the Sinhalese Buddhists, and even less with his teacher and superiors.

It was not apparent to him that he was stabbing himself in he back. It also did not occur to him that he was making himself unpopular through his conduct, and that it would have been better had he been more moderate in expressing himself. Everyone appeared to avoid him, but he did not notice until he was finally clearly told that it was better for him to leave. Thus he left shortly after his full ordination and went to Ratnapura, where he stayed in a large monastery and helped at the monastic college. But also there his stay was not long. He made no friends. On the contrary, he repelled people through his manner until he was told to go, and even to go immediately back to Europe, which they did not have to tell him twice. He had not been capable of exchanging his Jesuit attitude for the one of a bhikkhu when he exchanged his black frock for a yellow robe. Thus he took the money he carefully saved for the journey and went with visible relief back to his home country which had again become dear to him after the experiences he had undergone.

Many others underwent the same experience. There was a middle aged Pole, not as temperamental as the Catholic priest, but not more suited to the life at the Island Hermitage. He was not a Buddhist and did not appear to have much of an inclination towards Buddhism. He had taken to Indian Yoga teachings which he had come to study. He had only arrived at the Island Hermitage where he wanted to have a look around, but when he stumbled upon the unbearable heat and, even more so, the oppressive solitude which he compared to banishment, with great urgency he went on to the promised land, India. This was the shortest way most went after having stayed for some time at the Island Hermitage.

There was also an elderly, white-haired, gentleman, pharmacist by profession, and still the owner of a pharmacy in Lüneburg, which, heaven knows why, he had deserted many years ago to find a new home under the tropical sky here in Sri Lanka. He was one of the first students of the Pandita and lived since then in complete solitude in a small hut somewhere in the mountains in a desolate tea-plantation. Not as a real bhikkhu because, whether driven by good or bad motivations, he lived on the ten marks sent every month from his home country, until he finally, out of necessity, came to the conclusion that it was better to return to the Island Hermitage as a bhikkhu. But the already 75 year old monk couldn't bear this austere life for a long time. Increasingly his strength declined and his end seemed to be approaching. But then he suddenly decided to return to Germany and die there. His friends had to bring him onto the ship, because he could not go himself anymore, and no one believed that he would survive the journey. However, he survived it and arrived in his home country shortly before the start of the war, where, having been brought to a hospital, he managed to stay alive for a week.

There was also an elderly gentleman, a doctor of law, who had come to the Island Hermitage to close his life. But he did not stay long. The climate and the bugs were not for him—and then the oppressive solitude. Having read the letters and descriptions, etc., he had imagined everything to be different. Why did he have to wait so long for his ordination? Why all this rubbish? "I will become mad if I have to stay here any longer," he repeatedly said, and one could see that he suffered under the solitude. In fact he just waited until he was ordained and could wear the saffron robe to go to a hut in the cooler upcountry. Many came and went like this, but it is too time-consuming to report about each of them.

But most notable was a German married couple that stayed for three months in Dodanduva. It had been twelve years ago but the locals still remembered the strangers, and with reason, because they stirred up a lot of dust. The couple, who had never been in the tropics and perhaps not even over the border of Germany, could not adjust to the local conditions and took on a downright hostile attitude towards the natives that made their situation impossible. Finally, the police had to step in and the German Consulate had to order them to go back to Germany.

Seldom would a day pass that we didn't visit the Hermitage. Later we curtailed our visits, but it remained the most welcome change to our daily routine. There were no roads and it was a matter of course to stop over at the Hermitage when we were rowing to Parappaduva. Many times we would stop west of the steep gravel path to the cottage of the Pandita, which, being on the highest point, had the best location... Whenever we came we were welcomed by the elderly gentleman. He was always friendly, kind, helpful towards all. Notwithstanding his reservedness, he had something very captivating. Even at the first meeting, one felt one was in the presence of a mature sage, whom no storms could affect anymore.[183] It therefore comes to no surprise that all felt so attracted to him. They also knew that the Island Hermitage had become the way it was only through him, and that it would fall apart without him.

From near and far the native people came to see and pay respect to the great teacher. They came to be in his presence for a little while, to bow at his feet and then with lowered head, being fully satisfied, departed. This especially happened at full moons, the religious holiday of Buddhists, when everybody, old or young, dressed with clean white clothes, would go to the temple in the afternoon or evening to put down flowers in front of the image of the Buddha.

But he also had European visitors sometimes. Everybody knew him or had heard about him. Even the officers of a German warship stopping over in Galle for a few days did not neglect to honor the Island Hermitage and its bhikkhus with a visit. The island itself was worth a visit, although there were no special sights. The shady, old jungle trees, the well swept paths that crossed the island in various directions, the cottages of the bhikkhus hidden in the greenery, the wholesome silence—this all had a special attraction and created an atmosphere that spellbound each visitor. It felt as if time stood still here and that everyone who lived here lived life itself, timeless and desireless, without worries for today and tomorrow.

Unforgettable are the hours I spent within the little yellow cottage of the venerable master and scholar, who immediately put aside his books and work when I came, and welcomed me with friendly laughter. Whatever time of the day it was my visit never seemed inconvenient to him. We would talk about this or that, or discuss a theme that was close to both of us, or he would clarify an unclear point in the Buddhist teaching to me, in which he was unsurpassed.

We would often walk together along the shady path to visit another bhikkhu and inquire after his wellbeing. Such reserved, unobtrusive and selfless bonds connected me to him. That Parappaduva so quickly became my second home was last but not least thanks to the presence of the German Pandita, who gave me a great deal subconsciously through his personality, although he wasn't my teacher in the usual sense.

The third island, Mätiduwa, which means Clay-island, played a controversial role for a long time. It was a coconut and cinnamon grove and had an old derelict house, which could have become a ruin if it had not betimes occurred to the owners to maintain and repair it. A small, shallow channel separated it from Polgasduva, but today the islands have been linked so that one can go from one to the other without wetting one's feet. The residents of Polgasduva had their eye on Mätiduwa and awaited the moment that it would be presented to them or would be put at their disposal without conditions, but the owner was not yet inclined to do that. Nevertheless, he allowed the novices to live in the old house and pick the coconuts. This he thought was good enough. At the same time he also made promises that he would give it in the foreseeable future. Then, however, an unexpected misfortune happened.

A newly ordained novice[184] from Saarland, Germany, bought the adjoining island of Mätiduwa in a wave of enthusiasm without consulting his teacher and companions at all. For a long time the Pandita had had an eye on the Mätiduwa island and had tried to get it into the possession of the Sangha and the owner had assured him that this would happen. However, the Sinhalese character is that while they eagerly like to do good things and give, they also like to see that it is paid for. The one who has money bids, and this is how it is in Ceylon. Thus the deal was quickly settled.

The youngster should have known that he, the prospective bhikkhu, could not handle money, not to speak about buying land, and then solely in his own interest and not for the Sangha. Worst, he had already informed his parents and siblings of his intentions, and had asked them to come immediately to Ceylon where they could make their home on the island acquired by him and lead a carefree life. The Pandita tried to annul the deal, but to no avail.

Soon the family arrived: his elderly father, a much younger mother, and his two brothers. They had brought their whole household from Saarland as if one could not buy anything here. The arrival in Colombo, the reunion with their son who was now wearing a brick-red robe, then the moving in to the half derelict house on Mätiduwa—these were the first bitter disappointments for the family, even more so because their son had not informed them of how things were in reality. He had written about the beautiful vegetation, the delicious fruits, and the gentle brown people living a content, contemplative life, but he had not written about the Buddhist monastery on the adjoining island, and that he himself had already become a novice. This was all a surprise to them.

Disappointment after disappointment followed. Especially the elderly father was disappointed because his health already started to falter. But the mother was also disappointed. Musical as she was, she had at least hoped to find a piano. The brothers too were disappointed. They had no inclination towards Buddhism and the solitary life. What would they do here, how and where could they get a job?

No, their stay did not last long—one month in total. Then the whole family had enough of it. They returned to Saarland at the first opportunity. Only the owner of the island stayed for a while, although he had enough of his possession too and sold it in order to get at least some of his money back. He was lucky because he could have had to wait for decades. Soon after he had the money, his idea of following the Buddha was definitely gone. He disrobed and returned to Germany, which he had only left a few months earlier.

Now Mätiduwa was again in the possession of a Sinhalese. However, he was clever enough not to donate it straightaway to the German bhikkhu as there were ample indications of an impending war, of which the Pandita and other German monks would again become victims...

Editor's Note: *During WWII, Wirz continued coming to Ceylon, but there were only a few monks left on the Island Hermitage.*

Our friend, the caretaker of the house, wasn't coming anymore. Apparently, there had been a great row. Our other friend, a Sinhalese bhikkhu at the Island Hermitage, who had always warned us, who had always been right, found out about all kinds of small and large frauds that had been going on. As he was an informative person, he told us that our caretaker had got the cinnamon branches cut in our absence and when selling it, told the people that it was on our orders. Apparently, the theft was also our caretaker's work.

Indeed, the caretaker always spoke in unfavourable terms of the bhikkhus on the island, but had not found a ready ear with me. I knew that limitless envy was at the root of this disposition. He was not keen that we went there and that we were told how things truly were. His whole family was involved in this bad relationship. Each of them apparently had much to answer for, but the great crook amongst them was the recently deceased uncle who had at one time swindled a considerable amount of money that had been entrusted to him for the acquisition of the Island Hermitage for the Pandita.

He also spoke badly about the Sinhalese bhikkhu on the Island Hermitage who was of a low caste origin and had been adopted in his youth by the Pandita. This dislike was connected to caste-pride. After the white monks had been interned in India, the Sinhalese bhikkhu was on his own on the island, and so our caretaker believed that he could deal the monk a final blow. He accused him of degenerate conduct, also implicating us. Our good intentions had always been a thorn in his side. Moreover, he had already heard that if I and my family were to leave the country again, we would put our island at the disposal of the bhikkhus of the Island Hermitage. Due to the arrangements we had made, he was using all kinds of chicaneries and forms of blackmail against us, still hoping that when we left the country, he would become custodian of the island and could make money out of it, as he had done in our absence. Now, this hope had been squashed.

The whole Dodanduva village came to know about the matter and we had to be on our guard. This was of course the work of our "friend." Unfriendly glances followed us and children threw stones at us from behind. If our boat was left alone, it would be fouled or damaged. Our time here seemed finished too. We avoided the village and people whenever possible. Occasionally we would visit the Island Hermitage to inquire how the Pandita was doing and whether there was any news. The place had become even more quiet and silent. Shyly, the Czech monk went out of our way. Also the Sinhalese bhikkhu, because he was now lord and master here, was not the same.

The paths were overgrown with weeds, and all cottages, except one, were empty. For the second time the island had to suffer the mercilessness of fate; for the second time the creation and work of a noble man found an abrupt end. Locked and sealed was the door of his cottage, through the windows of which one often has seen light shining until deep at night, when working and bent over a thick book he would not rest until he had finished the work he had started.

Two policemen were keeping watch. Nobody knew what the next days or weeks would bring. It was said that Polgasduva, the possession of a German, would be confiscated by the government and auctioned. But there were also other rumours.

Indescribably quiet it was here and it was indescribably empty in me. What am I searching for here, what has been the purpose of my being here? But in my mind I see the tall figure walking on the path, laughing friendly and nodding at me. That is my last image of him..."

Editor's Note: *Earlier, Wirz had also visited Sister Uppalavaṇṇā in the Variyagoda hermitage in the Gampola mountains.*

"The road went up steeply. After leaving the hamlet behind, the landscape became more and more bleak. After walking for an hour we arrived. Before us a hill appeared with no vegetation except low tea bushes. Three small huts were on it. It is unbelievable how one could inhabit these uninviting blotches, however the land was given for free, and the cottages cost very little.

When we came close to the first cottage, we were received by a great number of barking dogs. A small shrunken, but in reality, much younger, small woman with a smoothly shaven head and wearing a brick-red robe came out of the door. It was the female German Buddhist from Hamburg about whom we had heard of before. Five years ago she had left her homeland and came to Ceylon to be accepted in the Sangha and to take on the homeless life. She was not yet disillusioned:

> 'I am happy with my lot, which I have chosen myself. There is no turning back for me. What I call my own are the robes I wear on my body, the shelter of my hut, some writing paper and books–all donated by good people–and not to forget the alms-bowl. What more do I need? The big life does not offer me anything anymore, but it would be more agreeable for me to be able to have more solitude. Too many people come here and most only out of curiosity. Already a cave has been assigned to me. It would be the most ideal living place; one which I have always wished for.'

We talked for a long time with the unusual woman, who, as we found out later, was the only one in Ceylon who had taken to this way.

In the second cottage lived the old pharmacist bhikkhu from Lüneburg. He had now been alone for several years too. This cottage, which was a bit bigger than the others, was built some years ago by a German lady doctor. She had lived there for some time and had then made it available to the German Buddhists. In a motherly manner she had adopted a young, enthusiastic German artist and writer [Govinda], who was likewise inclined to Buddhism. He decided to move to Northern India with his adoptive mother, where a more profitable and bearable field of work had opened up for him. There, with his paintings, he had succeeded to draw the attention of a Maharaja, who had given him some orders.

In the third cottage lived the oldest German monk, who had come first to Ceylon with the Pandita, but ,not being able to bear the coastal climate, had fled to the upcountry. This was the way which many had taken, but only very few were able to bear up for a long time. Not all are fit for a life of solitude and homelessness. In this monk a certain disillusion was noticeable. Too long he had lived the life of poverty and homelessness. One could infer from his words and behaviour that he had become weary of this eternal solitude, this permanent renunciation of all that makes life worth living, even though he did not openly admit this feeling in any way. Ever more frequently he looked for change in his monotonous life. He would suddenly appear at the Island Hermitage, and then suddenly would disappear. Eventually, he constantly commuted between the Island Hermitage and his home at the tea plantation.

One day, however, he spontaneously decided to go for good to Burma: "There the climate is much better, the people are more friendly and there is the possibility of getting a proper dwelling, much larger than here" he said with full conviction. "When I am there, I will not return. It has always been my wish to end my life in Burma." The money for the journey was provided by a supporter, who could not refuse this modest request of a bhikkhu, and for some time nothing was heard of the old monk. But only a few months had passed and then he suddenly appeared again on the Island Hermitage. Burma, the life in the monasteries, and the people there had disillusioned him. The people's generosity there was not much more than here and, so to say, rice too was the only thing put in his alms-bowl there. So here he was again commuting between the Island Hermitage and the tea plantation. This did not last long however, because the start of the war abruptly stopped him. He and the other Germans had to go unwillingly to the concentration camp."

Chapter 21: Internment in Dehra Dun, 1939–1946

Once the British Government declared war on Germany, on 3 September 1939, Ñāṇatiloka was immediately interned again.[185] Along with the other arrested Germans in Ceylon, forty-four men altogether, they were brought to Colombo and kept there for a short time before being sent to the internment camp in Diyatalāva, just like in 1914, and there they remained for over two years. Women were not interned and Sister Uppalavaṇṇā stayed on in Variyagoda. She acquired the property from Govinda in 1945 and stayed there until the 1970s, when she moved to a cave near Kandy.

In the camp in Diyatalāva, with the help of Ñāṇamālita, Ñāṇatiloka finally managed to finish his German translation of the *Visuddhimagga* (*The Path of Purity*). He had already done the first seven of the twenty-three chapters in Polgasduva in 1927. A cyclostyled edition of one hundred books was published.

When the Japanese occupied Singapore on 15 February 1942, Ceylon was declared a war zone and all Germans were brought to India; including Ñāṇatiloka together with seven other German monks.[186] They were taken by ship from Colombo to Bombay and from there by train to the Central Internment Camp near the town of Dehra Dun in north-western India, where they arrived in March 1942.

This internment camp was the biggest one in India, with several thousand inhabitants. It was situated on the upper reaches of the Ganges River, north of Delhi, up among the fore-mountains of the Himalayas and surrounded by tea plantations. Somewhat higher on the mountains was the hill station of Mussoorie. The area reminded Ñāṇatiloka of his stay in the Tessin in southern Switzerland in 1910.

The barrack camp was surrounded by a double barbed-wire fence. The British were fighting a hopeless war against the white termites that were continually eating up the wooden fence poles. Within this fence there were eight separate camp wings, each again surrounded by barbed wire, which housed different groups of people. Of the four wings that were for the Germans, one was for anti-National Socialists, and three for the Nazis. Of these three German Nazi wings, one wing was for Germans from India and Ceylon, one for Germans from Indonesia, and one for all other remaining.

The first of the other four wings was inhabited by Italian generals arrested in North Africa (they were further divided into fascist and anti-fascist sections), the second wing was for Italian Catholic missionaries, the third for others, and the fourth one was the hospital wing.

The first German wing, Wing One, housed the so-called "Bara Sahibs" ("Big Sahibs"), that is, members of the upper class, such as representatives of German companies, independent traders, doctors, missionaries (among whom were at first the Buddhist monks), teachers and scientists, such as the members of the Nanga-Parbat mountaineering expedition. The second German wing housed the so-called "Sumatra Heinis," the German rubber planters who had been arrested by the Dutch on the Indonesian island of Sumatra.

For most Germans who had been in other camps, the conditions in this camp seem to have been more humane than those camps run by the Dutch, Japanese, or Russians. The barracks were well built and the fresh air from the mountains was pleasant. However for the Germans from Ceylon things were different. In Diyatalāva they had been living in relative luxury with their own rooms and good food, but now the German monks were living in barracks and tents.

The internees were treated properly by the British, as they were cautious to preserve the natives' esteem for the whites. The camp was like a little town with a cinema, a soccer field and two tennis courts. There was a workshop, library, hospital, a canteen, an orchestra, and even a school with authorisation to give diplomas. Many internees kept animals and made gardens in front of their barracks. The internees were also given holidays once or twice a week on word of honour, so that they could go for walks in the beautiful surroundings.

The German Buddhists were not all in the same wing. Ñāṇatiloka and Vappo stayed in the "Bara sahib wing," while Ñāṇaponika together with Ñāṇakhetta and his brother Ñāṇamālita, were in the "anti-Nazi wing."

Govinda had been brought from another camp in India earlier on. Although Govinda was not a German anymore and had British citizenship, he was interned in 1940 due to his associations with "persons of anti-British sympathies," that is, with the Nehru family.[187] At first there was no place for Ñāṇaponika and the two other monks in the anti-Nazi wing and they had to wait for half a year in Wing One before they could join Govinda in his barrack.

Why did Ñāṇatiloka stay in Wing One? There appear to be several reasons for this. One ought to take into account that Ñāṇatiloka had grown up in a nationalistic, upper-class family during the founding years of modern Germany. When he returned in 1919–1920 to the so-called Weimar Republic, he only found chaos and the subversive activities of the Communists. Furthermore, he had repeatedly experienced the extreme anti-German attitude of the British, who treated him as a spy. For six years after the First World War, they did not allow him to come back to Ceylon. Perhaps due to these negative experiences he preferred to stay on the side of the German government. He definitely did not harbour anti-Jewish feelings because his disciples Ñāṇaponika, Ñāṇakhetta and Ñāṇamālita were of Jewish origin and he had Jewish friends in his youth. Nazis had caused troubles for him at the Island Hermitage in 1939 and it is quite unlikely that he had an affinity for Nazism.[188]

It is also to be noted that Wing One's official name was not "Nazi Wing" and was not solely inhabited by Nazis because even Ñāṇaponika, who had a Jewish background, stayed there initially. Like the Australian camp Ñāṇatiloka stayed in during WWI, the wing he stayed in was for upper class Germans such as managers, officials, etc. However, because many of its inmates were Nazi sympathizers and because these inmates had a large influence in this wing, it got to be called this way in the anti-Nazi wing.

The relative comfort and smooth organization of the "Big Sahib" wing, where he could get his own room and privacy, was probably the decisive factor that made him stay there, rather than at the anti-Nazi wing where he would have had to stay in a barrack and where things were not so well organized. His 1920 experience of the journey to Colombo on the ship with the disorganized and disobedient Communist crew would have put him off. In terms of the Buddhist monk's monastic discipline, there is no fault in talking to unvirtuous persons and teaching them Dhamma. If they are requested, Buddhist monks are even allowed to stay and teach for a few days in army camps near battle fields. In any case, Ñāṇatiloka stayed on in Wing One together with the loyal Vappo.

On the other hand, Ñāṇaponika, as a Jewish victim of Nazism had first-hand experience of harassment by Nazis. For that reason he had brought his mother to Ceylon and thus saved her from the Holocaust. So it was quite understandable that he decided to move to the anti-Fascist camp, though the separation from his beloved teacher would not have been easy for him, and apparently Ñāṇatiloka also was sad about it.

Both Ñāṇatiloka and Ñāṇaponika used the time in Dehra Dun to do a lot of literary work. Ñāṇatiloka wrote his *Buddhist Dictionary,* an authoritative manual which has been reprinted several times, and prepared German translations of the works he had written in English. Ñāṇaponika made the German translations of the *Suttanipāta, Dhammasaṅgaṇī, Atthasālinī* and some texts related to *satipaṭṭhāna* meditation.

The environment was not suitable for meditation since the other internees were often very noisy. Moreover fellow internees would make fun of meditators when they would see them sitting cross-legged.

Ñāṇatiloka was fortunate enough to have his own room with furniture and electricity, where he lived with Vappo. Behind a curtain in this room, Vappo had his own place. The monks in the anti-Nazi wing were less well off and had to stay in barracks without furniture. Electricity came to the anti-Nazi wing a long time after it came to the Nazi wing in 1943. With permission from the camp authorities, visits to other wings were possible and Ñāṇaponika and Govinda regularly visited Ñāṇatiloka.[189] Ñāṇaponika and Govinda became close friends despite having different views about the Dhamma.

Unlike his last imprisonment in 1916, this time Ñāṇatiloka did not try to escape. Others however did attempt to do so. The escape of seven Germans in broad daylight was quite spectacular. Two German businessmen, Rolf Magener and Heins von Have, who were accustomed to British upper class customs, dressed up as British officers, and the others including Heinrich Harrer—a member of the Nanga-Parbat mountaineering expedition—dressed up as Indian workmen. Pretending to be a wire repairs crew, the "officers" and their "crew" walked out through a guard post, and then escaped through the jungle. Magener and von Have traversed India first class, pretending to be British and then Swiss businessmen. In a month they reached Burma, where they were arrested by the Japanese as British spies. After three months of interrogation by the dreaded Japanese military police, they were released and sent to Tōkyō. Their experiences were written down by Magener in *Prisoner's Bluff*.[190] Harrer managed to travel all the way to Lhasa in Tibet, enduring much hardship on the way. He later wrote a book about his adventures called *Sieben Jahre in Tibet*,[191] translated into English as *Seven Years in Tibet*, and made into a romanticized Hollywood movie in 1997. The escapees who were caught by the British, as most escapees were, received a punishment of twenty-eight days solitary confinement.

The only Buddhist monk who ran away was Ñāṇakhetta. After having managed to get away from the guards,[192] he walked for days through the mountains until he happened to meet a Hindu yogi who allowed him to stay for a few weeks. The yogi successfully taught him how to reach the state of deep tranquillity (*samādhi*) he had earlier strived for in vain. This encounter and the experience of deep tranquillity, which he took to be full liberation, eventually made him abandon the Buddhist teachings and become a yogi himself.

Like most escapees, Ñāṇakhetta went back to the camp of his own free will. The solitary existence with the constant concern about being arrested was too stressful. He left the Saṅgha at the end of 1944 and later he became a Hindu swami with the name of Gauribala. In contrast with the many disrobals that took place during the internment in World War One, Ñāṇakhetta and his younger brother Ñāṇamālita were the only disciples of Ñāṇatiloka who disrobed during this period of internment.

Eidlitz on the Life in Dehra Dun

Editor's Note: *The following is an account of the life in the Dehra Dun camp by the Jewish Austrian writer Walther Eidlitz,*[193] *a part of his book called* Bhakta.[194] *In May 1938, Eidlitz came to India on a spiritual search and became a Hindu* bhakti-yogi *under a guru called Śri Mahāraj. When WWII broke out he was arrested, and except for a brief period of freedom just before the Germans invaded France, spent the rest of the war in the internment camps in India. In the camp he met a German Sanskrit scholar who was a* bhakta *and became his disciple. Eidlitz mentions that there were a few eminent and exemplary German scholar monks in the Dehra Dun camp, but instead he had to* *stay in a barrack with the rigid German monk Ñāṇasīsi with whom he and the other inmates could not get along. Although Eidlitz' account doesn't deal with Ñāṇatiloka directly, it describes the life in the camp in such a unique way that it is worth reproducing it here.*

"The Indian camps, in which I lived for almost six years, were mostly good camps. There were no gas-chambers, no cremation-ovens and no torture-and punishment-rooms. These camps could not be compared in any way to those of Germany and surrounding countries. The simple food was generally good and sufficient, but consisted almost solely of meat, which diet was certainly not the fault of the authorities because in many parts of India there was actually famine. That I personally suffered and occasionally starved was my own mistake, because I selfishly endeavoured to follow the strict vegetarian lifestyle I had learned in the house of my guru. But despite the good treatment, there was no one in the camp (and I was no exception) who was not at some time overcome by despair and close to committing suicide to end the suffering, concerns and problems of a tortured world.

Like God, the authorities in all countries wanted to see everywhere and therefore they built up ingenious secret police systems which looked with a hundred thousand prying eyes and listened with a hundred thousand crafty ears. The senses and extremities of these ghost-like monsters reached out all over the world, and also into the prison camp. When I arrived in the Indian camp, I was at once whispered to, "Take care. He's only friendly with you so that he can check you out. He is a spy, a Nazi agent. That one? He writes reports for the English. When he was drunk once, he told me himself. I have myself once seen he handed over a message to the sergeant. This one here? God save us! Don't you know? He is a communist, belonging to the GPU. Believe me, the Russians have their representatives and cells with the anti-nazis and the Nazis. Now they are looking already at what will happen when the war is finished."

Division and fear jerked and quivered in the entangled mass of several thousand people who lived in barbwire pens, without knowing anything about Shiva's dance from under whose steps the flames of destruction were flaring up.

Outside the camp lived large hoards of grey and brown monkeys, which were each led by one huge, old male monkey, a very controlling dictator, a real tyrant. Often a whole group of monkeys stood before the outer barbwire fence, and all the elderly and young ones, the males and females (which were carrying their babies on their chests), stared with sad, serious animal eyes into the fenced-off, strange world of humans.

Often we laughed, "We are doing really well. We also have a zoo." But then we would remember how things stood in reality—the monkeys outside were free and were staring curiously through the fence at us, the caged in humans.

What did the monkeys see? They saw humans inside the barbwire always teeming like ants. They dug the earth, planted bananas and other fruit shrubs and trees. They made small gardens in front of their barracks. They gave water to their flowerbeds. They sowed flowers and vegetables; they planted lettuce. They were doing carpentry, laying pipes, knitting, and plumbing; and they were sweating. They mixed concrete, built with bricks and stones. They fought a never-ending battle against the vermin in their beds and the holes in their socks and shirts. They played cards and let the gramophone run for hours. They chatted; they argued; they fought. Many lay dully for days on their bed-bugged braced-beds in the barracks and dreamed their difficult dreams.

The eight enclosures of the internment camp enjoyed autonomy behind barb-wire. Behind carefully guarded fences, there was a National-socialist state, which was further divided into three separately enclosed zones. There was a Führer (leader), Under-Führer, and an Inner Circle. Here there was an organization for "fortitude through joy," for music and theatre performances, and for education. Whoever wanted to, could get further education, from the basics of writing law to factory management and even examinations. There were also blacklists, secret acts, boycotts for disagreeable elements, the bringing into line of opposing groups, sometimes cane punishment, proposals for the censure of letters, and the Gestapo.

Adjacent, in the camp-wing of the anti national-socialists, there was a strict democratic form of government with regular elections and heated election agitation. Here, publicly and in many languages, there was prayer for the victory of the allied forces over their hated opponents. In this wing the inhabitants lived as in a waiting room of a railway station: "only a few days, only a few weeks, until the ordeal is finished." All waited for their early release. They celebrated behind barbwire the great victory celebration of the end of the war, and then waited much longer, full of grief and embitterment.

Another barbwire enclosure, only for Italian Catholic missionaries including two bishops, was a real church-state, two hundred and fifty meters wide, and three hundred meters long.

There was a camp wing for about one hundred Italian generals, who were arrested in Eastern Africa. This group of high military men was also internally divided into fascist and anti-fascist groups, which were fervently feuding against each other.

In one camp wing, groups of internees stood close to the barbwire, facing the neighbouring section in a hostile manner, and sang in unison and staccato: "*Du-ce! Du-ce! Du-ce!... Hit-ler! Hit-ler! Hit-ler!...*" In the neighbouring cage, where the anti-fascists were living, simultaneously a woodpile fire was lit in preparation of the coming events, followed by a life-size straw image of Mussolini being hung on a gallows in the flickering light. When the dangling dictator was about to be hauled down off the gallows and thrown into the fire–it was well after midnight–the English sergeant-major came marching in with some soldiers who were keeping watch. He was curt and uptight and called "Nutcracker." With his false teeth clacking, he asked friendly and politely, "Who is the artist? Who has arranged this so well?" Flattered, the main artists reported themselves, and, because they had disturbed the night's rest, were taken away under loud acclaim of the opposition on the yonder side of the barbwire.

We were cared for in every way. Even a big cinema barrack was erected for the internees, behind barbwire of course, but with buzzing fans against the heat. The cinema was also for the European guards and officers. When the cinema barrack burnt down, it was built up again by day and night labour in a few weeks of time. The Indian tenant did not want to give up his income. Arranged in rows of three, we marched under guard through the double barbwired towers of our camp wing, into the barbwire enclosure surrounding the cinema. The Nazis marched tightly in unison, while the anti-nazis did not do so out of protest.

Disturbed, the monkeys jumped from the street into the foliage of the trees and showed their teeth. Then we sat down on the benches, tightly crowded, surrounded by smoke from cheap Indian cigarettes, and watched the American sensation movies. We also saw the newsreel. We saw how a young queen gave flowers and sweets to injured young soldiers. We saw how humming bomber-planes dropped big bombs, which dug huge craters into the ground and threw up smoke, high into the sky. Before our eyes, unknown large cities were destroyed, sometimes also the cities in which we were born.

Everything was for us as though it were in the outside world. All the problems and misery and strife and hate of the world penetrated unhindered to us through the double barbwire fences into the strictly closed off camp: to believers and non-believers, Catholics and Protestants and adherents of all possible Christian denominations, to Jews and the lonely Mohammedans and Buddhists, to the men from about twenty European nations, to Germans, Austrians and Italians, Finns, Bulgarians and Rumanians, Estonians, Latvians and Lithuanians. But also those who were kept in our camp, although they belonged to allied nations: Czechs, Poles, Greeks, Yugoslavians, Danes, Norwegians... They were all people whom the war had caught by surprise in the distant tropical countries between New Guinea and Iraq, between Hong Kong and Ethiopia.

They all tried to live on as they had done before. They referred to themselves according to the titles they had had before: as Director or Study-counsellor. Among them were also many directors and managers of huge plantations who formerly had had phenomenally high incomes and important work-domains. The suitcases were regularly unpacked, in so far as that they had not been sunk by a Japanese submarine during the journey from the Dutch internment camp in Sumatra to India. The belongings were stacked in the fresh air and the night clothing was hung in the sun, so that they wouldn't get spoiled. Then, the snobbish suits and dinner jackets were hanging on washing lines and wafting in the wind. On Sunday afternoons, often one or the other would go walking between the barracks and the latrines in a dinner jacket and ironed shirt so as to become an elegant gentleman again for a few hours, before he would mothball the clothes once more and put on his khaki shorts.

Suitcases were unpacked and packed again. The memories were unpacked but never locked up. Because the present became bleaker and bleaker over the years and rhetorical constructions all collapsed, many thousands of these imprisoned people lived ever more passionately in their memories, wallowing in their memories. Hours and days they walked up and down along the barbwire and would tell each other what they had eaten in this or that restaurant, down to the minutest details about the sequence of dishes, the accompanying wines, and the intense relishing of the tastes. In the same manner they would talk about their adventures with women, the good and bad business deals they had pulled off, and how they had managed to cheat someone. Greedily they sought for new companions who had not yet heard their stories and jokes. Any newcomer from another camp would be visited and wooed as someone to be told stories to. Many people, because of living together for years in the same barrack, strongly avoided each other because they could not endure any longer the other's way of laughing and his stories.

Many internees kept pets. They, who were themselves kept inside barbwire fences, had put small cages with animals inside their own cages, and gave these animals all their love. A man, who proudly claimed that he diligently helped to ignite a number of synagogues in Germany, affectionately cherished his parrots, nightingales, and other birds. A good-hearted German musician in my barrack, a convinced anti-fascist, kept mice. Once he put a field mouse, who had taken a wrong turn, into a cage where already a family of mice was living. Shyly and fearfully the lean, strange mouse—a female—nestled itself in a corner of the cage. Attempting to make itself as little noticed as possible, but the father mouse, mother mouse, and small mice could smell her and felt disturbed, irritated, and betrayed by her presence So half an hour later the strange mouse, which possibly was of a different race of mice, was seen lying dead in a puddle of blood, bitten to death by sharp teeth. Probably the mice thought that their strange guest trembling with fear was a malignant intruder, who had sneaked into their own land full of ulterior motives.

By far the best place in the camp was the hospital, which was also fenced in by barbwire. It was communal to all parties in the camp. Nevertheless, one could find true peace in one of the wards of this hospital. When the patients were suffering severe pains, often the most fanatic faces would become fresh and human, like faces of children. Oh, how many strange misfortunes have been disclosed to me when old and young men, who had lived decades in the tropics, would tell the stories of their lives in the sleepless night before a difficult operation, or when they'd be waiting for death. Then they were grateful for the smallest favour; then they'd forget that a human who didn't belong to their party and belonged to a different race than them was lying in the next bed to them. But as soon as they'd get better, or as soon as a ray of false hope would shine for a slowly and miserably dying man, their faces again became hard, scornful and dismissive, and they would start to think about secret messages and boycott measures against their fellow sufferers.

The camp cemetery, from where one could best see the mountain ridge, was situated at the western edge of the camp and was not surrounded by barbwire. The graves were carefully kept by internees who were brought there under guard. However, the churned up political hate and the mutual antipathy among the prisoners did not even stop with the dead. The most powerful party in the camp was outraged that the dead of an opposing group of people were polluting their own dead by being in the neighbourhood in the earth of the cemetery. To avoid renewed unrest in the camp, the camp-commander felt obliged to have the anti-Nazis and anti-fascists buried in a far away cemetery in the next town.

Above on the roofs of the kitchen-barracks of all the eight wings of the camp, odious, vulture-like birds of prey were sitting in tight rows. They were the real lords of the camp. Barbwire did not hinder them; no watchman would shoot at them when they were hovering over the barbwire and would peek down unto the various folds of men. What did the birds see? They saw food. They did not bother whether the people who came out of the kitchen barracks were anti-fascists or fascists or priests. They'd swoop down violently in swarms and would snatch the morsels of meat for themselves. In their greed, they would even often strike next to the plate and tear the human hand holding it, which was dangerous because the greedy birds of prey also ate carrion and carried corpse poisons.

I too tried to live on and meditate in the barracks as I had done in the house of my guru and selfishly withdrew myself. There were some solitary rooms in the camp. To get such a room and to work and meditate there in peace was for some time my aim; or at least to get a corner place in a barrack, because this meant one would have a neighbour on one side only and on the other side a snug, protective wall. In the Bhagavadgīta I had read, "Without meditation, how can one get peace?" I tried to meditate in the midst of the noise and turmoil, put myself upright, crossed my legs, and became the object of laughter... Again in a corner of the camp where the grass had been trampled everywhere by many feet, I had found a reasonably secluded spot where I could find peace in meditation behind one of the small hutches for rabbits or cages for chickens or ducks that some of the internees had built. Afterwards, still a bit filled with happiness and light, I joined the long line at the food-distribution point where there often was a noise like from a pack of hungry dogs waiting for their meal. There some angry man would charge me, "Why are you always smiling like Mona Lisa? I can't understand why one can still smile in such a camp as we are in."...

A shrill whistle woke me in the morning; a shrill whistle called me to go and stand in line at the sports ground for the daily roll-call. Whistling from the kitchen called to go and stand in line for the distribution of food. Shrill whistling called for communal service, peeling potatoes, and so on. I was ordered to some kind of work, to clean windows, to wash the barracks... I was shouted at and also shouted many times at others. Yet where was I myself?

[*After being released for a short time and then being rearrested.*] ...I was lying in the dim barrack under a white mosquito-net within the narrow rows of sleepers who were moaning under the mounts of shards of their broken past and who were full of fear of the future. I couldn't sleep. The rush of images under my eyelids could not be extinguished. I too was full of restlessness like the others. I could not repress the concerns about my relatives, my mother, wife, and child, who were in ever increasing danger in Austria, perhaps living in worse camps than myself. I could not wrestle down the sorrow over my own fate, the grief that my spiritual training with a beloved teacher had been broken off twice in an apparently meaningless way. I sat up in bed and tried to meditate as I had learned with my guru. It worked, but when I at last lay down wearily, new agonizing images buzzed restlessly before my eyes and thoughts unrolled perforce.

Jackals howled around the camp. Then one pack stole into the camp and greedily dug around in the garbage pits, making cans rattle. My snoring neighbours turned around restlessly in their sleep; their beds were creaking. Often moaning filled the barrack, as if an alp was lying on the sleepers. I could not get rid of one agonizing thought: that all people, and I with them, in this big barrack, all people in the eight pens of this barrack-camp, no, all people on the whole earth were lying bound at the bottom of a dim cave. We were bound through the fetter of our own desires, prejudices, through our ignorance, through our lack of humility. I must have read about such a cave before. Wasn't it in a work of Plato? I couldn't remember well.

We, the prisoners in the dark cave, all stared with fearful eyes in one direction to a flickering shadow-play on one wall in the background of the cave. We only saw the dance of the distorted shadows and could not interpret the meaning of these movements. The play of the real live figures in the empire of primordial images, of which only a few hazy shadows fell into the cave, was inaccessible to us.

With a stroke of my hand I tried to dispel the images. I was thirsty and got up to go to the well and drink some water there. Quietly, not to wake the sleepers, I walked between the rows of beds to the door of the long barrack. Outside, the calls of the packs of jackals around the camp were even shriller. For hours they cried in choirs in the dark woods that surrounded the camp. Often the choir would fall silent and only one single animal would then stir itself in ever more wild, lurid laughter, as if it was madly laughing at the strange shadow-world in which we humans lived."

Release from Dehra Dun

Germany capitulated on 8 May 1945 and the internees of Dehra Dun hoped to be released soon. However, the war against Japan continued, and this was why the internees were kept on in Dehra Dun. Govinda was fortunate though, because he had a British passport and he was released on 14 July 1945. When Japan finally capitulated, the internees hoped to be released soon, but again in vain. The problem was that according to law they could only be released once there was a peace treaty, and in actuality there never would be one with Germany.

Besides this legal reason for not releasing the internees, there was a more practical one. Similarly to the end of the First World War, the British intended to repatriate all Germans, but while in 1919 there was the German Empire which had the obligation to receive all the repatriated, now there were four occupation zones with rather different conditions. The commander of the British zone had no interest to receive more people as there was already a constant flow of refugees from the east into his overpopulated zone. The goal of the British, however, remained to repatriate all Germans in order to prevent the re-establishment of German influence in Asia.

Finally in November 1946, after much deliberation most of the German inhabitants of Dehra Dun were repatriated to Hamburg in the British occupied area of Germany. Thanks to the efforts of the Sinhalese Buddhists and several of their increasingly politically powerful organizations, Ñāṇatiloka, the other Buddhist monks, and Gauribala and his brother Ñāṇamālita (who had disrobed but remained Buddhist[195]) were spared the return to the misery of a bomb-ravaged Germany. The organizations asked the Prime Minister of Ceylon, D. S. Senanayaka, to put pressure on the British government to allow the German monks to return to Ceylon, which at that time was taking its first steps towards independence. Senanayaka's intervention was successful and thus, in September 1946, Ñāṇatiloka and the others were able to return to Ceylon.

In 1946, just before his departure from the internment camp, Ñāṇatiloka finished the introduction to the English edition of his *Buddhist Dictionary*. Already by 1941, in Diyatalāva, he had completed the German version. Thus, the popular and authoritative *Buddhist Dictionary* was the main fruit of his time spent in Dehra Dun.

Chapter 22: Last years, 1946–1957

The last ten years of Ñāṇatiloka's life are not as eventful as his earlier life. The most important event is his participation in the Sixth Council in Burma.

After seven years of exile, Ñāṇatiloka was able to return to the Island Hermitage together with Vappo and Ñāṇaponika. This time, the Island Hermitage had been kept in good condition. Ñāṇāloka had looked after the island together with the Ceylonese monks Soma and Kheminda, the two friends of Ñāṇaponika from his time in Gampola and Bandaraväla. Ñāṇaponika had brought them to the Island Hermitage just after the outbreak of the war in order to use their help taking care of the place. During the time they had been away the adjoining island called Mätiduva had been donated to the Island Hermitage by its owner, Evadne de Silva, a member of the organization called Sāsanadhāra Kantha Samitiya which supported the Island Hermitage. A little causeway had been built to connect the two islands so it was now possible to walk from one island to the next. This was a nice welcome present for Ñāṇatiloka.

A false report that Ñāṇatiloka had died was spread in Germany in 1947. It appeared in the newspapers and even on the radio. Condolence letters flooded the Island Hermitage until the report was declared to be false. However, ten years later, when Ñāṇatiloka had really died, the German press did not take any notice of it.

In 1949, with the help of his supporter in Colombo, Mr. J. K. Fernando, Ñāṇatiloka had started the Island Hermitage Publications in order to publish his works and the works of other monks staying at the Island Hermitage. The only publications that were published were his *Buddhist Dictionary* and Ñāṇaponika's *Abhidhamma Studies*.

Ñāṇatiloka's second anthology of discourses called *The Path to Deliverance* was published in 1952. It is larger than the *Word of the Buddha* and has a different arrangement. Instead of being based on the Four Noble Truths, it combines the seven Stages of Purification with the three categories of the Eightfold Path. Although it was written in English, it was the one Ñāṇatiloka liked the most of all works that he had written. His most popular work, however, remained the *Word of the Buddha*. This modern classic of Buddhist literature has gone through many editions and has been translated into many languages. Many were introduced to the Buddha's teaching or gained a clear understanding of it from this book.

Ñāṇavīra and Ñāṇamoli

In 1949 two educated, upper-class English Buddhists, Harold Musson[196] and Osbert Moore[197], came to the Island Hermitage and were accepted by Ñāṇatiloka under the names of Ñāṇavīra and Ñāṇamoli.

Musson came from a well-to-do family. When he was nine years old, his father, a colonel in the British army, was stationed in Burma and there the young Musson received his first impressions of Buddhism. At Magdalene College at Cambridge, he first studied mathematics and later modern languages, including Italian, in which he graduated.

Moore grew up in the Scilly Isles. His father had once been an explorer. Having a gift for the Italian and French languages, Moore entered Exeter College at Oxford, where, like Musson, he studied modern languages. Because of his expert knowledge of antiques and his ability to find rare and unusual objects, he became a partner in an antiques shop that a rich university friend opened after their graduation.

When WWII broke out, Moore was enlisted into the army and because of his skill in Italian became an intelligence officer working in a large internment camp for Italian prisoners of war. In 1944 he was transferred to Italy, where he interrogated important Italian spies and saboteurs. Here he first met Musson, who, because of his fluency in Italian, had also become an officer interrogating spies. The colleagues became good friends and had long, deep discussions about literature and philosophy in the officers' mess.

Their interest in Buddhism was roused after having read a Nietzschean book about Buddhism called *The Doctrine of*

Awakening.[198] Written by the artist, fascist, and esotericist Julius Evola, the book greatly impressed them. Evola wrote the aim of the book was to "illuminate the true nature of original Buddhism which had been weakened to the point of unrecognisability in most of its subsequent forms." For Evola the essential spirit of Buddhist doctrine was "determined by a will for the unconditioned, affirmed in its most radical form, and by investigation into that which leads to mastery over life as much as death."[199] Musson translated Evola's book into English and eventually got it published by Luzac & Co.

Having returned to England after the war, Moore joined the Italian section of the BBC. In 1948, Moore and Musson, who shared a flat in London, came to the conclusion the lives they were leading were utterly pointless. They therefore decided to go to Ceylon to practice Buddhism. They arrived in April 1949 in Colombo where they visited Vajirārāmaya and then the Island Hermitage.

After having been at the Island Hermitage for a few weeks, Moore wrote the following description of the life at the Island Hermitage in a letter to a relative:

> The hermitage really consists of two islands joined by a causeway. Polgasduva (coconut tree island) has been the hermitage since before the first World War, whilst Madiduwa (round island) was a cinnamon garden which was given to the hermitage by the owner.
>
> The original hermitage is covered with a forest jungle of mangroves, palms, creepers and what not amongst which are seven isolated 'houses' (one room each) and a refectory. Madiduwa is more open and covered with cinnamon bushes and coconut palms. Both are surrounded and the causeway arched over with a narrow belt of mangroves... The lake is large, about two-and-a-half miles across and brackish as it connects with the sea, and is entirely surrounded by hillocks covered with coconut palms. A huge colony of cranes which spend the night feeding in the countryside among the rice fields, roost by day and squawk in the island mangroves. Iguanas wander among the bushes, some three feet long and oddly prehistoric-looking, whilst similar looking water lizards

swim in the lake. Large birds whoop and shriek and small birds sing rather saccharine and sentimental songs–often indeed tunes rather than songs. Drums beat for long periods from many places on the mainland, sometimes all night and sometimes all day, with complicated rhythms.[200] All day from the nearest mainland comes the monotonous pounding of coconut husks being beaten into fibre.

The weather is always summer. The sun is now overhead. It is apt to be very heavy at midday but there are always clouds about and the sky looks absurdly English. Often it rains, and what rain! Clouds pile up with thunder and lightning. Then you hear a strange roaring like a waterfall across the lake and soon the rain bursts on the island with astonishing violence.

The day at present is spent like this: I aim to get up at four and meditate till about seven. Then sweep the room (the only manual work allowed to monks) and make tea in the kitchen. Breakfast arrives brought by one of the four lay attendants. It consists of rice gruel made with coconut milk, rice cakes with spiced sauce, sweets and bananas and papaws. I spend the morning between learning Pali, meditation or cooking. Sometimes food is brought and sometimes not, in which case I cook it from supplies I keep in hand.

In the afternoon one sleeps for a bit, bathes in the lake and meditates afterwards. At seven or so there is tea in the refectory for anyone who wants to go there. Here one has cups of tea and lemon and talks of doctrine with the monks, or Pali discourses are recited. It is dark at this time and the refectory is open on two sides to the air. Strangely when the doctrine is discussed or Pali recited, large toads come out on to the floor to listen, their large golden eyes unblinking. When it is over, they go away. The atmosphere is almost Franciscan, especially when the rain roars so loud that you have to shout to be heard and the feeble light of naked oil wicks is drowned by the almost continuous blue lightning accompanied by the crashing of thunder–or again on one of those incredibly grandiose nights of the full moon when soft strong light streams down through the dense trees.

> One goes to bed at about ten. As you see one does not eat after midday, a habit which I have taken to kindly. I sleep on a board with a thin mattress which is also reasonable as I have always liked hard beds ...
>
> Two things impress me about the monks here, Sinhalese, German and Burmese,–that is their extraordinary kindness, solicitude and cheerfulness and that there are no subjects which are taboo for discussion or anything which you have to take on trust.[201]

Towards the end of the same letter Moore announced that he and Musson had decided to become monks and would be accepted as novices in a few weeks. Thus, on April 24 1949, the Englishmen received the going forth, *pabbajjā*, from Ñāṇatiloka at the Island Hermitage. In 1950 they got the full acceptance, *upasampadā*, at Vajirārāma monastery in Colombo under Venerable Pelene Vajirañāṇa Mahāthera.

Except for occasional interruptions such as pilgrimages and visits to other monasteries, Ñāṇamoli spent the eleven years of his monk life at the Island Hermitage. After having been taught the basics of Pali by Ñāṇatiloka Thera, he acquired a remarkable command of the Pali language and a wide knowledge of the canonical scriptures within a comparatively very short time. He became a renowned scholar and a prolific translator of mostly abstruse Pali texts such as the *Visuddhimagga* (*The Path of Purification*) and the *Nettipakaraṇa* (*The Guide*). In 1960 he died of a heart attack while doing a walking pilgrimage with Kheminda Thera.

Ñāṇavīra left the Island Hermitage after five years due to health problems and a desire for more solitude. Eventually he moved to a hut in a more suitable, dry, remote jungle area, near a coastal village called Bundala, in the deep south of Ceylon. Here he lived as a hermit. He kept up a continuous correspondence with Ñāṇamoli, and also several other people, wherein they would extensively discuss the Buddha's teaching and its relation to Western philosophy and literature.

Based on the understanding he had gained of the Buddha's discourses and of Western existentialist philosophers such as Nietzsche and Heidegger, Ñāṇavira wrote a polemical work called

Notes on Dhamma,[202] which he published in a private, cyclostyled edition in 1965. Among other views he argues, for a "one-life interpretation" of dependent origination (*paṭiccasamuppāda*) and strongly rejects the "three-life interpretation" and other interpretations of the Buddha's teachings as propounded in the Abhidhamma and the Pali commentaries.

Due to severe, chronic health problems, Ñāṇavīra committed suicide in 1965. In a letter, which was supposed to be opened after his death, he claimed that in 1959 he had become a stream-enterer while doing walking meditation and reflecting on the Dhamma.

Ñāṇavimala

In 1953 a pupil of Ñāṇatiloka called Friedrich Möller returned to Ceylon from Germany after a long absence. Möller had met Ñāṇatiloka in the Dehra Dun internment camp and became his disciple.

Born in 1911 in Hessendorf bei Rinteln, Möller was spiritually inclined from an early age. Although he was first a Christian, a meeting with an Indian medical student in Germany aroused his interest in yoga and Hinduism, so he decided that he wanted to go to India to further his new religious pursuits. Because the German military was preparing for war and needed many recruits, it was generally quite difficult for German men to leave the country, but three or four years before World War II, Möller managed to arrange for the trading house in Hamburg at which he was employed to send him to Bombay in India to work as a trader. About a year before the war started, Möller was appointed the director of a German trading house in Colombo. In Colombo he led a pleasant and luxurious life which came to an abrupt end with the outbreak of war in 1939. Along with many other German male nationals living in British colonies, Möller was arrested by the British government as an enemy. He was first interned in Diyatalāva in the Ceylon hill country and then early in 1942 was sent to the large and fairly comfortable Central Internment Camp near Dehra Dun in northwest India. He was placed in the same wing as Ñāṇatiloka and his German pupil Vappo, where they became friends.

Being a strict vegetarian, Möller refused to eat the non-vegetarian food served in the camp and almost died because of this. On the brink of death, he took the advice of his Buddhist friends to give up his vegetarian views and quickly recovered. Later, while recounting this experience he said he then understood the wisdom of the Buddha in not promoting vegetarianism. During his time in the internment camp, he became a pupil of Ñāṇatiloka and a devout Buddhist.

Friedrich Möller had to go to back to Germany after being released from the internment camp despite his strong desire to become a Buddhist monk in Ceylon. He was not eligible to do so because he had not been a Buddhist monk in Ceylon before the war. He first worked on a farm in the countryside near Hamburg. The only remuneration he received was free food and lodging, but this was his only alternative to going hungry. After some time he found work as an English teacher in Hamburg and could stay with his former landlady, who treated him like the son she had lost during the war. Many German men had died during the war and the large majority of Möller's pupils were females. Nevertheless, Möller was able to resist the temptations of sensuality and romance because he was firmly determined to return to Ceylon and become a monk.

He became involved with a local Buddhist group. One day in 1953, in a hotel in Hamburg, he had to translate from English into German a speech given by Asoka Weeraratna, the founder of the German Buddhist Missionary Society (Lanka Dharmadhuta Society) in Colombo. At this meeting, Weeraratna and Möller agreed that he would come to Ceylon with the support of the Dharmadhuta Society, which would arrange for him to train in missionary work for three years before returning to Germany with the first German Buddhist Mission.

After an absence of almost thirteen years, Möller returned to Ceylon, arriving in Colombo in June 1953. He lived for a year at the Dharmadhuta Society in Colombo and also spent time at the Forest Hermitage in Kandy. He moved from Colombo to the Island Hermitage and at the age of forty-three was accepted as a novice by Ñāṇatiloka on 19 September 1955, taking the Pāli name of Ñāṇavimala. As Ñāṇatiloka's health was declining, he put the novice under the care of Ñāṇāloka, the abbot of the Island

Hermitage. It was the English bhikkhu Ñāṇamoli, however, who especially helped by teaching him Pāli and explaining the monk's rules and other aspects of the monk's life. Exactly two months after becoming a novice, he received full acceptance into the Sangha with Madiha Paññāsīha as his preceptor. He then realized that he first had to work on himself and did not regard himself capable of being a teacher for others yet. He decided to stay on in Ceylon. He later related that this change of mind had been brought about by conversations he had with Ñāṇamoli. The Dharmadhuta Society respected his wish.

For ten years Ñāṇavimala lived quietly at the Island Hermitage, completely dedicating himself to study and meditation. He studied the Pāli suttas and put the understanding he gained into practice. He generally kept to himself and had little contact with others. Then, in 1966, he left the Island Hermitage to go on a walking tour (*cārikā*) through Ceylon. For about twenty-five years he walked all over Ceylon, from south to north and back, from west to east and back. He would normally stay in monasteries and other places on the way for at most three days at a time and would then continue walking. The aim of his austere practice was to avoid accumulating possessions and mental attachments to places and people. When staying in a place for a long time, various attachments can easily build up that can be in conflict with the Buddhist monk's state of being a homeless one. Ñāṇavimala would only carry his alms bowl and a small bag with some essential requisites. He did not even use sandals. Once, robbers came up to him and investigated his bag, but finding nothing of value left empty-handed.

To be even more free and detached inside, Ñāṇavimala would normally have no fixed destination. Once he had been staying for a few weeks at the Vajirārāma temple in Colombo. One morning he left the monastery and was walking down Vajira Road towards Galle Road. A supporter of Vajirārāma saw him walking down the road, came up to him and greeted him. Seeing his bag and bowl slung over his shoulder, he realized that he had left the monastery and said to him: "Well, venerable sir, I see you've decided to leave the monastery and resume your travels. Where are you heading?" Ñāṇavimala promptly replied: "I haven't decided yet. I'll decide when I get to the corner."

He would collect his food by going on alms-round (*piṇḍapāta*) in villages and towns along the way. Only during the rainy season retreat (*vassa*) would he stay put in a monastery for three continuous months, in accordance with the prescribed rule; most often he would spend the rains period at the Island Hermitage. To undertake such a difficult ascetic practice for a long time can be quite physically demanding even for young monks, how much more so for an elderly monk. Nevertheless, Ñāṇavimala persisted with this practice up to 1991, although after 1987 a hip affliction prevented him from walking for long stretches at a time. He then spent four years in Colombo at Vajirārāmaya Monastery. In 1995 he returned to the Island Hermitage, and later moved to the more secluded island, Parappaduva, where he subsequently passed away in during the rains retreat of 2005.

When he met people, Ñāṇavimala would encourage them to practice the Dhamma with the suttas as a guide. Again and again he emphasized that the practice of the Dhamma, a simple renunciant lifestyle, and the giving up of all worldly attachments will lead one to the supreme bliss of Nibbāna. His own renunciant lifestyle and mental well-being certainly exemplified his advice to others. He inspired many younger monks and, when he still had physical strength, was happy to give wise counsel to them on how to live the bhikkhu life to best advantage.

The Forest Hermitage

On 26 December 1950, Ñāṇatiloka and Ñāṇaponika became Sinhalese citizens of the newly independent Ceylon. Ñāṇatiloka left the Island Hermitage for the third and last time in 1951, this time due to old age. He had turned seventy in 1948 and it became difficult to bear the humid, sultry climate of the coastal area, so he looked for a different place to live. At first he stayed in a few places upcountry such as Diyatalāva, where he had been interned earlier, then in Bandaravāla with his Czech student Ñāṇasatta, and also in Välimada.

Ñāṇaponika also had some health problems due to the hot and humid climate of the Island Hermitage and he too decided to look for a place in the more pleasant upcountry where he had stayed before the war. While visiting Kandy in 1950, he met the elderly American nun Dhammadinnā,[203] who was living in a cottage in the ancient royal forest called the Udavattakälē, situated on a hill ridge right behind the famous temple with the Buddha's tooth. The name of the cottage was the Forest Hermitage. As she was about to go and live in Australia, Dhammadinnā offered him the Forest Hermitage, if the owner, Mrs Senanāyake, would agree. Mrs Senanāyake then kindly donated the Forest Hermitage to the Saṅgha. Thus, the German monks could move from the Island Hermitage to the more agreeable climate and conditions of the Forest Hermitage. In 1951, Ñāṇatiloka and Vappo went to live there and in 1952 Ñāṇaponika joined them. The hermitage became known among the locals as the "German Pansala," or the "German Monastery." Ñāṇaponika continued staying at the Forest Hermitage until his death in 1993. In 1958 he co-founded the Buddhist Publication Society, of which he was the editor and president.

The Sixth Council

In the meantime, the following had happened: On 2 February 1950, U Nu,[204] the devout Buddhist prime minister of Burma, had visited the Island Hermitage and met Ñāṇatiloka and his students. As a result of this visit, Ñāṇatiloka and Ñāṇaponika were soon after invited to participate in the preparations for the Sixth Buddhist Council in Rangoon.[205]

Ñāṇatiloka went by ship with Ñāṇaponika to Rangoon where they arrived on 30 January 1952. They had discussions with U Nu regarding his grand plans to bring Buddhism to the West and to translate the entire Pali Canon into English.[206] His ideas were only partly realized as he was ousted by the Burmese military in 1962.

Ñāṇatiloka stayed for some days at the monastery in Rangoon where he had been accepted in 1903. He returned to Colombo on 17 February 1952 by ship and then went to Kandy. Ñāṇaponika, however, remained for a longer time in Burma. He visited Mandalay and Moulmein and participated in a Vipassanā meditation course under the famous Mahāsi Sayādaw, before following Ñāṇatiloka to the Forest Hermitage in Kandy.

The Sixth Buddhist Council was opened with festivities in Yagu, near Rangoon, on the Vesak of 1954. It was held in a large hall inside a huge manmade mount which was to resemble the cave in which the First Council was held. It was called the Mahā Pāsāṇa Guhā, the "Great Sacred Cave." The purpose of the Council was to prepare and then recite a new purified official edition of the Tipiṭaka, the so-called "Sixth Council Edition" (*Chaṭṭhasaṅgāyana*). The text of the Burmese Fifth Council edition, which was held about one hundred years earlier and was inscribed completely on large granite slabs in Mandalay, was compared with the editions existing in other Buddhist countries, that is, Cambodia, Ceylon and Thailand. At this Council, twenty-five hundred Buddhist monks participated, including Ñāṇatiloka and Ñāṇaponika. They were the only Western bhikkhus to participate in the Council and perhaps the first ones in any of the councils, unless there had been Greeks from Central Asia at the Third Council. There were numerous monks from Ceylon and other Theravāda Buddhist countries who helped with preparing this new official edition.

This time they flew to Burma. Due to a throat ailment, Ñāṇatiloka was not able to deliver the message that he was supposed to give to the Council and Ñāṇaponika read it out in the presence of Ñāṇatiloka while standing on a podium in front of the large assembly of monks and lay people:

> With permission of the Mahā Sangha. The Venerable Ñāṇatiloka Mahāthera regrets it very much that a throat ailment prevents him from addressing the Mahā Sangha directly. He has requested me to read his message on his behalf. The Mahāthera says:
>
> "We are very happy to be present at an event of such great importance for the Sāsana as the Chaṭṭha Saṅgāyana, and we are full of admiration for the faith, courage and sacrifice that has gone into its realization. We have all reason to be grateful to the Sangha, the Government and the laity of the Union of Burma for making all this possible.
>
> The Saṅgāyana has the task to preserve the purity of our traditional texts containing the words of the Enlightened One. It is a very important task, indeed, to see to it that the reliability of our traditional texts inspires confidence in those who

study them, and that the texts give no chance for distortions, additions and misinterpretations. There may be so-called 'modern minds' who may think that this amounts just to a cult of mere words. But they forget that we are dealing here with the clear, unambiguous words of an Enlightened One, deserving to be protected in their purity as a contrast to the mass of ambiguous verbiage and theories that confuse and mislead modern man today. Only the pure Dhamma that retains the precious flavour of Enlightenment will be a reliable guide to wise understanding and noble action. In an unambiguous teaching (*ekaṃsika-desana*), the purity of understanding is based on the purity of the wording. It is, therefore, my heartfelt wish that this important task of the Chaṭṭha Saṅgāyana may be completed successfully, and bestow its blessings on those who perform it, and help in performing it.

I have no doubt that these will also be the wishes of the Buddhists of Germany, the country of my birth, and that all German-speaking Buddhists, in Germany itself, in Austria and Switzerland, will also join me in my homage to the Mahā Sangha assembled here, and in the joy that fills us in this happy hour.

It was my good Kamma to become the first German Buddhist monk, having been ordained here, in Burma, 50 years ago. I believe that it is not without meaning and consequence that this is the first Saṅgāyana in which Western Bhikkhus take part. This fact fills me with hope and confidence that the '*Catuddisa-Sangha*', the Sangha of the four quarters of the world, will extend also to the West and take firm roots there. I am happy to tell you that enthusiastic and devoted Buddhists of Ceylon have formed a 'Lanka Dharmaduta Society,' with the intention to send, before Vesak 2500, a mission to Germany, and to establish the Sangha there. It is hoped that the year 2500 will see the first Upasampada on German soil. The realization of these plans will be a notable contribution to the hopes we cherish for the year 2500, regarding the spreading of the Sāsana. May I beg the Mahā Sangha for its blessings to that Sāsana work in my home country, Germany."[207]

They stayed for three weeks in Rangoon and, returning by boat, arrived in Colombo in June 1954. Ñāṇatiloka had a last look at the Shwe Dagon Pagoda before leaving Burma, on the ferry bringing mostly British passengers leaving the newly independent Burma for good. He was deeply moved and said to the Burmese layman accompanying him that, although he was born in Germany, he was born as a monk in Rangoon, adding that perhaps this would be the last time he would see this pagoda—and so it was.

Swami Gauribala

After WWII, Peter Schönfeldt, Ex-Ñāṇakhetta, became a Hindu sanyasi in the Shaivaite Dasanami monastic order under the name Gauribala Giri. In Ceylon the people called him the "German Swami." Initially, he regularly travelled to India meeting saints and sages but eventually found his guru in the anti-traditionalist Yogaswami of Jaffna.

A German reporter, who was a youth friend and had seen him and Feniger off when they departed for Ceylon, visited Gauribala in Ceylon after having seen a picture of Gauribala doing firewalking at Kataragama in an American magazine. He wrote an article about Gauribala which was published in the German magazine *Stern*.[208] They visited Ñāṇatiloka at the Forest Hermitage:

> In Kandy we visited, accompanied by the German Swami, the old German Buddhist monk. I noticed the cordial relation between the Hindu Swami and his former Buddhist Guru and tried, as a comparison, to imagine how a Catholic monk would receive a monastic brother who had gone over to Protestantism. I voiced this thought. The calm, clear eyes of Ñāṇatiloka looked pensively through me. "This cannot be compared with each other," he answered slowly, as if he had to consider every word. "Surely, Buddhism has come out of Hinduism like Protestantism has come out of the Catholic Church, but don't forget that the Buddhist reformation has not given rise to religious wars." After a short pause he added: "Tolerance is considered to be the highest law in both Buddhism and Hinduism since thousands of years." Up in the hermitage of the German Swami we learnt more of this tolerance. For example, that he, the renegade, could come back into a Buddhist monastery at any time.

In the 1960s, the son of the British Lord Soulbury[209] became a pupil of Gauribala and built him a small ashram (hermitage) at Selva Sannidhi Kovil on the Jaffna Peninsula in the far north of Ceylon. The unorthodox "German Swami" practised tantrism and rejected all conventions, dogmas and concepts. He had a taste for fine cigars and liquors, and was known for his Bohemian ways.[210] In 1984, not long after the civil conflict broke out, the Swami passed away. He had predicted his death three days in advance. A few months later, his ashram was bulldozed away during an army-campaign.

Last Days of Ñāṇatiloka

In July 1954, Ñāṇatiloka became ill. He had problems with his prostate and was brought to the hospital in Kandy. He stayed in the hospital for six months, during which time Ñāṇaponika came to visit him every second day. A Sinhalese novice and a student of Ñāṇatiloka stayed in the hospital and looked after him. In January 1955 Ñāṇatiloka was taken from Kandy to a hospital in Colombo, where he was operated on. His condition improved swiftly and soon he was brought back to the Forest Hermitage in Kandy.

In the spring of 1956, Ñāṇaponika went without Ñāṇatiloka to Burma in order to participate in the conclusion of the Sixth Council at Vesak. After his return in the summer of 1956, he went with Ñāṇatiloka to Colombo, in order to have better facilities for looking after him than were available in the Forest Hermitage.

From 22 July onwards, they lived together with Vappo as guests in the new building of the German Dharmaduta Society in Colombo. Ñāṇatiloka, Vappo and five other monks spent the rains retreat here. The German Dharmaduta Society had the aim to spread Sinhalese Theravada Buddhism in Germany, and Ñāṇatiloka was supportive of its mission, seeing a well-established mission to Germany as the culmination of his life.[211] The society still manages Das Buddhistische Haus or the Berlin Vihāra in Berlin, which it acquired in 1957 from the relatives of Dr. Paul Dahlke.

Nearby the German Dharmaduta Society there was the large Colombo Central Cemetery. Ñāṇatiloka could see the numerous funeral processions passing by and had ample opportunity to practise contemplation of death and impermanence. This was to be Ñāṇatiloka's last rains retreat. Ñāṇaponika carefully looked after him during his last months.

On 28 May, at 10:15 pm, Ñāṇatiloka passed away peacefully and without pain. During his last fourteen days, he had become weaker and had a light fever. The day before, he had come down with pneumonia, which his very weak body could not fight off.

The cremation took place on June 2 1957, at the Independence Square, Colombo, as an official State Funeral given in tribute to a great monk and an eminent exponent of the Dhamma to the West. Vast crowds gathered for the occasion. Among the speakers were leading monks of the three monastic orders of Ceylon; the Venerable Ñāṇasatta Thera—an experienced speaker who regularly gave public Dhamma speeches—was representing the late Mahāthera's pupils, and among lay speakers, Ceylon's Prime Minister, Mr. S. W. D. Bandaranaike, and the German Ambassador. On June 9, 1957, the ashes were brought to the Island Hermitage, Dodanduva, and interred near the late Mahāthera's hut. A monument was later erected, on which the famous stanza of Assaji which had brought the Venerable Sāriputta to the Dhamma was engraved in four languages, Pali, Sinhala, German and English:

Of things that proceed from a cause,
Their cause the Tathāgata proclaimed;
And also their cessation,
Thus taught the Great Sage.

hra Dun, 1993

Ñāṇasatta, Kheminda, Ñāṇaponika, Soma, 194

aponika, P. Schönfeldt, Govinda,
xner, Ñāṇamālita. Dehra Dun, Jan. 1943

Ñāṇatiloka at private house, Morawaka, 1935

: ?, F. Möller,Asoka Weeraratna, Nyanatiloka,
aponika, G. Anuruddha (?). Between June 1953 &
955 at the Lanka Dharmaduta Society, Colombo.

Ñāṇatiloka at Forest Hermitage, 1955

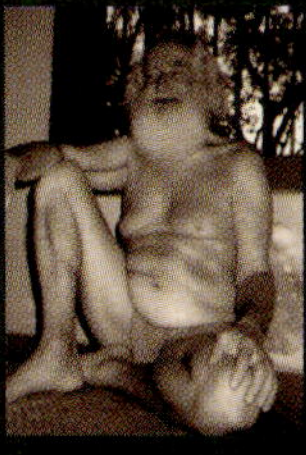

Swami Gauribala and his brother.

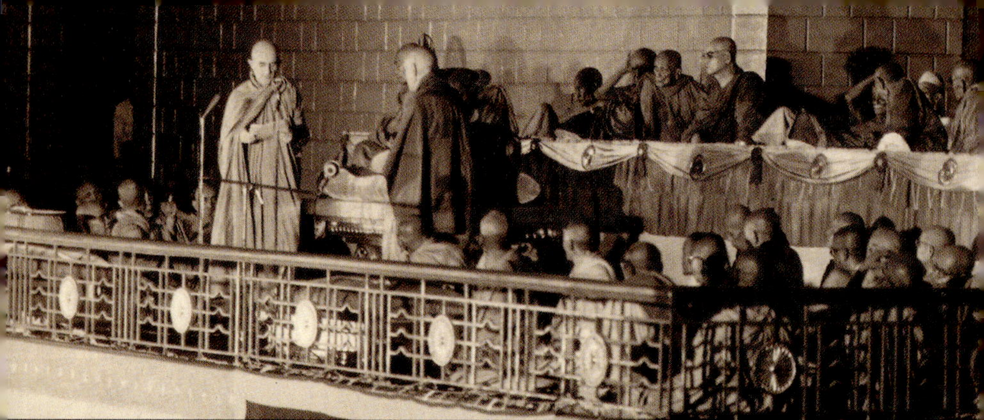

Ñāṇaponika reading out the address of Ñāṇatiloka at the opening of the Sixth Council, 18.5.195

The opening of the Sixth Council in the Great Sacred Cave. Below: The exterior of the cave.

aypeople entering the cave from the side of the Vorld Peace Pagoda.

ıks entering the cave from their living quarters.

Monks attending the council.

Venerable Vicittasāra, who could recite the whole Pali Canon by heart. During the whole Council he was the regular "Answerer of Questions."

Venerable Nyaungyan Sayādaw, the President of the Council, sitting on his golden throne in the sacred cave. He had the title "Teacher of the Country," In 1955 he was 81 years old.

Prime minister U Nu paying respect to the mahātheras.

The cremation of Ñāṇatiloka on 2.6.1957

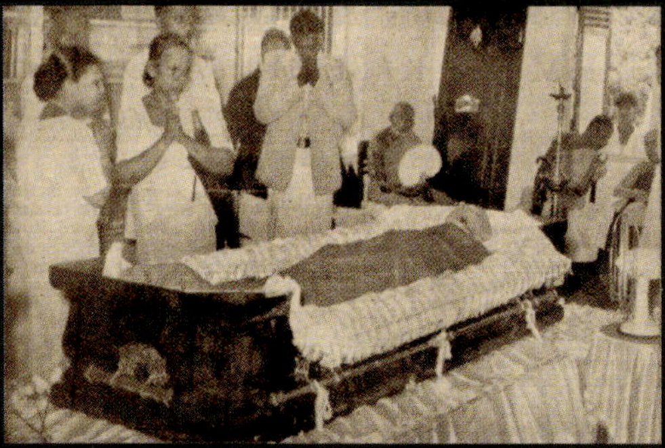

Devotees and monks paying their last respects

Ñāṇavīra, Ñāṇamoli, Ñāṇaponika, early 1950s

Tombstone of Ñāṇatiloka

Ñāṇavimala, Vajirārāma, late 1980s

Vajirārāma and IH monks at an almsging, perhaps in

APPENDIX I

LIFE SKETCH OF VENERABLE ÑĀṆAPONIKA

Ven. Bhikkhu Bodhi[212]

The person who was to become known as the Venerable Ñāṇaponika Mahāthera was born on 21st July 1901 in Germany—at Hanau, near Frankfurt—as the only child of a Jewish couple, Isaak and Sophie Feniger. His lay name was Siegmund Feniger. When he was six years old, his parents moved to an industrial town in Upper Silesia called Königshutte, whose economy was dominated by coal mines and iron foundries. There his father operated a shoe shop.

The young Siegmund attended school in Königshutte, where he studied Latin, Greek, and French. His parents were moderately religious Jews devoted principally to the ethical ideals and humane values of Judaism. Siegmund received a religious upbringing and even from an early age he evinced a keen personal interest in religion. On his own initiative he enrolled for extra lessons in Hebrew and studied Jewish religious texts under the guidance of a rabbi.

When he finished his secondary-school education, at the age of sixteen, he went to work as an apprentice in a bookshop in a neighbouring town, where he learned various aspects of the book trade. From childhood he was a voracious reader. Although his family situation did not permit him to pursue a university education, he was a fervent lover of books and was consumed with a burning intellectual curiosity which impelled him to read many of the great classics of Western literature and philosophy. His avid reading opened up to him new intellectual landscapes, which planted in his tender mind disturbing doubts concerning the traditional Jewish religious beliefs that he had hitherto accepted uncritically. These doubts spurred young Siegmund to an intense religious search by way of books, the only access he had to intellectual stimulation in this middle-sized industrial town.

In the course of his reading Siegmund came upon books on the wisdom of the East, including books about Buddhism and translations of Buddhist texts. Buddhism had an immediate appeal to him, an appeal which grew stronger the more he read. He found that Buddhism presented him with a balanced teaching that could satisfy both the critical demands of his intellect and the religious urges of his heart. Its lucidly realistic doctrine resolved his doubts about the origins of suffering and inspired him with its lofty conception of the goal of deliverance and the way to its realization. Although he had to pursue his Buddhist studies alone, without a teacher or even a friend to share his interests, so firm did his conviction in the truth of the Buddha's Teaching become that by his twentieth year he already considered himself a convinced Buddhist.

In 1922 he moved with his parents to Berlin, where he met other Buddhists, joined a Buddhist group, and gained access to a much greater range of Buddhist literature. It was here too that he first learned of a person who was to play a key role in his later life. This was the German Buddhist monk Venerable Ñāṇatiloka, who had been ordained in Burma in 1903 and in 1911 had established a retreat centre for Western Buddhist monks called Island Hermitage in a lagoon in south-western Ceylon. Ñāṇatiloka was a prolific translator of Pali Buddhist texts, and his writings and translations, which Siegmund encountered in Berlin, impressed him with their authenticity and clear rendition of the Buddha's teachings.

In 1924 the Fenigers moved to Königsberg, in East Prussia (present Kaliningrad, in Russia). At a public lecture on Buddhism Siegmund met a convinced Buddhist who introduced him to a wider circle of Buddhist acquaintances. Together with his friends he formed a Buddhist study circle in the city which met for regular sutta readings and Dhamma discussions. He also started a Buddhist lending library quartered at his father's shop. This library brought Siegmund into contact with Professor Helmuth von Glasenapp, the famous German Indologist, who was then teaching at the University of Königsberg.

One former member of a Buddhist circle in Berlin, Conrad Nell, had gone to Ceylon and taken ordination as a monk at Island Hermitage under Ñāṇatiloka with the name Bhikkhu

Ñāṇādhāra. From Ceylon and Burma Ñāṇādhāra wrote letters back to his friends in Germany describing his monk's life in the East. These letters helped to crystallize in Siegmund's mind an idea that had already been vaguely taking shape: the idea of becoming a monk himself. He now knew that there were other Western Buddhist monks living in the East, that there was a qualified Western elder to guide him, and that there were suitable facilities for his support as a monk.

This idea however could not be acted upon for some time. In 1932 his father died after a long illness and Siegmund did not wish to leave his newly widowed mother alone. In 1932 mother and son moved back to Berlin, and there Siegmund rejoined the Buddhist friends he had met during his first stay in the city. But dark clouds lay on the horizon. In 1933 Hitler came to power in Germany and began his heartless program of persecuting German Jews. At first Siegmund tried his best to stand ground in the expectation, shared by many, that the persecutions would not continue long. When he lost his job with a book association because of the spreading policy of anti-Jewish discrimination, he joined the Central Committee of German Jews for Help and Self-Protection (Zentralausschuss der deutschen Juden für Hilfe und Aufbau), a Jewish organization formed to protect the vital interests of German Jews. In time, however, it became clear to him that the waves of hatred, ignorance, and violence unleashed by the Nazis were gaining momentum at an alarming rate, and he realized that neither he nor his mother could safely remain in Germany. Hence in December 1935 he left Germany with his mother, heading for Vienna, where relatives of theirs were living.

Earlier Siegmund had spoken to his mother about his wish to become a Buddhist monk, and his mother, sympathetically responsive to her son's keen desire, told him that she would allow him to do so when their situation was secure. Siegmund had also written to Ñāṇatiloka, requesting acceptance as a candidate for ordination when conditions allowed him to come to Ceylon. The older monk had replied giving his consent. Now that mother and son were outside the immediate danger zone of Nazi persecution, Siegmund felt free to act upon his resolution. He arranged for his mother to remain in Vienna at the home of their relatives who had promised to look after her, and then set out on his journey to the East.

From Vienna Siegmund proceeded to Marseilles, where on 16th January 1936 he embarked on a ship bound for distant Asia, scheduled to stop at the port of Colombo. When the ship reached port on 4th February 1936, a launch came out to meet it bearing on board a stately light-skinned figure clad in saffron robes. This was Ñāṇatiloka Mahāthera who had come to Colombo to welcome his prospective pupil. That same day, after lunch, the party left by car for Dodanduva, the coastal town near Island Hermitage. The great venture had begun.

For several months Siegmund lived at Island Hermitage as an upāsaka, a lay disciple, preparing for ordination. On 4th June 1936, the Poson Poya day, along with three other postulants he received at the hermitage the novice ordination (*pabbajjā*). His teacher named him Ñāṇaponika, meaning "inclined to knowledge." (In conferring Pali names Ñāṇatiloka would sometimes attempt to "Palicize" part of the civilian name, and in this case he considered *ponika* the closest phonological equivalent of Feniger, the *f* turning to *p* in Pali, which lacks an *f* sound.) The following year, on 29th June 1937, in a mainland temple he received the higher ordination (*upasampadā*) as a bhikkhu.

At Island Hermitage, Bhikkhu Ñāṇaponika took regular lessons from his teacher in the Buddhist teachings and in the Pali language; on his own, he also studied English, which he had not studied earlier. Ñāṇatiloka, in his system of teaching, combined instructions in Dhamma with lessons in Pali, which he insisted all his pupils learn until they had acquired at least a rudimentary acquaintance with the language. His standard course of instruction lasted between six and nine months. Thereafter he left his pupils to pursue their Dhamma studies and meditation practice on their own, while he himself was always prepared to answer their questions and to provide advice and guidance.

In 1938, feeling the effects of the coastal heat, Ñāṇaponika moved to the temperate upcountry town of Gampola. Here he lived alone in a converted brick kiln in the middle of a paddy field, obtaining his food by going on alms round (*piṇḍapāta*) in the nearby village and started to translate selections from the Saṃyutta Nikāya from Pali into German. Soon after his move to

Gampola, on a trip to Colombo, Ñāṇaponika befriended two English-educated Ceylonese bhikkhus who had been ordained in Burma in 1936, Soma and Kheminda. The three friends decided to live together and to establish a hermitage in the Gampola area, outside the village of Gampolawela, on the banks of the Mahaveli River. Soon, with the aid of lay supporters, they built their "Mahānadi Ashram," which consisted of three huts and a hexagonal pavilion for meals overlooking the river. There the three monks lived happily in ascetic simplicity, sleeping on mats, using low tables, and living only on food collected on alms round.

The stay in Gampola lasted from late 1938 to mid-1939. Ñāṇaponika considered this period to be one of the happiest in his monk's life. Each evening the three friends would watch the beauty of the sunset reflected in the river, and on full-moon nights they would meditate quietly while the splendour of the full moon was reflected in the waters and on the sands of the riverbed. He continued with his scholarly work, translating the Satipaṭṭhāna Sutta and its commentary into German, while Ven. Soma translated the same texts into English (the early draft of his book, *The Way of Mindfulness*, first published in 1941).

When the Nazis invaded Austria in late 1938, his mother had to leave the country along with her relatives, and Ñāṇaponika made arrangements for them to take asylum in Ceylon. The entire party arrived in Colombo in March 1939. After their arrival, Mrs. Feniger first lived in Gampola with a Ceylonese lawyer who was a lay supporter of her bhikkhu-son. During this time Ñāṇaponika would sometimes share his almsfood with his mother, as the Buddha had permitted bhikkhus to give almsfood to their parents in time of need.

The idyllic sojourn in Gampola, like everything else enjoyable in this world of impermanence, was not to last. In the summer of 1939 malaria broke out. Ven. Soma suffered a bad attack and had to be hospitalized, and Ven. Kheminda also later contracted the disease. Ñāṇaponika managed to escape, but the danger posed by the epidemic made continued residence in Gampola impossible. When Ven. Soma recovered, the three friends moved to Bandarawela. Until Ven. Kheminda had recovered from his bout of malaria they lived in a vacant house, after which they moved into an abandoned tea factory. Meanwhile his mother had moved to Kandy, and from there to Colombo, where she lived with the distinguished Ceylonese couple, Sir Ernest and Lady De Silva, patrons of the Island Hermitage. The De Silvas offered to be guarantors for his mother, thereby enabling her to obtain a residence visa for Ceylon. During this period Ñāṇaponika came to visit her every four to six weeks. As a result of the explanations of the Dhamma given by her son, and the impressive example of her Ceylonese sponsors, she herself embraced Buddhism, taking the Three Refuges, the Five Precepts for regular observance, and the Eight Precepts on Uposatha days.

When war erupted between England and Germany, all men of German nationality living in the British colony of Ceylon were taken to civil internment camp at Diyatalāva, in the Uva province near Bandarawela. Ñāṇaponika and his teacher, Ñāṇatiloka, were interned at the camp from September 1939 through a large part of 1940. Being of Jewish origin, Ñāṇaponika was temporarily released in the spring of 1940. During this brief respite, he brought the Ceylonese bhikkhus Soma and Kheminda to Island Hermitage to look after the premises during the war and to provide good companionship for Ven. Ñāṇaloka Thera, the senior Ceylonese disciple of Ñāṇatiloka. After the fall of France in June 1940, the British Crown reversed its lenient policy towards Jewish refugees, apprehensive that the refugees could in some way pose a danger to security. Hence the German Jews, including Ñāṇaponika, were again arrested after their three weeks of freedom and were taken back to the camp at Diyatalāva.

After the Japanese captured Singapore, Ceylon was considered to be in a war zone. Consequently all civil internees had to be moved to a region of safety. The German bhikkhus too were sent in late 1940 to the large civil internment camp in north India, at Dehra Dun in the Himalayan foothills. It was in this camp that Ñāṇaponika spent the next five years of his life (1941–1946), the bitter and trying years of World War II. But the periods of internment did not deter the indefatigable scholar-monk from his work. During the stay at Diyatalāva he prepared a German translation of the Sutta Nipāta, to which he later added extensive notes. When he was sent to India, he brought along many books and continued his studies and translations. While the outside world was embroiled in deadly conflict, Ñāṇaponika, safely if not always comfortably ensconced in the camp at Dehra Dun, quietly translated into German the entire *Dhammasaṅgaṇī*, the first book of the Abhidhamma Piṭaka, along with its commentary, the *Atthasālinī*. While engaged in these translations, he also wrote down his reflections on the Abhidhamma philosophy, notes which became the nucleus for his later *Abhidhamma Studies*, written in English after the war. He prepared, too, in German an anthology of texts on Satipaṭṭhāna meditation which, with some alterations and additions, was later incorporated into *The Heart of Buddhist Meditation*.

At Dehra Dun Ñāṇaponika found himself assigned to the same barracks as another German, a few years older than himself, who had also immersed himself in the Buddhist traditions of the East. This was Lama Anāgārika Govinda, who had first lived as a Theravādin lay ascetic in Sri Lanka and then had relocated to India, where he had taken up the study and practice of Tibetan Buddhism. The two men quickly became fast friends. Their friendship deepened over long walks together in the hills and valleys of Dehra Dun (which the camp authorities permitted them) and over intense Dhamma discussions, which often closed with the two "agreeing to disagree." From Lama Govinda, Ñāṇaponika learned Sanskrit, and the two scholars cooperated in translating, from the reconstructed Sanskrit, portions of the philosophical treatise *Catuśataka*, by the Madhyamika philosopher Āryadeva. Their warm friendship continued through the years, with periodic exchanges of letters and a meeting in Europe in 1972, until the death of Lama Govinda in early 1985.

In September 1946, a full year after the war had ended, Ñāṇaponika and his teacher, Ñāṇatiloka, as well as the other internees, were released from the camp. On his return to Ceylon, after a short reunion with his mother in Colombo, he proceeded to Island Hermitage. He and Ñāṇatiloka found that in their absence the hermitage had been maintained in very good condition by the Vens. Ñāṇaloka, Soma, and Kheminda.

Resettled at the hermitage, he continued his work on the Abhidhamma, writing up the results of his investigations in his book *Abhidhamma Studies*. In early 1951 both Ñāṇatiloka and

Ñāṇaponika were made citizens of Ceylon, the country of their adoption, towards which they both always cherished a deep sense of affection and gratitude.

In January 1952, Ñāṇatiloka and Ñāṇaponika travelled to Burma for consultations preparatory to the convening of a "great Buddhist council," the sixth in Theravada Buddhist history, to be held in Rangoon starting in 1954. The two German theras were asked to help formulate plans for propagating Buddhism in the West and for producing fresh translations of the Pali Canon into English. In Rangoon, Ñāṇaponika discussed his concerns with the devout Buddhist Prime Minister, U Nu. He lodged at Thathana Yeiktha, the famous centre for Vipassanā meditation run by the renowned meditation master, Ven. Mahāsi Sayādaw. When the conference was over, Ñāṇatiloka returned to Ceylon, but Ñāṇaponika stayed on for a period of meditation training under Mahāsi Sayādaw. This experience impressed him deeply, inspiring him to write a book about this system of Vipassanā practice for the benefit of others seeking clear instructions in Buddhist meditation.

Before his trip to Burma, already in 1948 Ñāṇaponika had written a book in German on meditation (*Satipaṭṭhāna*, Christiani Verlag, 1950), in which the directions for practice were derived from information he had received from Ven. Soma and Ven. Kheminda, who had undergone training in meditation in Burma in 1937. This book also contained the Satipaṭṭhāna Sutta in Pali and in German translation, along with its commentary and a long introductory essay. Following his experience in Burma, Ñāṇaponika rewrote this book in English, incorporating into it instructions for practice based on the experiences and guidance he had gathered under Ven. Mahāsi Sayādaw at Thathana Yeiktha. The result was *The Heart of Buddhist Meditation*, first published in Ceylon in 1954 and, in 1962, in a revised and enlarged edition in England. This book, translated into seven languages and still maintained in print after 33 years, has achieved the status of a modern Buddhist classic. It is generally regarded as the finest treatment of Satipaṭṭhāna meditation in English.

In 1951 Ñāṇatiloka moved from the Island Hermitage to a cottage compound in Udawattakele Forest Reserve, on a wooded hill just above Kandy, a region whose temperate climate he found more congenial to his health in his advanced years. This compound, called Forest Hermitage, had been gifted to the Sangha by its owner, Mrs. F. R. Senanayake. When Ñāṇaponika returned from Burma in 1952, he joined his teacher at his new residence, which subsequently became known among the townsfolk as "the German temple." In 1954 the two theras returned to Burma for the opening of the Sixth Great Council. As Ñāṇatiloka had laryngitis on the opening day, Ñāṇaponika read his teacher's message to the assembly. After a short stay in Burma they returned to Ceylon. Ñāṇaponika made several subsequent trips to Burma during the Council and attended the closing session in 1956, alone as his teacher's health was failing. Unless there were Greek monks present at one of the earlier Buddhist councils held in India, the two German elders had the unique honour of being the only monks of Western origin ever to participate in a major synod of Theravada Buddhism.

In 1956 his mother, who had still been living in Colombo, passed away at the age of 89, and in 1957 Ñāṇatiloka expired, aged 79. As a token of gratitude to his teacher, Ñāṇaponika, at the latter's request, edited his German translation of the complete Aṅguttara Nikāya, consisting of five volumes, which he retyped in full himself. He also compiled forty pages of indexes to the work.

The most significant turning point in Ñāṇaponika's life as a Buddhist monk came on New Year's day 1958 when, along with two lay Buddhist friends from Kandy, he founded the Buddhist Publication Society. Ñāṇaponika became the Editor and Honorary Secretary of the Society (and later its first President). One friend, Richard Abeyasekera, became the Assistant Secretary; and the other friend, A. S. Karunaratna, became the Honorary Treasurer. Originally the founders intended to issue only a limited number of small booklets in English on various aspects of Buddhism, chiefly for distribution abroad; after completing a series of about twenty-five booklets they would end this venture into the publishing world. However the enthusiasm with which their first publications were received encouraged them to continue with their efforts, and thus the BPS continued to grow and expand into the prolific organization it is today.

From the time of its birth, Ñāṇaponika dedicated himself without reservation to the work of the Society. While Mr. Abeyasekera, with great devotion and dauntless energy, attended to the numerous details of the Society's administration, Ñāṇaponika supervised the editorial and production wings. As Editor he examined all manuscripts himself, endeavouring to ensure that they faithfully reflected the authentic spirit of Theravada Buddhism. In the early days of the Society not only did he attend to his editorial responsibilities, but he also performed such menial tasks as typing address labels, pasting stamps on envelopes, walking to the printers two or three times a week, and arranging the mailing list. While an enlarged staff soon relieved him of these chores, through the years he personally oversaw every detail in the actual process of book production—from the solicitation of manuscripts to the review of cover designs—until the finished product was in his hands.

He himself wrote a good number of the Society's *Wheel* publications and also elicited from other authors works which he nurtured to completion with encouragement, suggestions, advice, and constructive criticism. He expended an enormous amount of labour, almost invisible in the end product, in bringing to light the works of several Dhamma companions of his who had predeceased him. Several times he edited, revised, and enlarged Ñāṇatiloka's *Buddhist Dictionary* and *Guide through the Abhidhamma Piṭaka* as well as his major German books. He collected, edited, and organized the scattered writings of his friend Francis Story[213], producing the three volumes of this writer's collected works published by BPS. He edited Mahāsi Sayādaw's *Practical Insight Meditation* and translated from the Pali the same meditation master's treatise *The Progress of Insight*. He also edited and prepared for publication Bhikkhu Ñāṇamoli's *The Life of the Buddha according to the Pali Canon* and *A Thinker's Notebook*. Indeed, so complete has been Ñāṇaponika's dedication to the dissemination of the Buddha's Teaching in the world through the Buddhist Publication Society that from 1958 until his retirement his personal biography virtually merges into the history of the Society he helped to found.

Starting in 1968, each year Ñāṇaponika made a trip of one or two months' duration to Switzerland. He originally went on the invitation of an old friend from the Jewish self-defence movement in Nazi Germany, Dr. Max Kreutzberger. During his trips to Europe Ñāṇaponika visited Buddhist groups, particularly in Switzerland, and thus came to be regarded by many as a "spiritual advisor" for Theravada Buddhism in Europe. These annual trips ended in 1981, when weakening legs made travel difficult.

As advancing age began to sap his strength and a long-standing glaucoma condition limited his ability to read, in 1984 he retired as Editor of the BPS, handing over this responsibility to the present writer. He continued actively as President of the Society until 1988, when he retired from this position as well, accepting appointment as the BPS's distinguished Patron. During his later years his work brought him the recognition he so well deserved, both internationally and in the country of his adoption. In 1967 he was made an honorary fellow of the World Academy of Art and Science. In 1978 the German Oriental Society appointed him an honorary member in recognition of his combination of objective scholarship with religious practice as a Buddhist monk. In 1987 the Buddhist and Pali University of Sri Lanka, at its first convocation, conferred on him its first-ever honorary degree of Doctor of Literature. In 1990 he received the honorary degree of Doctor of Letters from the University of Peradeniya. And in 1993 the Amarapura Nikāya, the chapter of the Buddhist monastic order into which he was ordained 56 years earlier, conferred on him the honorary title of Amarapura Mahā Mahopadhyaya Sāsana Sobhana, Great Mentor of the Amarapura Nikāya, Ornament of the Teaching.

Despite minor infirmities and advancing blindness over the last four years of his life, Ñāṇaponika had enjoyed remarkably good health through his 93rd birthday on 21st July 1994. His last birthday was celebrated joyously by his friends and the BPS staff with the release of the BPS edition of his book *The Vision of Dhamma,* a collection of his writings from the Society's *Wheel* and *Bodhi Leaves* series. In late August, however, the inexorable process of aging suddenly accelerated, ushering in a combination of ailments that signalled the approaching end. Ñāṇaponika was brought to a private hospital for medical treatment in late September, but at his own request he was returned to the Forest

Hermitage after a week. Three weeks later, in the hushed quiet of the pre-dawn forest, he breathed his last.

The body of Ñāṇaponika was cremated on 23rd October at the Mahaiyawa Cemetery in Kandy at a funeral attended by religious and lay dignitaries as well as by his many friends and admirers. On 29th January, after the traditional "three-month alms offering," his remains were interred at the Island Hermitage in Dodanduva, where he had spent his formative years as a monk. And there they rest, near the remains of his revered teacher, Ñāṇatiloka Mahāthera, and his former Dhamma companions, Ñāṇamoli Thera and Ven. Soma Thera.

The entire Buddhist world, and in particular the English- and German-reading followers of Theravada Buddhism, will forever be indebted to Ñāṇaponika Mahāthera for his life of selfless service in transmitting the wisdom of the Buddha to humanity.

APPENDIX II

THE LITERARY WORK OF ÑĀṆATILOKA THERA

Ñāṇaponika Thera[214]

Though the Ñāṇatiloka Mahāthera's external life was quite varied due to the vicissitudes of the times, his personality expresses itself pre-eminently in his literary work and in the serene quietude and simplicity of his monk's life.

The mere quantity of his literary work in English and German commands respect and would have been remarkable even if it had been done in an entirely undisturbed and sheltered life, furnished with all the study aids which are now easily accessible. To appreciate fully the Mahāthera's achievement, it must be remembered that a good part of his voluminous early work was done under very trying circumstances. He worked indefatigably under the primitive and noisy living conditions of his first internment and during the hardships, deprivations and frequent illnesses experienced after the first war when he travelled or was forcibly sent from one country to another, before he could again reach the quiet haven of Ceylon. In the first years of his studies and when doing his first translations from the Pali, large dictionaries and well edited and printed Pali texts did not exist, or were not accessible to him. Often he had to use, with critical caution, Burmese and Sinhalese palm-leaf manuscripts, which were sometimes full of errors and hard to read.

His first publication, appearing in 1906, was the German version of *The Word of the Buddha (An Outline of the Teaching of the Buddha in the Words of the Pali Canon, with explanatory notes)*. This slender but substantial book was destined to become a classic of Buddhist literature and had, in the course of the years, a world-wide circulation in thirteen languages. It cannot be estimated how many were introduced to the Buddha's Teaching or gained a clear understanding of it through that book. There were some who even learned it by heart. Its potential for spreading and clarifying the Buddha Word is by far not yet exhausted, and it would merit further effort to circulate it still more widely and methodically. In view of the importance of this book, some bibliographical details on it follow.

A first, shorter version of *The Word of the Buddha*, compiled in German in 1905, was serialized in the very first German Buddhist journal *Der Buddhist* and appeared in the issues of 1905–1906, under the title *"Die Lehre des Buddha oder Die vierheiligen Wahrheiten"* ("The Teaching of the Buddha or The Four Noble Truths"). An enlarged and revised version of it—now with the title *Das Wort des Buddha*—was printed in book form in 1906 (Th. Grieben Verlag). After the First World War, an edition of 10,000 copies was issued by the German Buddhist publisher Oskar Schloss. The presently available German edition, published by Verlag Christiani, Konstanz, appeared in 1953.

The first English version of *The Word of the Buddha* was originally translated from the German by the Sāmaṇera Sāsanavaṃsa (later Bhikkhu Sīlācāra), and was published in Rangoon in 1907. Later on, the Mahāthera's own English translation was used in all subsequent publications of the book. The 11th English edition was issued in Sri Lanka in 10,000 copies by "The Word of the Buddha Publishing Committee of the Sāsanadhāra Kantha Samitiya." The Sāsanadhāra Kantha Samitiya was a Buddhist ladies' society supporting the Island Hermitage. The book is now in its 15th English edition, of which the last three impressions had been issued by the Buddhist Publication Society. Three reprints appeared in the U.S.A., and one in the Philippines, issued by a Chinese Buddhist Temple in Manila. Translations have appeared in Bengali, Czech, Finnish, French, Hindi, Italian, Japanese, Javanese, Polish, Russian, Sinhalese and Thai. The original Pali of the texts selected in the book was published in Sinhalese script (*Sacca-Saṅgaha*; Colombo 1914), in Devanagari in India, and in Roman script in Sri Lanka (*Buddha-Vacanaṃ*; Kandy 1968, Buddhist Publication Society).

The Russian translation of *The Word of the Buddha* had been published in 1907, sponsored by the Lamaist Temple in St. Petersburg. It was banned twice by the Russian authorities. One copy of this Russian version had a remarkable history which was told in a letter to the present writer and is worth re-telling. This letter was written by a lady, a member and supporter of the Buddhist Publication Society, who was Russian on her father's side and a Mongolian Buddhist on her mother's side. In early 1933, as a young girl, she was sent to Berlin for her higher education, and her grandmother, a devout Buddhist, gave her a copy of the Russian Word of the Buddha as a farewell gift. When she was in the first year of her medical studies in Berlin, Russia became involved in the war and the girl was arrested and sent to various concentration camps. She had the book with her in all the camps and in two prisons, hiding it close to her body. In the first camps she was allowed to keep it, but when she was sent to Torgau (Elbe), a camp matron started tearing it up. Precisely at that moment, the young adjutant of the Camp Commander passed by. "I rushed towards him," so she tells, "begging him to let me keep my only possession, a 'prayer book'. I fell at his feet—a gesture totally unknown to a Western male and which confused him greatly. Being too young and inexperienced for handling such unusual situations, he picked me up, addressed me politely, stammering some meaningless words. Having finally composed himself, he ordered the matron to have the book mended and returned to me." When he learned that she had been a medical student, she was made a nursing attendant in the sick barrack and she retained this function until she was released at the end of the war. When she met her future husband at a Displaced Persons Camp, this very book helped her to introduce him to Buddhism, and as a result he finally became a greatly devoted and deeply understanding Buddhist. When, after marriage, she went with her husband to live in Canada, this book, which had gone through such a strange and moving history, was placed in their shrine room. She says in her letter, "The marvel of all this is that all those people, without knowing it, had touched and set eyes upon the greatest treasure this world has to offer—the pure word of the Buddha. I am extremely happy, after having come with this treasure from so very far and undergone hardships and humiliation due to my bad Karma, to bring this glorious word to my husband."

After this excursion into one book's adventures, we now resume our record of the Ñāṇatiloka's literary work.

As early as 1905 he started to translate into German the most voluminous of the four great Collections (Nikāya) of the Buddha's Discourses, the *Aṅguttara Nikāya* (*Gradual Sayings*; in German: *Angereihte Sammlung*): The first part, the Book of the Ones, appeared in 1907 (Walter Markgraf Verlag), and in the following years additional parts were translated up to the Book of the Fours. The first complete edition was published in 1922, in five volumes (Oskar Schloss Verlag). A new edition, revised by the present writer, appeared in 1969, likewise in five volumes (Verlag M. DuMont Schauberg, Köln).

In the years before the first world war the Ñāṇatiloka wrote and published, all in German: *Das Buch der Charaktere* (1910; translation of the *Puggalapaññatti* of the Abhidhamma Piṭaka); a *Systematic Pali Grammar* (1911); *Die Fragen des Königs Milindo* (*Milindapañhā*; Vol. I: 1913/14; Vol. I/II: 1924).

In 1928 appeared, in German, *A Pali Anthology and Glossary*, and in 1931 the first volume of the *Visuddhi Magga* (*"Der Weg zur Reinheit"*). When he completed the German translation of this voluminous work, it was first cyclostyled, with the help of a pupil monk, during internment at Diyatalāva (Sri Lanka). It appeared in print first in 1952 (Verlag Christiani, Konstanz); a second, revised edition was published in 1976.

1938: *Guide through the Ahhidhamma Pitaka* (English); reprinted in 1957 and 1971 (BPS). A German version of this work, translated by the author, is unpublished. This applies also to his German translation of the *Abhidhammatthasaṅgaha* (a compendium of the Abhidhamma philosophy) and his German translation of the Dhammapada, with the explanatory sections of the ancient commentary:

1949: *Fundamentals of Buddhism*. Four Lectures (in English).

Two important works were published in English, in 1952: (1) *Buddhist Dictionary. A Manual of Buddhist Terms and Doctrines* (2nd Ed.: Colombo 1956; 3rd Ed., revised and enlarged by Ñāṇaponika: 1972): German version: 1953; 2nd Ed. 1976 (Verlag Christiani, Konstanz). A French version, translated by Suzanne Karpeles, was published by "Adyar," Paris, in 1961 (*Vocabulaire Bouddhique de Termes et Doctrines du Canon Pali*).

(2) *The Path to Deliverance*, in its Threefold Division and Seven Stages of Purity (Second revised ed. 1959). German version: 1956,

Verlag Christiani). Indonesian translation: Second Edition, Surabaya 1970. This is again an annotated anthology, and may be regarded as an advanced supplement to *The Word of the Buddha*. It is rich in instructive and inspiring texts.

Some shorter essays in English have been issued as reprints by the Buddhist Publication Society, Kandy: *The Influence of Buddhism on a People* (BLA 2); *Karma and Rebirth; The Significance of the Dependent Origination* (Now both republished in *Fundamentals of Buddhism*, Wheel 394); *Egolessness;* with extracts from the Saṃyutta Nikāya (in *The Wheel* No. 202/204).

It is befitting to remember here those publishers—all Buddhists by conviction—who have served the literary work of the Mahāthera in a dedicated way.

In German language: Walter Markgraf, Oskar Schloss, Ferdinand Schwab; and since 1952, Verlag Christiani (Konstanz), which continues to issue reprints. The late Dr. Ing. Paul Christiani, himself a long-time Buddhist, had been a great admirer of the Mahāthera.

In English language: Bauddha Sahitiya Sabha (Buddhist Literature Society), Colombo; The Word of the Buddha Publishing Committee of the Sāsanadhāra Kantha Samitiya, Colombo; and the Buddhist Publication Society, Kandy.

The Mahāthera had shown a great sagacity in the choice of the subjects of his writings and translations, which were meant to give the greatest benefit to a serious study and correct understanding of the Buddhist doctrine. His books provide reliable guidance to the study of Theravada Buddhism. Many misinterpretations in modern writings and translations could have been avoided by consulting the Mahāthera's *Buddhist Dictionary*.

His way of writing mirrored his way of life and his character. His literary style, as befitting the Pali scriptures, was simple and dignified, and so was his life. He was no friend of embellishments and verbosity, be it in print or in talk. He cherished clarity of thought and language, and disliked vagueness and ambiguity. When meeting with books or people, he always insisted, "Define your terms!"—a wholesome intellectual discipline, which, as he gratefully remembered, he had inherited from his father. He was filled with a deep respect for the enlightened words of the Enlightened One, and in the genuine spirit of cautious scholarship he was very wary with regard to facile attempts of "interpreting" the words of the Buddha, being distrustful of the excess of subjective opinion in the Buddhist literature of our time. Similarly, he refrained from "interpreting" or judging lightly other peoples' thoughts, words or actions, and he never indulged in sweeping condemnations. In the true and practical spirit of the doctrine of not-self (*anattā*), he used to say, "There are no bad people, only bad qualities"–implying that any qualities of human beings are of an impermanent nature and can be changed. He was never harsh to people and he disliked argument or excessive criticism in writings or talk. He was more in favour of stating what was good and true, allowing it to yield its steady, though sometimes slow, influence on minds ripe for it. Therefore, the rare instances when he wielded a sharp critical pen against misinterpretations of two salient Buddhist doctrines, *anattā* and *paṭiccasamuppāda*, carry a special emphasis and are deserving of the student's earnest consideration.

As much as he could, he avoided the "inner and outer noise" of modern life, and characteristic of his love of nature and stillness was the choice of his hermitages: on islands, hills and in forests. He shunned publicity and, gladly renounced the honours and burdens of public activities. He did not disparage them in the case of others, but he himself preferred to remain detached and keep to his own simple way of life, congenial to him and to the ideals of Buddhist monkhood. He did so also from the additional motive of single-minded devotion to his work and the practice of the Dhamma. From that great quality of single-mindedness stem his outstanding achievements in the service of the Dhamma as well as the harmony and composure of his character. All these guidelines of his life and work have an important message for everyone, particularly vital in our turbulent times of not only violent but also wordy conflicts: silent and single-minded devotion to productive work of any kind that is beneficial to individual and society.

Ñāṇatiloka Bibliography

Prefatory Note

This is a translation of the bibliography prepared by Dr Hecker in *Lebensbilder Deutscher Buddhisten: Ein bio-bibliographisches Handbuch, Band I: Die Gründer,* Konstanz, 1996, pp. 65–79. The reviews of books of Ñāṇatiloka which were listed by Hecker have been omitted here. A few texts in French and Italian have been added by the BPS editor; they are marked with an asterisk (*).

Hecker: Prof. Rolf Hennequel wrote on 31 March 1959 to Max Ladner in Zurich: "I am the translator of the only existing complete Nyanatiloka Biography, which I have written in 1927 at the Island Hermitage."

Hennequel was a Professor Emeritus in Philosophy in Launceston, Tasmania, from where he wrote in 1959. Hecker's inquiries in Tasmania remained unanswered. At present the literary legacy of Prof. Rolf Hennequel is at the National Archives of Australia, Canberra. But, according to the National Archives librarian, the manuscript is not among Hennequel's papers. Inquiries at the State Library of Tasmania, where some (other?) of Hennequel's papers are kept, also had no result.

In *Buddhistische Monatshefte* 1953, pp. 27 Ankenbrand mentions that he was working on a biography of Ñāṇatiloka and was intending to publish it. More is unknown.

Literary Inheritance

All the following papers, except perhaps the ones marked with an asterisk (*), are kept at the Institut für Indologie und Buddhismus (Institute of Indology and Buddhism) of the University of Göttingen, Germany.

Commemoration Volume

Nyanatiloka Centenary Volume. On the occasion of the 100th Birth Anniversary of the Venerable Nyānatiloka Mahathera, 19th February 1978. Edited by Ñāṇaponika Thera, Kandy, 1978, 71 pp.

Autobiography

Ñāṇatiloka wrote an autobiography (in German) in 1948, which only reaches until 1926. It consists of 64 pages, of which are lacking pp. 3-4 and 46[215], which are stored at the Seminar für Indologie in Göttingen. Published in Dr Hecker's *Der Erste Deutsche Bhikkhu*, pp. 3-143.

About Ñāṇatiloka in General

Ankenbrand, Ludwig: "Zum 75. Geburtstag Nyanatiloka Mahatheras. Aus seinem Leben und seiner Bedeutung fur uns," *Buddhistische Monatshefte* (Ind.Welt) 1953, pp. 21-28 (with preface of Dr. v. Meng) = *Mitteilungsblatt der BG Hamburg*, 1957, pp. 359-365.

Auster, Guido: "A teacher of German Buddhists," *Nyanatiloka Centenary Volume*, Kandy, 1978, pp. 25-27 (BPS).

Carrithers, Michael: *The Forest Monks of Sri Lanka. An Anthropological and Historical Sketch*, Delhi, 1983, pp. 26-45, in the chapter "European monks."

Hecker, Hellmuth. *Buddhismus in Deutschland. Eine Chronik*, Hamburg, 1. Publ. 1974, pp. 16-17 = 2. Print 1978, pp. 16-17

—. *Chronik des Buddhismus in Deutschland*, 3d print of the preceding, Plochingen 1985, pp. 17-20 = Publ. Nyt. No. 5 (*Dhammapadam*), pp. 361-367.

—. "Deutsche Buddhisten als britische Zivilinternierte auf Ceylon und in Australian 1914-1919," Spirits 1992, No. 1, pp. 27-31.

Krauskopf, Georg: "A German Pilgrim in Ceylon" (transl. by Soni), *Light of Buddha* 1956, No. 7, pp. 20-26 und No. 8, pp. 32-39.

Ladner, Max: "Bhadanta Nyanatiloka Mahathera zu seinem 75. Geburtstag," *Einsicht*, 1953, pp. 1-2.

—. "Ehrung fur Nyanatiloka Mahathera," ditto 1956, pp. 30-31.

Ñāṇaponika: "Biographie und Bibliographie," translated on request of the Auslands-Instituts Stuttgart, and which was supposed to be published in the bilingual *India Magazine* (as he wrote to Frau Dr. Kell vom 28. 1. 1955). (Dr. Hecker was not able to find out more about this work, but it probably it is the unfinished English draft found at the Forest Hermitage archives; see Introduction p. 10)

"Nyanatiloka Mahāthera. 'His Life and Work,'" Nyanatiloka *Centenary Volume*, Kandy, 1978, pp. 1-16.

Nyānasatta: "Nyanatiloka and his Methods of teaching Dhamma," ditto, pp. 17-24.

Persian, Walter: "Nyanatiloka" *La Pensee Bouddhique* III/2, April 1947.

–. Nyanatiloka "A Biography of the German Buddhist monk," in *Middle Way* 1947/48 (Vol. 22), pp. 131–34.

–. "Der Nestor des deutschen buddhistischen Lebens und Denkens," *Buddhistischen Weltschau* (Dü), Jan. 1948, Anlage p. 8.

–. "Geiger wurde Eremit," *Zeit* v. 19. 2. 53, p. 8.

–. "Der älteste europäische Buddhamönch," *Stuttgarter Zeitung*, 26.2.53.

–. "Dem Geheimnis der deutschen Buddhisten auf der Spur: Der Mann im gelben Gewande," *Heim und Welt*, No. 16 v. 16. 4. 54, pp. 8–9 (anonymous).

Spannring, Hermann: "Erinnerungen an Nyanatiloka" *Einsicht*, 1961, pp. 154–156.

Stacke-Rosen, Valentina: "Nyanatiloka" in *German Indologists*, Delhi, 1981, pp. 204–205.

Tin, Myanaung U: "A Humble Tribute," *Nyanatiloka Centenary Volume*, Kandy, 1978, pp. 28–30.

Obituaries 1957

Ñāṇaponika: "Leben, Werk und Persönlichkeit," *Einsicht*, 1957, pp. 97–106.

Obituary in *Light of Dhamma*, 1957, No. 3, p. 65.

Nyānasatta: "In memory of the Ven. Nyanatiloka," *The Maha Bodhi*, 1957, pp. 301–303 = *Light of the Buddha*, 1957, No. 7, pp. 38 f.

Stegemann, Wilhelm: "Zum Tode Nyanatilokas," *Mitteilungsblatt der BG*, Hamburg, 1957, p. 368.

Veljavic, Chedomil: Obituary in Krugovi (Zagreb), 7.6.57, pp. 632–635.

Wilson Dias, S.A.: "In Memoriam—the first German Bhikkhu. Musical Lectures drew him to Buddhism," *Sunday Times* (Colombo), 2.6.57, p. 12.

o.V.: Obituary in *Ceylon Daily News*, 1.6.57.

–. Death of Ven. Nyanatiloka Mahathera, *Morning Times* (Colombo), 29. 5. 57 = also *World Buddhism* 1956/57, No. 11, pp. 11 ff. = *Forschungsberichte* 10, pp. 321 f.

–. Nachruf, *Light of Buddha*, 1957, No. 10, pp. 41.

Books

Translations from the Pāli

1. Puggala Paññatti

Des Buch der Charaktere. Aus dem buddhistischen Pāli-Kanon (Abhidhammo) zum ersten Male ubersetzt. Breslau, 1910, XII, 124.

pp. (Publ. by the Deutschen Pāli-Gesellschaft No. 1), Reprint = Neubiberg um 1924 (Oscar Schloss Verlag). Ed. 2., Capelle (Nd), 1995, 136 pp. (Oscar Schloss Verlag)

2. Die Reden des Buddha.

Aus der "Angereihten Sammlung" (Aṅguttara-Nikāyo) des Pāli-Kanons übersetzt und erläutert

Ed. 1: First volume, Leipzig, 1907, 96 pp. (Buddhistische Verlag). Second volume, Breslau, 1911, 79 pp. (Verlag der Deutschen Pāli-Gesellschaft, No. 4). Third volume, Leipzig, 1914, 383 pp. (Neue Ver. a.d. Gebiet des Pāli-Buddhismus No. 10). Fourth book, Breslau 1912, 518 5. (Verlag der Deutschen Pāli-Gesellschaft, No. 7), Fifth book, Lpz. o.J., 254 pp. (Theosophische Verlagshaus)

Ed. 2: *Die Reden des Buddha. Aus dem "Anguttara-Nikāya." Aus dem Pāli zum ersten Male übers. und erl. durch Nyanatiloka,* Neubiberg, 1922-1923 (Oscar Schloss Verlag), Vol. I, 1923, 472 pp.; Vol. II, 1922, 412 pp.; Vol. III, 1922, 254 pp.; Vol. IV, 1922, 292 pp.; Vol. V, 1922, 536 pp.

Ed. 3: *Die Lehrreden des Buddha aus der Angereihten Sammlung. Anguttara-Nikāya. Aus dem Pāli ubersetzt durch Nyanatiloka. Überarbeitet und herausgegeben durch Nyanaponika,* Köln 1969, (Verlag DuMont) Vol. I, Einer- bis Dreier-Buch, 273 pp. Vol. II, Vierer-Buch, 228 pp. Vol. III, Funfer- bis Sechser-Buch, 277 pp. Vol. IV, Siebener- bis Neuner-Buch, 252 pp. Vol. V, Zehner- bis Elfer-Buch, 201 pp. (with index).

Ed. 4. Reworked Edition: ditto, Freiburg, 1984 (Aurum-Verlag).

Ed. 5. (Printing-errrors corrected), Braunschweig, 1993 (Aurum).

3. Die Fragen des Milindo

Ein historischer Roman, enthaltend Zwiegespräche zwischen einem Griechenkönige und einem buddh. Monche über wichtige Punkte der buddh. Lehre. Aus dem Pāli zum ersten Male vollständig ins Deutsche übersetzt durch Bhikkhu Nyanatiloka (aber einige Änderungen!)

Ed. 1, Breslau 1913, only Vol. I, (Markgraf). Ed. 2, Leipzig, 1919, Vol. I, X, 340 pp. (Altmann). Ed. 3, Neubiberg, 1924, Vol. I, X, 340 pp.; Vol. II, VIII, 268 pp. (first time) (Oscar Schloss Verlag). Ed. 4, Interlaken 1985, 396 pp.: *Die Fragen des Könings Milinda (überarbeitet durch Nyanaponika: 55 pp. ausgelassen, viele neue*

Anmerkungen, Pāli-Anmerkungen weggelassen, zahlreiche Veränderungen der Übersetzung, Ergänzung der Auslassungen Nyanatilokas), Ansata Verlag. Reprinted 1998.

Visuddhimagga

a) Extract: *Aus dem Visuddhimagga. Aus dem Pāli zum ersten Male ins Deutsche ubersetzt und erläutert durch Nyanatiloka*, Neubiberg, 1926, 30 pp. (Untersuchungen zur Geschichte des Buddhismus Vol. 18) (Oscar Schloss Verlag)
b) Preprint: *Buddhaghosa, Der Weg zur Reinheit. Erstmalige deutsche Übersetzung durch Buddhagosas Visuddhimagga, der größten systematischen Darstellung der Lehre des Buddha. Aus dem Urtext durch Nyanatiloka*, Vol. I. *Zeitschrift für Buddhismus*, 1928, pp. 31–61, 163–187, 309–337.
c) First print of Vol. I: *Visuddhimagga oder "Der Weg zur Reinheit." Die größte und älteste systematische Darstellung des Buddhismus. Zum ersten Male aus dem Pāli ubersetzt durch Nyanatiloka*, Neubiberg, 1931, XVI, 287 pp. (Benares-Verlag Ferd. Schwab).
d) First bookprint of Vol. II (Chap. V-VII/2), Hamburg, 1936, 80 pp. Buddh. Gem. Hamburg
e) Cyclostyled Edition. *Der Weg zur Reinheit, aus dem Pāli ubersetzt durch Nyanatiloka*, Diyatalāva 1941, 494 pp. Continuation of 1936 Hamburg Edition, containing Ch. VII/3-XXII, i.e., until the end, but without footnotes. 100 copies cyclostyled in the Diyatalāva camp with the help of Bhikkhu Ñāṇamālita.
f) First complete edition, in one volume, *Der Weg zur Reinheit. Die großte und älteste Darstellung des Buddhismus. Zum ersten Male vollständig aus dem Pāli ubersetzt von Nyanatiloka*, Konstanz, 1952, XVI, 981 pp., Verlag Christiani.
g) Reprint 1975. At the same time, reprint of the second edition with corrections from Ñāṇatiloka's own copy and by Ñāṇaponika. Two identical reprints appeared as the 4th and 5th Edition.
h) Reprint (?) 1997 Oy-Mittelberg, 1006 pp. (Jhana Verlag)

5. Dhammapada

Des Buddha Weg zur Weisheit und Kommentar. Palitext, wortliche metrische Übersetzung und Kommentar zu der eltesten buddhistischen Spruchsammlung. Geleitwort durch Nyanaponika, Oy-Mittelberg, 1992, 371 pp. (Jhana Verlag).

Nyanatiloka, Mahathera, Dhammapada, wortliche metrische Übersetzung der ältesten buddhistischen Spruchsammlung, Oy-Mittelberg, 1995, 109 pp. (Jhana Verlag). Only the verses, without Pali and commentary.

6. Abhidhammatthasaṅgaha

Handbuch der buddhistischen Philosophie (Abhidhammatthasangaha). Übersetzt und erläutert von Nyantiloka Mahathera, Oy-Mittelberg, 1995, 157pp. (Jhana Verlag)

7. Kleine Systematische Pāli-Grammatik

1. Publ. Breslau 1911, VIII, 119 pp.: Veröff. der Deutschen Pāli-Gesellschaft No. 5
2. Publ., Reprint of Oscar Schloss Verlag, Neubiberg um 1924, 120 pp.
3. Republished, newly typeset and revised, by the Deutsche Buddhistische Union, Munchen, 2002.

8. Pāli Anthologie und Wörterbuch

Eine Sammlung progressiv angeordneter Pālitexte mit einem nach wissenschaftlichen Grundsätzen verfaßten und mit ethymologischen Anmerkungen versehenen Wörterbuch, Neubiberg, 1928.

Part A: *Wörterbuch,* XII, 128 pp. Part B: *Anthologie,* 71 pp.

2. Ed. in one volume, Capelle (Nd), 1995, 212 pp. (Oscar Schloss Verlag).

9. Buddhistisches Wörterbuch

a) **English**: (28 August 1946, translated in Dehra Dun).

1. Publ.: *Buddhist Dictionary, Manual of Buddhist Terms and Doctrines,* Colombo, 1950, 189 pp. (Island Hermitage Publication No. 1). 2. Publ.: Kandy, 1952 = 1956, 198 pp. (BPS). 3. Ed.: Kandy, 1972, revised and enlarged by Ñāṇaponika Thera, 274 pp.. Reprint 1980, 1988, 1997, 2004 (BPS). Reprint: Singapore, 1987, 220 pp.

b) **German**: *Buddhistisches Wörterbuch. Kurz gefaßtes Handbuch der buddhistischen Lehren und Begriffe in alphabetischer Anordnung,* Konstanz, 1953, 277 pp.; Second revised. edition published by Ñāṇaponika, 1976, 280 pp. (BHB No. 3).

c) **French**: Suzanne Karpeles (translator), *Vocabulaire Pali-Française des Termes Bouddhiques,* Paris, 1961 (Verlag Adyar).

Preview: *La Pensée Bouddhique* IV/6, April 1952, pp. 12–14 (Extracts).

III. Other Books

10. *Das Wort des Buddha*

Eine Übersicht über das ethisch-philosophische System des Buddha in den Worten des Sutta-Piṭakam des Pāli-Kanons nebst Erläuterungen. Mit einer Einleitung versehen durch Karl Seidenstucker, Leipzig, 1906, XX, 72 pp. (Th. Grieben).

2. Ed.: *Das Wort des Buddha. Eine Übersicht über das ethischphil. System des Buddha, in den Worten des Sutta-Pitaka. Zusammengestellt, übersetzt und erläutert*, Neubiberg, 1923, XI, 110 pp. (Oscar Schloss Verlag).
3. Ed.: *Das Wort des Buddha. Eine systematische Ubersicht der Lehre des Buddha in seinen eigenen Worten. Ausgewählt, übersetzt und erläutert*, Konstanz, 1953, 116 pp. (BHB No. 1).
4. Ed.: republished by Ñāṇaponika, Konstanz, 1978, 118 pp. (BHB 1).
5. Ed.: ditto.

b) English

The Word of the Buddha. An outline of the ethic-philosophical system of Buddha in words of Pali canon. Translated from the German by J. F. McKechnie, Rangoon 1907, XI, 52 pp.

2. Print. London, 1914, 69 pp. (Republished by the Buddhist Society.)

From now on own translation by Nyanatiloka

3. Enlarged edition, Colombo, 1927, VII, 67 pp. (Foreword, Dodanduva, 26.6.1927)

Ed. 5, Dodanduva, 1935, 64 pp. = Included in Goddard, *A Buddhist Bible*, 1938, 1966 and Boston, 1970, pp. 22–60.

Ed. 6 rev. ed., Dodanduva, 1937, 70 pp.

Ed. 8. Abridged Student's Edition, Colombo, 1948 (Young Men's Buddhist Association)

Ed. 9., rev. ed., Colombo, 1950, VIII, 70 pp. (Bauddha Sahitya Sabhā/ Buddhist Literature Society)

Ed. 10, Santa Barbara (USA), 1950.

Ed. 11. rev. and enlarged ed., Colombo, 1952, XIV, 97 pp. (The Word of the Buddha Publishing Committee of the Sāsanadhāra Kantha Samitiya.)

Ed. 12., in *The Path of Buddhism*, Colombo, 1955, pp. 199–292.

ed. 13, Colombo, 1959. (Lanka Buddha Mandalaya)

ed. 14, *The Word of the Buddha. An outline of the teaching of the*

Buddha in the words of the Pali Canon, Kandy, 1967, 101 pp. (BPS) with foreword from Ed. 11 as well as new foreword

15–16. Edition, ditto 1971, 1981, 2001, 101 pp.

c) Catalan

La Paraula del Buda, Barcelona 1984 (Transl. by Amadeo Sole-Leris. Publicacions de l'Abadia de Montserrat).

d) Czech

Slovo Buddhovo, 1935 (Transl. anonymous and publisher not mentioned.)

Slovo Buddhovo, Prague 1993 (Transl. Mirko Fryba. Stratos.)

e) French

La Parole du Bouddha, Paris, 1935. Second edition: Paris, 1948, 108 pp. (Transl. by M. La Fuente. Publ. by Adrien-Maisonneuve.)

f) Italian

La Parole del Buddo, Atanor, 1919 (Transl. by G. B. Fenne).

g) Javanese

Sabdha Pandita—Pokoking Adjaran Agami Buddha. 80pp. Salatiga, 1969. (Transl. Sariputra Soedjas. Persaudaraan Umat Buddha.)

h) Pali

Saccasaṅgaha. Colombo, 1914, 53 pp. In Sinhala characters. Also in Devanagari characters in the Indian edition.

Buddhavacanam. Original Pāli text in Roman script as translated in *The Word of Buddha*, Kandy, 1968, 84 pp. (BPS).

i) Russian

Publ. in St. Petersburg 1907 as supplement to the magazine *Birzevoje Vedomostva.*

j) Sinhala

Buddha Vacanaya, Colombo, 1964.

k) Spanish

La Palabra del Buddho (Gautama el Buddha). Buenos Aires, 1943, 186 pp. (Transl. by A.M.D.).

La Palabra del Buda. Madrid 1982 (Transl. Amadeo Sole-Leris, Altalena Editores), 143 pp.

l) Thai

คจามจริงอันประเลริฐตามผุทธฮาลนะ, (Thailand), 1974 (Transl. Prasert Ruangskul)

Ed. 2. Bilingual: English & Thai. Bangkok, 2008, 220pp.

m) Other languages

Bengali, Finnish, Hindi, Japanese, Polish.

1. Guide through the Abhidhamma Piṭaka

Synopsis of the Philosophical collections belonging to the Pali Buddhist Canon, followed by an essay on the Paṭicca Samuppāda (from *The Maha Bodhi*, 1934, No. 9).

Ed. 1: Colombo and Bombay, 1938, 179 pp.

Ed. 2: Colombo, 1957, XIV, 179 pp., rev. and enlarged by Ñāṇaponika.

Ed. 3: Kandy, 1971, 178 pp. Reprint 1983.

a) Recensions:

The Maha Bodhi 1938, pp. 508. *Vishva Bharati Quarterly*, Nov. 38 (N.A. Sastri), *Wiener Zeitschrift für die Kunde Süd- und Ostasiens* 1939, pp. 159 (Frauwallner). *Buddhism in England* 1939/40 (Vol. 19), pp. 167. *Orientalische Literatur Zeitung*, 1942, pp. 376–378 (F. Weller) *World Buddhism* 1957/58, No. 5, pp. 16 (W.F.J.) *Light of Dhamma*, V/1, Jan. 1958, pp. 70 f. *East and West*, 1958 (Vol. 9), pp. 110 (G. Tucci) *Light of Buddha*, 1959, pp. 119 f. (Tha Kyaw).

B. * German: *Führer durch das Abhidhamma-Piṭaka.* (In Ms.)[216]

12. Fundamentals of Buddhism: Four lectures

Ed. 1: Colombo, 1949, 113 pp., publ. by Bauddha Sahitya Sabha Publications. Ed. 2: Colombo, 1956. Ed. 3: Kandy, 1968 (BPS). Ed. 4: Kandy, 1994.

a) *Contains the following lectures:*

I. "The essence of Buddhism." Lecture for Radio Colombo, 1933. Preprint: *Peace* 1934/35, pp. 174–183 = *Wheel* IV, No. 4–5, April–May 1938, 11 pp. Pamphlet, Colombo, 1944, *Buddhist Herald* Vol. I, No. 9, Aug.-Sept. 1948, pp. 6–18. German lecture Tokyo, 1920 expanded by a foreword.

II. "Kamma and Rebirth," Lecture at the Ceylon University 1947. Reprint as *Wheel* No. 9, Kandy, 1959 und 1964, 23 pp.

III. "Paṭicca Samuppāda," Lecture at Dona Alpina Ratnanayake University College, Colombo, 1938. Not to be confused with Pamphlet no. 20 below.

IV. "Mental Culture," Lecture Tokyo, 1920.

13. The Path to Deliverance:

The Path to Deliverance in its threefold division and seven stages of purity being a systematic exposition in the words of the Sutta Piṭaka, with explanation.

Ed. 1: Colombo, 1952, 198 pp. (Bauddha Sahitya Sabha).

Ed. 2: revised, Kandy, 1959, 80 pp. (BPS).

Ed. 3: Kandy, 1969 (BPS).

Ed. 4: Kandy, 1982 (BPS). New title: *The Buddha's Path to Deliverance. A Systematic Exposition in the Words of the Sutta Piṭaka.*

Ed. 5. 2000, Kandy (BPS).

a) *b. German:*

Der Weg zur Erlosung in den Worten der buddhistische Urschriften. Ausgewählt, übersetzt und eingeleitet, Konstanz, 1956, 266 pp., Reprint 1980 (BHB No. 8).

Indonesian translation of Ed. 2, Soerabaya, 1970.

14. Grundlagen des Buddhismus

Ed. 1 *Vier Vorträge des Ehrw. Nyanatiloka,* Oy-Mittelberg 1995. (Jhana Verlag). Foreword by Ayyā Khemā, pp. 7.

I. "Quintessence des Buddhismus," Lecture in Tokyo, in German. Published:

1. *Der Pfad* 1923/24, pp. 1–22.
2. 1924 in Pamphlet No. 17, pp. 16–37.
3. as: *Grundlehren des Buddhismus,* München 1953, 12 pp. *Aufklärungsschrift* No. 2
4. Here pp. 9–30 (with the introduction of the English ed. of Colombo Lecture 1933, see above No. 11).

II. "Karma und Wiedergeburt," here pp. 31–51.

III. "Bedingte Entstehung," here pp. 52–92.

IV. "Entfaltung by Ruhe und Klarblick" (engl.: "Mental Culture"), here pp. 93–121.

Appendix: "Die Unpersönlichkeit alles Seins: Zitate aus Saṃyutta-Nikāya," here pp. 122–137, Hecker, *Nyanatiloka–Sein Leben,* here pp. 138–147.

Ed. 2 Oy-Mittelberg 2003, 152pp. (Jhana Verlag).

IV. Pamphlets

15. De L'influence du Bouddhisme sur la formation du caractère Traduction de l'Allemand par R. A. Bergier. Lugano 1911, 15 pp. (Casa editrice Coenobium). *Also published in the journal *Coenobium*, Anno V, Fasc. I-II, Lugano, 1911, pp. 78–88.

Influence of Buddhism on a people, published by "Word of the Buddha Publishing Committee of the Sasanadhara Kantha Samitiya," Nugegoda, 1955, 10 pp.

Republished as *Bodhi Leaves* No. A 2, Kandy, 1959, 18 pp. (before and after published at least in six Buddhist magazines 1950–1964).

German original only in *Mitteilungsblatt der BG Hamburg*, 1956, pp. 160–162, 174–176.

16. Die vier heiligen Wahrheiten

Breslau 1911, 26 pp. (Verlag Markgraf). Partial Preprint: "Der Gelbe Erzahler," 1911, pp. 160–164. Full-Preprint: IBW 1911/12 (Vol. 5), pp. 28–34, 41–59.

French: *"Les Quatre Vérités du Bouddhisme," *Coenobium*, Anno V, Fasc. IX, Sept. 1911, pp. 4–22.

17. The Quintessence of Buddhism

Nettipakaraṇa (in English and German), Colombo, 1913, III, 18 pp. Reprint: *Buddhist Review* 1914, pp. 15–37. German only: *Buddhism and World Peace* (Colombo), Vol. I, No. 1, April-Juni 1977, pp. 55–65.

18. Zwei buddhistische Essays

Neubiberg, 1924, 37 pp. (*Untersuchungen zur Geschichte des Buddhismus* No. 10) (Oscar Schloss Verlag).

1. "Über die buddhistische Meditation," from: *Zeitschrift für Buddhismus*, 1923, pp. 100–115 (from Mil).
2. "Quintessenz des Buddhismus," from: *Pfad* 1923/24, pp. 1–22 (Lecture in Tokyo), see also below No. 20.

19. Der buddhistische Mönchsorden

Lecture in Tokyo. Neubiberg, 1925, 36 pp. (*Buddh. Volksbibliothek* Vol. 23), together with: Sīlācāra, *Der Buddha, ein Dialog* (Transl. from Engl.) (Oscar Schloss Verlag).

20. Paṭicca Samuppāda

The law of "Dependent origination" of all Phenomena of Existence, explained in accordance with the Pali tradition.

Ed. 1: Calcutta, 1934. Preprint: *Peace* 1934/35, pp. 344–363.

Ed. 2: republ. by Buddhist Brotherhood, Kandy, 1937, 30 pp.

Ed. 3: Colombo und Bombay, 1938, expanded as appendix to book No. 10.

Ed. 4: Kandy, 1969, 41 pp. (Wheel 140), Reprint of the Ed. 3, with title: *The significance of Dependent origination in Theravada Buddhism*. Not to be confused with the radio lecture 1938, see above No. 11, Part III.

Preliminary essay: "Dependent origination (Paṭiccasamuppāda)," *Buddhist review* (London) 1913, pp. 267–271 = *The Maha Bodhi* 1927, pp. 250 ff.

21. The Need for a Buddhist literature society

Colombo, 1940, 8 pp.

(d) Magazine Articles

Articles which have not appeared in book form.

I. Der Buddhist

1. "Die Lehre des Buddha oder die vier heiligen Wahrheiten," 1905/06, pp. 164–167, 194–197, 228, 230, 265–270, 295–303, 326–336, 362–370.
2. "Ein Spezimen des Eka-Nipato (AN)," 1906–1910, pp. 13–20.
3. "Das Girimananda-Suttam. Aus dem Samyutta-Nikaya des Pāli-Kanons ins Deutsche ubersetzt," pp. 175–180.
4. "Des Meisters letzte Tage," pp. 180–193.
5. "Paticcasamuppada oder die Entstehung aus Ursachen. Aus dem Abhisamaya-Samyutta des Pali Kanons ubersetzt und erlautert," pp. 289–300.
6. "Das Vasettha-Suttam," pp. 300–306.
7. "Analyse des materiellen Daseins," pp. 369–378.

II. Buddhistische Warte

1. "Zwei Sutten aus dem Eka-Nipato des Anguttara-Nikayo. Ins Deutsche übertragen und mit Erläuterungen versehen," 1907/08, pp. 152–156, 206–209.
2. "Meditation (Kammatthanam). Freie Übersetzung aus dem Abhidhammatthasangaho und mit Erlauterungen versehen," 1907/08, pp. 289–299; 1908/11, pp. 164–169.

III. Die Buddhistische Welt

1. "Drei Pāli-Sutten (AN IV, 182, 204, 211). Aus dem Urtext übertragen," 1909/10, pp. 4 f.
2. "Die Übung der Konzentration (AN IV, 91). Aus dem Pali übertragen," ditto, pp. 10 f.
3. "Die Primären Eigenschaften der Materiellen Welt," ditto, pp. 62–64.

4. "Frei by jeder Theorie," ditto, pp. 116 f.
5. "Die Rede an die Kalamer, AN III, 65," 1910/11, pp. 85-90.
6. "Zwei Sutten aus dem Viererbuch des AN, IV/185-186," ditto, pp. 169-173.
7. "AN 111,61: Die Drei Glaubensgebiete," ditto, pp. 189-194.
8. "AN IV,174: Die Grenzen des Erklärbaren," 1911/12, pp. 283-285.
9. "Der Paticcasamuppado," ditto, pp. 393-397.

IV. Zeitschrift fur Buddhismus

1. "Zum Problem des Ich (Ubersetzung aus M 22)," 1920, pp. 9-15
2. "Sollen nur Fortgeschrittene Aufnahme im Orden finden?" (from Mil), 1920, pp. 73-80.
3. "Die Uberwindung der Ich-Illusion," 1921, pp. 6-11.
4. "Metta-Bhavana, die Erweckung der Liebe," 1922, pp. 52-55.
5. "Die Betrachtung Ober den Tod (Vsm)," 1926, pp. 75-91.

V. Buddhistische Monatshefte (Indische Welt)

1. "Der Buddha als Friedenstifter (D 16.1, abbreviated in AN)," 1949, pp. 22-24.
2. "Das Gleichnis by der Schlange" (M 22)," pp. 84-91.
3. "Ober die buddhistische Meditation," pp. 91-93, 113-115 = *Mitteilungsblatt der BG Hamburg, 1*955, pp. 74-76, 86-88.
4. "Aus Milindapañha," 1949, pp. 94-95; 1951, pp. 24-25.
5. "Das Wort des Buddha (Extract)," 1949, pp. 105-108.
6. "Das Eiserne Gesetz der Natur (A V/49)," pp. 169.
7. "Die Anatta-Wahrheit, Buddhas Lehre vom 'Nicht-Ich'," pp. 137-141.
8. "Aus Visuddhimagga," 1950, pp. 133-135, 171-178.
9. "Mahayañña-Sutta: A IV/39," pp. 149.
10. "Des Achtpfades 5-8 Glied," 1951, pp. 180-182.
11. "Geistesentfaltung" (from *Grundlehre des Buddhismus*), 1952, pp. 8-10, 22-23, 42-43, 60-62, 93-95, 113-114; 1953, pp. 121-129.
12. "Die drei Merkmale," A III,134: 1952, pp. 17-18.
13. "Gestalte deine eigne Zukunft," 1952, p. 69 = *Mitteilungsblatt der BG Hamburg, 1*960, p. 38.

VI. Die Einsicht

"Übersetzungen aus AN," 1953, pp. 97; 1951, pp. 1-3; 1949, No. 5, pp. 1; 1951, 5. 50; 1958, pp. 161 f.; 1951, pp. 38; 1949 No. 4, pp. 2-5.

"Die Unpersönlichkeit allen Daseins (Anatta), Stellenlese aus SN," 1954, pp. 2-6, 18-21.

"Die drei Meister" (aus Pug), 1954, pp. 65–66.

VII. Mitteilungsblatt der BG Hamburg (SPB)

1. "Ichlosigkeit," SPB 1953, pp. 126–129 = *Mitteilungsblatt der BG Hamburg,* 1957, pp. 286–290 (Above Engl.).
2. "Ober die buddh. Meditation," 1955, pp. 74–7,6, 86–88.
3. "Der Keim allen Daseins," 1956, pp. 197–203.
4. "Der Einfluß des Buddhismus auf ein Volk" (For the Engl. See below), 1956, pp. 160–162, 174–176.
5. "Geistesentfaltung," 1958, pp. 123–134 (Lecture Tokyo, 1920).

VIII. Various German

1. "Vor Uruvela (A IV/21)," *Theosoph. Kultur* (Leipzig) 1912 (4. Jg.), pp. 227–228.
2. "Kaccāna: Nettipakaraṇa" (Auszug), "Des Zustandekommen der Darstellungsmethoden: Kap. 3 (*naya-samuṭṭhāna*)," *World Buddhism* 1931/32, pp. 3741, 49–52; 1932/33, 5. 2–9.
3. "Beilage zur 'Buddh. Weltschau, Vierteljahresmitt. der BGD,'" Jan, 1948.

"Die Quintessenz des Buddhismus," pp. 1–3, "Gedanken über die buddh. Meditation," pp. 3–5, "Gedanken über das Karma im Buddhismus," pp. 5–7.

IX. English articles

Buddhist Annual of Ceylon

1. "Some Hints on the Control and Culture of Mind," 1921 (Vol. 1/2), pp. 27–29.
2. "An Outline of the Method of Meditation," 1927 (Vol. III/1), pp. 49–52.
3. "How to Balance the Mind, 1929 (Vol. III/3), pp. 206–213.
4. "A Concise Summary of the Abhidhamma Piṭaka," 1932 (Vol. IV/2), pp. 137–149.

Other English

5. "The Message of Buddhism," *Buddhist Review* (London) 1910, pp. 307–314.
6. "The Primary Properties of the Material World," ditto, 1913, pp. 192–194 (after *Abhidhammatthasaṅgaha* Ch. 6).
7. "Dependent Origination (Paṭiccasamuppāda)," ditto, pp. 267–271.
8. "The Only Specific Buddhist Doctrine. An Exposition of Anatta," *Ceylon Daily News,* May 1934, Vesak-Number.

9. "The Word of the Buddha," *Peace* (Singapore) 1934/35 (Vol. 3), pp. 50–60.
10. "The Five Groups or Khandhas," *The Maha Bodhi,* 1937, pp. 129–140.
11. "The First Link of the Path," *Middle Way,* 1942/43 (Vol. 17), pp. 86 ff.
12. "The Buddhist Way of Thinking," *Buddhist China,* Winter 1943, pp. 7–11.
13. "Message to Lanka Dharmaduta Society," Asoka Weeraratna, *Buddhism in Germany,* Colombo, 1953, pp. 1f.
14. "The Egolessness of all existence (*anattā*), extracted from the Saṃyutta-Nikāya, translated and explained," *Light of Dhamma,* 1953/ 54 (Vol. 2), pp. 35–39 = *Wheel* No. 202–204, 1974, pp. 37–48.
15. "Egolessness," *Light of Buddha,* April 1958 (Vol. III/1), pp. 3–7 = *Wheel* No. 202–204, pp. 1–8.
16. "On 'Reality in Mind,' A Comparison of Western Opinion with Abhidhamma," *Light of Buddha,* 1958 (Vol. III,4), pp. 115–118.

French

17. "L'Essence de L'Enseignement du Buddha," *France-Asie,* No. 153157, *Présence du Bouddhism,* Februar-Juni 1959, pp. 241 -250 = Reprint Paris 1987.
18. "Resumé de Methode de Meditation," *La Pensée Bouddhique* I/2, Okt. 1939.
19. "L'Attitude de Pensée Bouddhique," *La Pensée Bouddhique* II/12, Okt. 1947.

Italian

* "Per il Progettato Eremiaggio Buddhista," *Coenobium,* Anno IV, Fas. II, 1910, pp. 145–147.

APPENDIX III

THE MONK DISCIPLES OF ÑĀṆATILOKA

This is a list of all those who became monks under Ñāṇatiloka.

Ñāṇatiloka's first disciples were named after the first five monk disciples of the Buddha (who were arahants): Koṇḍañño, Vappo, Bhaddiyo, Mahānāmo, and Assaji.

Initially, the names were given in the masculine form, ending in *-o*, as used in Thailand. After WWI, Ñāṇatiloka used the uninflected stem-form ending in *-a*, as used in Burma, Sri Lanka and India, which does not show the gender.

Later Ñāṇatiloka started to give his disciples names starting with Ñāṇa- or Nyāna- (the latter being the Burmese spelling) to mark the monastic connection and the origin of the monk. The first was Ñāṇāloka (1914), the next was Ñāṇādhāra (1932).

Because only a senior monk, one who has completed ten rains-retreats, can give the full acceptance, Ñāṇatiloka only started doing so in 1913.

Sam. = Sāmaṇera (novice), the initial acceptance into the Sangha (*pabbajjā* = going forth); Bh = bhikkhu (monk), the second, full acceptance into the Sangha (*upasampadā* = full acceptance); Disr. = disrobed.

Period I: 1905–1907

1. Suñño. N. Bergendahl (Dutch). Died as a monk, perhaps in Burma (see Koṇḍañño's letter in note 45), 1915. Sam.: end 1905 on Culla Lanka near Mātara. Upasampadā in Burma in 191? (see Koṇḍañño's letter).
2. Saddhānusāri (Sumano). Fritz Stange (German). Born 5 December 1874 Sprottau. Died 31 January 1910 in Bandarawela. Sam.: End 1905 on Culla Lanka. Bh: End 1906 in Bandarawela as Sāmaṇera Sumano.
3. Sīlācāra. J. F. McKechnie (English). 1871 Hull – 27 January 1951 Sussex. Sam.: 1906 Kyaundaw Kyaung (Burma), as Sāsanavaṃsa. Bh: 1906 by U Kumara, Ñāṇatiloka as assistant,

as Sīlācāra. Disr. 1925 and returned to England.

4. Dhammānusāri. Walter Markgraf (German). Sam.: 1907 Kyaundaw Kyaung. Disr.: half a year later. Fallen in the autumn of 1915 in Flanders, Belgium.

Period II: 1910–1914

5. Koṇḍañño. Bartholomäus Bauer (German). 20 April 1887 Waldthurn – 30 August 1940 Heidelberg. Sam.: 23 October 1910 Lausanne. Bh: 1912 Burma. Disr.: 1915.
6. Vappo. Ludwig Stolz (German). 1873 Elberfeld – 11 June 1960 Kandy Sam.: 9 June 1911 as Assaji. Bh: 1913 Burma as Vappo
7. Mahanāmo (I). Karl Hilliges (German). Sam.: 4 November 1911 Polgasduva. Disr. 21 or 22 December 1911.
8. Assaji (I). Franklin (American). Sam.: 1 May 1912 Polgasduva.
9. Bhaddiyo. Friedrich Beck (German/American). Died Dec. 1914 Gonamatara. Sam.: 9 August 1912, Polgasduva. Bh: 14 February 1913 Polgasduva.
10. Mahanāmo (II). Victor Stomps (German). 1864 Finnentrop – 1939 Westfalen Sam.: 24 May 1913, Polgasduva. Bh: 14 February 1914 Polgasduva. Disr.: 1915, again monk spring 1928 – summer 1939.
11. Soṇo. Dr. Arthur Fitz (Austrian). Sam.: 17 September 1913, Polgasduva. Bh: 28 August 1913. Disr.: 1916
12. Yaso. Julius Lenga (German). 16. 7. 1890 Heidenberg (East-Prussia) – 7 February 1965 Gengenbach. Sam.: 14 February 1914 Bh: 13 June 1914. Disr.: 1916.
13. Vimalo. Franz Josef Bauer (German). 20 April 1887 Waldthurn – 4 April 1956 München. Sam.: 14 February 1914. Bh: 13. 6. 1914 Disr.: 1915.
14. Puṇṇaji. Phurpa Dongrub (= Indrakhila Siddhartha) (Tibetan from Sikkim). Sam.: 13 June 1914. Disr.
15. Subāhu. Jampa Rinzin (Lepcha from Sikkim). Sam.: 13 June 1914. Disr.
16. Ñāṇāloka. Rājasinha (Sinhalese Rodiya). 1900 – 22 February 1976 Polgasduva. Sam.: Vesak 1914. Bh: April 1920; not with Ñāṇatiloka.

Period III: 1926–1939

17. Cunda. Friedrich Boll (German). On 19 February 1929 Mangelsdorf met him as monk on the Island Hermitage.

18. Sīlava. Silva (Portuguese/American). Disr.
19. Upāli (English). Disr.
20. Assaji (II). Dr. M. T. Kirby (English). Disr. (Ñāṇatiloka, in his brief handwritten notes intended as suggestions for his biography after 1926, gives "Nyanakavi, Dr. Kirby + Col.)"
21. Khema. Gugemos (German). Arrived in Ceylon 11. 1. 1929. Disr.
22. Ñāṇādhāra. Conrad Nell (German). 5. 10. 1897 Berlin – 17. 5. 1935 Mogok (Burma). Sam.: 1932. Polgasduva. Bh: 26. 11. 1933 Rangoon.
23. Ñāṇamanika. Walter Meinecke (German). Sam.: April 1933, Polgasduva. Disr.
24. Ñāṇapiya. Joseph Pistor (German). 1895 Frankfurt/M – 1976 Baddegama Sam.: 4 June 1936. Polgasduva. Bh: Juli 1937 Polgasduva. Disr.: 31 January 1939. Sam.: August 1951 Batapola as Vajirabuddhi. Bh: Juli 1952 there again. (Both not with Ñāṇatiloka.)
25. Ñāṇavipula. Mr. Ferdinand (Burgher, i.e. of Sinhalese-Dutch descent). Died 1971 on Polgasduva. Sam. and. Bh on Polgasduva.
26. Ñāṇavimala (I). Mr. Ferdinand (Burgher). Disr.
27. Ñāṇāvāsa. Sinhalese Sāmaṇera who took care of Ñāṇatiloka in Kandy, 1954.
28. Ñāṇasīsi. Otto Krauskopf (German). 3 October 1884 Rastenburg – 13 August 1950 Colombo. Sam.: 4 June 1936, Polgasduva. Bh: Juli 1937 Polgasduva.
29. Ñāṇaponika. Siegmand Feniger (German). 20 July 1901 Hanau – 19 October 1994 Kandy. Sam.: 4 June 1936 Polgasduva. Bh: 29 June 1937 Ovakande.
30. Ñāṇakkhetta. Peter Idu/Joachim Schönfeldt (German). 15 September 1906 Breslau – 1 May 1984, Jaffna. Sam.: 4 June 1936. Polgasduva Bh: Juli 1937. Polgesduwa Disr.: 1944 Dehra Dun. Then Swami Gauribala.
31. Ñāṇabrūhana. Dr. Max Bruno (German). 8 June 1915 Plicken (East-Prussian) – 24 June 1951 Colombo. Sam.: August 1936 Polgasduva. Bh: Juli 1937 Polgasduva. After leaving Ñāṇatiloka, he reordained as Anuruddho. Bh: 1947, Galle.
32. Ñāṇasīla. William A. Ellis (Australian). Disr.
33. Ñāṇagutta. Alfred Günther (German). Sam.: 15 June 1936. Disr.: Juli 1936.

34. Ñāṇatissa. Dr. Leslie (Australian/Hungarian). Supreme judge. Sam.: 1936. Disr.: November 1936.
35. Ñāṇamālita. Malte Schönfeldt (German). 11 January 1917 Berlin - 1989 Colombo. Sam.: 7 August 1937. Bh: 19 February 1938. Disr.: 1 January 1945, Dehra Dun.
36. Ñāṇasatta. Martin Novosad. (Moravian/Czech) 25 January 1908 Vizovice - 25 September 1984 Polgasduva. Sam.: 15 May 1938 Polgasduva. Bh: 20 August 1939 Polgasduva.
37. Ñāṇasiri. Sachvit Runjan Roy (Bengali) Sam.: 1938. Disr.
38. Ñāṇasukho. Alexis Sankowline (Ukrainian) Sam.: 1939. Disr.

Period IV: 1946–1957

39. Ñāṇavīra. Harold Musson (English). 1920 Aldershot - 5 July 1965 Bundala. Sam.: 24 April 1949, Polgasduva. Bh: 1950 Vajirārāma (Colombo).
40. Ñāṇamoli. Osbert Moore (English). 25 June 1905 England - 8 March 1960 Veheragama. Sam.: 24 April 1949, Polgasduva. Bh: 1950 Vajirārāma (Colombo).
41. Ñāṇakitti. Ronald K. F. Rose (English). Journalist. Listed in Visitors Book on 12 September 1949. Sam.: bei Ñāṇatiloka. Bh: 1950 with Ñāṇasatta. Disr.
42. Ñāṇavimala (II). Friedrich Möller (German). 23 November 1911 Hessendorf b. Rinteln - August 2005, Polgaduwa. Sam.: 19 September 1955 by Ñāṇatiloka. Then given over to Ñāṇāloka. Bh: 19 November 1955 on a sīmā on Ratgama-Lagoon by Madhihe Paññasīha.

ENDNOTES

1. *Ceylon Daily News*, Vesak Number, 1938.

2. The biographical parts on Ñāṇatiloka have been omitted here as they are also found in the autobiography.

3. The preceding part is from a shorter version of this essay by W. Persian called "Buddhism in Germany," published in *The British Buddhist*, 1931/32, Nr. 6, pp. 69–71.

4. "Buddhism is a hundred times colder, more truthful, more objective." (*The Antichrist*, Aph. 22–23.) See "Nietzsche's Critique of Buddhism," William Loftus Hare, *The Buddhist Review*, Vol. VIII, 1916, No. 1, pp. 21–35. (BPS ed.)

5. F. Zimmermann, a.k.a Subhadra Bhikshu, writes the following about the Christian antagonism towards Buddhism in the late 19th century in his introduction to the 1907 edition of the *Buddhistischen Katechismus*, translated by C. T. Strauss as *Buddhist Catechism*, Wheel 152–154, BPS, Kandy:

> In recent years a great many works have been published in favour of and against Buddhism: Everywhere comparisons are being made between Christianity and Buddhism, and the Church looks uneasily at the new adversary. The Christian Church is far-seeing enough to observe that from no quarter is its supremacy menaced so strongly as from the teaching of the Indian Prince of the tribe of the Sakyas. Even the German Emperor was moved to call Christendom to a united battle against Buddhism in an allegorical painting, wherein he depicts the same as a disastrous, destructive power. But the truth promulgated by the Buddha is not destructive to the civilization of Europe, as the Emperor ignorantly imagines; it is a destroyer only of error, delusion, superstition, and of mental and moral bondage; and only those have occasion to become alarmed to whose advantage it is, when darkness reigns instead of light.

Zimmermann refers to the drawing of H. Knackfuß *"Völker Europas, wahret Eure heiligsten Güter"* ("People of Europe, guard your holiest Goods"), after a design by Kaiser Wilhelm II, who gave it to the Czar of Russia. The picture is shown on picture page 1.

6. In German the words "professor" and "doctor" do not have the same advanced connotation as in English and are also used for teachers

at high schools.

7. The Gymnasium is the most advanced type of secondary school in European countries. It prepares students for university. Both Greek and Latin are taught.

8. Ludwig Friedrich Wilhelm, a.k.a. Ludwig II, was the King of Bayern. He is known as the "fairy tale king" due to his liking for the fairy tale world of Wagner's operas and his extravagant fairy tale like castles.

9. Here a small part of the manuscript has been eaten by cockroaches.

10. This was not King Ludwig, but a nephew (*vetter*) of her father.

11. Pablo M. M. de Sarasate y Navascuéz (1844-1908), a Spanish violin virtuoso and composer of the Romantic period.

12. C. A. Schuricht (1880–1967) was an influential orchestra conductor.

13 J. B. J. M. Reger (1873–1916) was a composer, organist, pianist and teacher.

14. 1877–1906.

15. F. Zimmermann (1852–1911) had actually never been a monk, but nevertheless published his book under the name of Bhikshu Subhadra. The first German edition of the *Buddhistischen Katechismus* was published in 1888 and the first edition of the English translation by C. T. Strauss was published in 1907 as *A Buddhist Catechism.* The popularity of this work is shown by the many German editions and the translations into several languages such as French, Russian and Japanese, and also by the official approval by the renowned Sinhalese scholar-monk Hikkaduve Sumaṅgala.

16. Arthur Joseph Pfungst, (1864-1912). The actual title is *Der Buddhismus: Eine Darstellung von dem Leben und den Lehren Gautamas, des Buddhas.* It was published in 1899 and is a translation of the 17th edition of T. W. Rhys Davids' *Buddhism: being a sketch of the life and teachings of Gautama, the Buddha,* 1887.

17 Jules Massenet (1842–1912). His most famous operas were *Manon* and *Werther.*

18. Charles-Marie Widor (1845–1937).

19. Konrad Bercovici/Berkovici (1882–1961), resident in the USA from 1916.

20. E. F. von Feuchtersleben (1806–1849) was a doctor and teacher of medical psychology in Vienna. His main work, *Zur Diätetik der Seele (The Dietetics of the Soul)*, was published in 1838 in Vienna.

21. Probably the Rumanian composer Ioan (or Ion) Scarlatescu (1872–1922).

22. The artist name of Queen Elizabeth of Rumania (1843–1916), the spouse of King Karl I. She was a prolific writer and musician.

23. Moritz Moczowski (1854-1925), a German Jewish composer, concert pianist and conductor.

24. Eugène Ysaÿe (1858-1931), a Belgian violinist, composer and conductor.

25. Gustaf Nagel (1874-1952), a promoter of natural health and vegetarianism, political activist and poet. After wandering barefoot around Europe, Palestinia and Egypt, he founded a health center (*kurort*) at his beloved Arendsee lake. His criticisms of the Nazi and Soviet regimes caused him to be put twice in a mental hospital, where he finally died. See http://www.vegetarierbund.de/nv/nv_1999_4__Gustav_Nagel.htm.

26. Ānanda Metteyya (C. H. A. Bennett, gen. McGregor, 1872-1923), was the second British monk. See *Ānanda Metteyya: His Life and Mission* by Elizabeth Harris, Wheel Series no. 420-22, BPS, Kandy. A year before Ānanda Metteyya's acceptance into the Sangha in 1900, Gordon Douglas became a monk, named Asoka, in Burma. He passed away in the same year. Thirty years before, c. 1870, an Austrian, whose name is unknown, temporarily ordained as a bhikkhu at Wat Pichaiyat in Thonburi, during the reign of King Chulalongkorn (Rāma V). At the time of his ordination he was employed by the Siamese government. See *Banner of the Arahants,* by Bhikkhu Khantipālo, Kandy, 1979.

27. The part of Colombo where the Vajirārāma Monastery is situated.

28. Mrs. Mah May Hlā Oung is the author of the article "The Women of Burma," published in *The Buddhist,* Vol. 1, 1903, pp. 62-82. A biography of this Burmese philantropist is found in *The Buddhist Review,* Vol. II, Oct.-Dec. 1910, No. 4, pp. 16-17.

29. R. Rost (1822-1896) was for many years the head of the Indian Office Library in London.

30. He was also the son of the scholar Reinhard Rost to whom Childers's *Pāli Dictionary* is dedicated. R. C. Childers (1838-1876) published the first ever Pāli-English dictionary in London, 1872-1875.

31. *The Soul of the People,* H. Fielding-Hall, London, 1898. Fielding-Hall (1859-1917) was a British judge in Burma. The charming book, which was reprinted several times, provides insights into Burmese thought, religion, and culture.

32. *Ñāṇa-ti-loka* = "Knower (*ñāṇa*) of the three (*ti*) worlds (*loka*)." The three worlds are the sensual world, the world of form (the jhānas), and the formless world (the formless spheres). All possible realms of existence are included in these three worlds.

33. Ñāṇatiloka was not aware of the little known fact that there was an Austrian who undertook temporary ordination in Thailand 30 years earlier; see note 26.

34. Ven. Dhammānanda Kosambi (1876–1947) was an important Pali scholar. He was born in Goa, India. As a child he was impressed with the stories of the Buddha in a children's book and later went to study Sanskrit and Buddhism at Poona and Varanasi. While travelling around India and Nepal, several monks advised him to go to study in Ceylon and in 1906 he received upasampadā there with Ven. Sumaṅgala Mahāthera as preceptor. Later he returned to India, gave up the bhikkhu training, got married in his home village and had a son named D. D. Kosambi, who became a distinguished Indian scientist. In 1910 he received *upasampadā* again. He travelled and studied more and got his doctorate at Harvard University in America. Upon returning from America, he founded the Bahujana Buddhavihāra in Bombay in 1937. He wrote many books, including *Bhagvān Buddhā*, the book responsible for arousing Dr. Ambedkar's interest in Buddhism. At the end of his life he entrusted his vihāra to the Mahā Bodhi Society of India.

35. On 10 February 1905 Ānanda Metteyya in Rangoon wrote the following about Ñāṇatiloka in a letter to Dr. Cassius Pereira in Colombo:

> He wants to learn Pali properly, and he cannot do this except for private study here; and I agree with him that in thinking it likely that he might find some English-speaking Bhikkhu, as Palita-thera, in Ceylon, who might help him. He is a very good monk, and since he has been in Burma has made as deep a study of Buddhism as is possible through the medium of translation… He is an easily-contented mortal, with a very gentle and considerate nature.

36. There is a question mark in colons here in the German edition. Later in the autobiography, in the Bangkok 1921 section, Ñāṇatiloka says that he met the prince in 1906. The colophons to the pictures of Ñāṇatiloka and Suñño in the prince's autobiography—see next note—state that the pictures were made in 1905. The date of the letter in the preceding note also suggests that Ñāṇatiloka returned to Ceylon in 1905. Suñño became monk at Cullalaṅkā Island.

37. Chulalongkorn, or Rāma V, was King of Siam from 1868 to 1910. The bright, but radical Prince Prisdung Jumsai (or Chumsai) (1851–1935), was the first ever Thai graduate from a Western university (King's College, London), and then became the first ever permanent Thai consul in the West. In this position in 1885 he made the first ever proposal for a constitutional government in Thailand to the King. The petition, conceived with the intention to save Siam from looming Western colonization, was co-signed by several other fellow princes, but was not received well by the King due to its non-secrecy and its criticism of polygamy. Jumsai was therefore called back from England in 1886. He fled from Siam in 1890 and came to Ceylon in 1895, where he became a

monk named Jinavaravaṃsa in 1896 under the renowned scholar monk Vaskaduvē Subhūti. He lived as an ascetic until 1905, and then became abbot of the Dīpaduttarārāma monastery in Colombo. In 1911 he returned to Thailand for King Chulalongkorn's funeral and was forced to disrobe by Prince Damrong (see note 123), perhaps to humiliate him or to prevent him from giving problems to the government while being protected by the robes. He was not allowed to reordain in Siam by Saṅgharāja Vajirañāṇa nor was he allowed to return to Ceylon by the new King. See www.geocities.com/RainForest/Vines/8769/Prisdang.htm; Brailey, Nigel. *Two Views of Siam on the Eve of the Chakri Reformation.* Whiting Bay, Scotland: Kiscadale Publication, 1989; Sumet Jumsai, "The Ratna Chetiya Dīpaduttārāma, Colombo", *Journal of the Royal Asiatic Society of Sri Lanka,* Vol. XLVIII, 2003.

38. Sumet Jumsai, see note 16, writes: "...he led an austere life of an ascetic, culminating in a period of meditation on a small island near Mātara. The island, which he named Cullalaṅkā in honour of King Chulalonkorn, was a place where snakes were released and human bones deposited, and his stay caused a considerable stir amongst the populace."

39. R. Sobczak was born on 13 July 1868 in Prussia.

40. Before WWI, Ñāṇatiloka employed the nominative masculine ending in *-o* in the Pali names of disciples such as Vappo, as is normal in Thailand, afterwards he changed to the uninflected stem-form in *-a* (e.g. Nyanaponika), as is normal in Sri Lanka, Burma, and India.

41. A. Besant (1847–1933).

42. The *Word of the Buddha* was published in German in 1906 in Leipzig.

43. The *Khandhaparitta.* The verses are found in several places in the Pali Canon, such as AN 4:67. Chanting the verses is supposed to protect one against the bites of snakes and other venomous creatures.

44. J. F. McKechnie (1871–1951). This Scotsman became a prolific writer. While a novice by the name of Sāsanavaṃsa, he translated from the German Bhikkhu Ñāṇatiloka's first literary work, *The Word of the Buddha* (first English edition: Rangoon 1907).

45. An extract from a German letter by Bhikkhu Koṇḍañño, given at http://www.payer.de/neobuddhismus/neobud0203.htm. Dr. Payer does not give the source, but he mentions 10 February 1910. However this can't be correct because Ñāṇatiloka and Koṇḍañño were then still in Europe. As Koṇḍañño mentions in his letter, it was written in Burma, which means that it was written between late 1911 and mid 1913; see note 65. It might have been published in the article "Der feste Ruhepunkt," *Zeitschrift für Buddhismus* 1913/1914, pp. 125–152; see "Bartel

Bauer" in *Lebensbilder Deutscher Buddhisten, Band II, Die Nachfolger* by Hellmuth Hecker.

What I can say about Sumano's death is the following: In the autumn of last year, Bhikkhu Ñāṇatiloka, the Burmese monk Sīlavaṃsa and I made a walking tour for a week through the Southwest of Ceylon. We went over the Adam's Peak, and came to Bandarawela. First, the three of us went to the small mud-hut, hardly 3 by 4 meters in size, where Sumano had lived and died. The hut is situated in a very lonely place, outside of the village, in the midst of bare grassy hillocks so that no sound can be heard from the village, and no human habitation can be seen right around. It is barren and desolate there, as rarely anywhere else. The second hut which, when Sumano died, was inhabited by Suñño, had already fallen into decay, and the rain had washed away nearly every vestige of it. Afterwards we wanted also to go to the site of the cremation, but we missed the place. Hence I went once more there, without Ñāṇatiloka, but together with the Thera of the Bandarawela Monastery. I found, besides some pieces of molten glass, a few small unburnt splinters of bone. I picked them up and handed them over to Ñāṇatiloka who still keeps them at Dodanduwa as a memento.

The site of the cremation is on the top of one of those grassy hillocks, about 10 minutes distance from the hut. Boys have planted a Bodhi tree at that spot. A great gathering is said to have been present at the cremation, amongst them hundreds of Christians and Mohammedans who secretly respected the ascetic way of life led by Sumano and then paid their respects at the day of the cremation. The Buddhists did *not* pay to the severely sick monk, mostly at the instigation of the well-known Dhammapāla (in Colombo) who seemed to pay only respects to learned monks and believed that Sumano was a European runaway. Sumano would not have passed away if he would have had better food-support, and could have been completely healthy with the food in Dodanduwa. A monk in the vicinity, who had room enough and also good food, sent Sumano away in a severely ill state just because he was ill and the sixty-year old monk feared the disease. Otherwise this monk is a good person, but he had no love and altruism, although he was living dependent on others since his youth.

After the cremation, the ashes were distributed among the lay people, and many a Christian, Mohammedan, and Hindu took them as gladly as a Buddhist. Suñño went to Burma shortly after this and became bhikkhu. Soon after he fell ill in the same monastery where I am living now, although he has good support from Mandalay. We are really no tropical plants.

The hut in which Sumano died was built on government land. Ñāṇatiloka came to measure the plot of land surrounding the hut. This plot was also advertised for bids and then auctioned. Sumano must have been a thorn in the side of the Catholic Missionary Society because many new Christians respected the ascetic life of Sumano much more than the Christian missionaries, who go hunting, wear polished boots, walking sticks, tropical hats and nice clothes, don't forsake anything, drink alcohol, and receive 60 Rupees monthly (about 100 Mark), besides free housing and various other benefits. In order to prevent the further inhabitation of this hut and to prevent it from becoming known further, the Christians offered 300 Rupees for the hut and the plot of land, although it altogether is not worth 50 Rupees and the Christians can't do anything with it. More is not known to me about this.

46. Perhaps in Burma, see the letter by Koṇḍañño in note 45.

47. Sumana Sāmaṇera's work, together with five letters on Buddhism by him and some biographical material, has been published by the BPS as *Going Forth–A Call to Buddhist Monkhood,* no. 27/28 in the *Wheel* series.

48. There appear to have been various reasons why Southern Switzerland was chosen as the site of the monastery and not Germany. First, it was not considered possible to get permission from the German government to found a monastery (*Die buddhistische Welt* 3, No 11, May 1910, p.108). Second, there was an invitation from the publisher of *Coenobium* who lived in Lugano. Third, there was a sort of freehaven for spiritual seekers near Mount Verita, Ascona, not far from Lugano (see note 57). Fourth, Fifth, Switzerland is centrally located in Europe. Land was cheap because the area was fairly remote (see the following letter to Arthur Pfungst). Sixth, perhaps the climate was considered more suitable.

The following is a translation of a letter by Ñāṇatiloka to Arthur Pfungst, reproduced in *Arthur Pfungst, Gesammelte Werke,* Bd. 3 II, Frankfurt, 1927, S. 318–319.

Rangoon, 13 January 1908
1 Pagoda Road

Dear Sir,

You should have received the English translation of my work *Das Wort des Buddha,* which I sent you.

As you might have heard from Leipzig, I have the plan to come and settle next year in Switzerland at the Lago di Lugano together with four other bhikkhus, namely two Germans, a wise and renunciant Burmese Saradaw (U. Tejavaṃsamahātthero, Shwezetee-Saradaw of Akyab) and a learned Ceylonese Thero. For this goal I intend to found a hermitage suitable for meditation and serious labour in a really remote place, and thus to lay the foundation for the Sangha in the Europe. For each individual bhikkhu a very primitive hut made of stone should be constructed. The land should not be too costly, because a square meter of land in remote areas is available from only 50 cents onwards. A German who is living here at the moment as a Samanero is going to accompany us as Upasako and intends to buy part of the necessary land out of his own means. He also will care for the utilization and cultivation of the land, so that eventually we would be able to live off our own land.

The publisher of the monthly magazine *Coenobium* in Lugano has offered to help in any way with the carrying out of this plan.

Mr. St. from Mexico, who visited me twice here in our hermitage, has also offered me his support. He thinks that on his return journey, which he might start soon, he will talk to the gentlemen in Lugano while stopping over in Europe and will then visit them in Frankfurt.

Thus, I request you too, dear sir, to take part in this very meritorious work of founding a Buddhist Viharo in Europe. All donations should be sent to the editor of *Coenobium,* Lugano, (Villa Conza); with the notice "For the foundation of a Buddhist monastery in Tessin by Bhikkhu Nyanatiloka."

Namo Tassa Bhagavato Arahato Sammāsambuddhassa!

With sincere Buddhist greetings,

Nyanatiloka

Dhammānusāri, Sāmanero.

Silācāra. (lately G. J. M.' Kechnie)

Cf. *"Was bringt uns die Zukunft? Zur Frage der Einführung eines Sangha im Abendland"* ("What will the future bring us? On the question of the introduction of a Sangha in the Occident") in the German Buddhist journal *Die Buddhistische Warte* Vol. I , 1907/08, pp. 257–269. In this article Karl Seidenstücker (1876–1936), the founder of the Buddhistischer-Missionsverein in Deutschland (German Buddhist Missionary Society), relates that Ñāṇatiloka had been in contact with the Coenobium group regarding the founding of a monastery near Lugano and that the response had been positive.

He mentions that Markgraf (ex-Dhammānusārī) had sent a letter to him (see note 51 below) in which he requested him to put a notice in the journal about this monastery and the establishment of a fund for buying a large plot of land on which huts were to be built. Seidenstücker, although sympathetic, had considerable reservations about the practicality of the plan. He was concerned that large numbers of "shady and opportunistic characters"—of whom (according to him) there were many in Theosophical circles, etc.—would be attracted to the vihāra.

Ñāṇatiloka had suggested that bhikkhus staying in the monastery would travel around Germany and Europe to give lectures in large cities, but Seidenstücker had doubts about them being qualified enough to do so. Another concern of Seidenstücker was the adaptation of the monks to Occidental conditions and how they would support themselves. In his opinion the time was not ready: "...a bhikkhu working in Germany as a missionary... will not have an easy time here. Certainly, a strong backing and guardianship is necessary, and here I come to the core question: Is it not opportune to wait with the foundation of a Vihāro and the missionary activity connected with it until we have a fairly strong Buddhist lay-community?" Seidenstücker also had the view that the Buddhist Community was to be completely undogmatic and was not to belong to a particular creed or current in Buddhism: "For heaven's sake, no scholastism, no dogmatism, nothing churchly!"

In *Die Buddhistische Warte* of July 1907 (pp. 370–71) the writer of an anonymous letter, introduced by the editor of the magazine, had other doubts:

> ...the writer then turns against the import of Asian bhikkhus, because, "then the cause will be hopelessly compromised and will be categorised as an exotic curiosity, seen as a Zulu caravan or the nature-people at Monte Verità near Locarno, but not taken seriously. Because the matter is urgent, I will immediately propose some, for orthodox ears, heretical ideas that form the foundation program for working with Buddhism in Europe in the first place ...:
>
> 1. The Buddhist Canon, which got into shape over a period of thousands of years, is of no use for Europe in form, expression, and size. Able men, familiar with Buddhism, modern philosophy, and science, have to extract the useful and put it into modern form to make it more accessible. *Only the inner spirit of the Teaching is lasting, the form ages and becomes invalid.*
>
> 2. The rules of the Brotherhood are an *Indian* product, archaic, born out of the climate of a past epoch. And therefore they need to be *completely revised.* The clothes, lifestyle, occupation of the bhikkhu

need to be readapted to the climate and changed conditions of living, etc.

3. Only Europeans can do this, and if this is not done through capable minds and through some kind of agreement between the European Buddhists, at least in the main points, one cannot consider the foundation of a Vihāro without damaging the matter seriously.

4. Any importing of Asian lifestyles and monks rules, mental exercises, etc, as well as brown brothers, is completely unallowable, and should be opposed by anyone who is sincerely concerned about the spreading of reformed Buddhist ideas and who has enough insight to foresee the effect of such a wrong start."

The well-known German translator Karl Eugen Neumann was strongly ridiculing the plan in a letter (23 March 1910) to Georg Grimm:

"...those quaint brothers in Lugano, who as unexperienced childlike enthusiasts make a great thing ridiculous with their hocus-pocus."

To his best friend, the Italian Prof. Giuseppe De Lorenzo (1871–1957) he expressed similar sentiments in a letter dated 21 July 1910:

...we absolutely don't want anything to do with any unworthy, childish hocus-pocus propaganda with barbarian pillars, symbolic carriage-wheels, tiaras, rosaries, white elephant cantilevers, and similar modern gewgaw, polished with a Persian saying taken from Schopenhauer and mutilated in bad French to boot. Much more, we feel that we have to raise our voice, without wanting to do so, to warn against such a puppet play with spiritual matters, in that we label it as *abusus optimi pessimus*. The establishment in Noviaggio will die in a dreadful disgrace...

And in a letter dated 18 May 1910 he wrote:

The brothers in Lugano are not up to Gotamistic as well as scientific standards. Firstly, because their head is a former Catholic seminarian and priest, and no one can purify himself from so thoroughly rubbed in "ecclesiastical, sacred oil of the Spirit" (*oleo sancti Spiritus ecclesiastici*). Secondly, those brothers lack clearly any vein of aesthetic culture, a lack that they, of course, don't feel.

Neumann and Lorenzo (who wrote negatively about Ñāṇatiloka in the introduction of his book *India e Buddismo Antico*, see *Coenobium* 1910, 5, p.83f.) might have had a grudge against Ñāṇatiloka because they felt offended by a remark by Walter Markgraf, the publisher, that Ñāṇatiloka's translation of the *Puggalapaññatti* was correct, in contrast to other translations which contain distortions and errors. Neumann took this to refer to his translations. (See Hellmuth Hecker, *Karl Eugen*

Neumann: Erstübersetzer der Reden des Buddha, Anreger zu abendländischer Spiritualität, Hamburg, 1986, p.116f.)

On 12 September 1909 the German Pali Society (Deutsche Pali Gesellschaft [DPG]) was founded by Walter Markgraf and Friedrich Zimmermann (1852–1917). Several well known German and European Buddhists (Rhys Davids, Sīlācāra, Ñāṇatiloka, etc.) became honorary members. One of the official aims of the society was the "Support for a Vihāro (hermitage) in Europe in a German language area." On 9 October 1910 at the following annual General Meeting this statute was changed to "For the general support of European Buddhist endeavours... Reason: many, even completely Buddhist minded Europeans, do not sympathize with the support of a Vihāro in Europe, therefore one should not put this explicitly into the statutes. This motion was unanimously accepted." From *Die Buddhistische Welt* 4 (1910), p.121, the journal of the DPG, which was edited first by Seidenstucker and then by Waltgraf.

The German versions of the above passages are online at http://www.payer.de/neobuddhismus/neobud0304.htm and http://www.payer.de/neobuddhismus/neobud0203.htm

49. *Coenobium,* a journal in Italian and French of a "society of educated and learned men." Twelve volumes appeared from 1906 to 1919. In this journal there are a few articles and letters by Ñāṇatiloka, such as a French translation of "The Influence of Buddhism" by R. A. Bergier.

50. The Italian patriot whose conquest of Sicily and Naples led to the formation of the Italian state (1807–1882)

51. This is the Deutsche Pali Gesellschaft, founded by Waltgraf and Zimmermann.

In *Buddhistischen Welt* issue of September 1909 there is he following in article called "The Foundation of a European Vihāro in the Tessin canton (Switzerland)." *("Die Gründung eines europäischen Vihâro im Kanton Tessin [Schweiz]")* by Walter Markgraf:

> In February 1908 I, as Sāmaṇero Dhammānusārī in Rangoon, and in association with Ven. Ñāṇatiloka, sent several hundreds of copies of a circular letter to all known Buddhists in the Old and New World. The letter promoted the foundation of a Vihāro (Hermitage) in Europe. In Germany thirty copies of this writing were distributed too. In *Die Buddhistischen Warte* a longer article appeared that was dealing with the matter, but, regrettably, it only had negative results. The letter of a someone interested in Buddhism in Germany, was written in such a tone, that it was difficult to see any Buddhist orientation in it.
>
> A few sympathetic letters came from America, Italy, and Switzerland, but with regards money... That not much could be expected from Europe was clear to us beforehand, but a complete lack

of any help is painful. Things were better in Asia. The Royal princes of Siam gave 300 Rupees, and Yeo Eng Biam Esq, Rangoon, a rich Chinese businessman, Rs. 400, for which they are thanked by this means. Thus 1000 marks have been gathered, and are deposited in the bank in Colombo for future use.

Meanwhile, this amount is insignificant, because the project cannot be undertaken in any manner with it... About 10000 marks* are needed for the building of a Vihāro. With it a small piece of land is to be bought in a very secluded place in the Southern Alps. Here for each monk, a hut is to be built out of stone, which can be built light because it is always warm near Lake Lugano. Food and clothing are to be supplied by volunteer donors as well as a Society. However, the food for the most part is to be gotten easily from the fertility of the land itself, through cultivation of crops, beekeeping, etc. For the purpose a good Buddhist has to take on the management of more worldly affairs of the Hermitage. That, on one hand, the site is very remote, and that, on the other hand, an energetic person experienced in worldly affairs takes on external matters is very important, because through this the Bhikkhus and novices can be guaranteed of the essential quiet and silence, which, we in the worldly life often search in vain throughout our whole lives.

According to the plans of my dear teacher, Venerable Ñāṇatiloka, each bhikkhu is obliged to study Pali diligently and also to make translations of old Buddhist texts into European languages, and just this will soon have a great influence to the spreading of the Teaching. One shouldn't forget that the climatic conditions in Burma are quite unhealthy and that it requires a sheer superhuman effort to set oneself to work in temperatures above 30° C. Moreover, because of the fever, bad drinking water, and poor food (rice with some vegetables, and that only before 12 a.m.), the body of a bhikkhu originally from Northern regions has to be from steel in order to endure for long. When we call ourselves Buddhists and sincerely endeavour to reach the objectives, we should also provide a place to work in peace for our trailblazers, who have at first made us attentive of the teachings by their translations and publications.

Ven. Ñāṇatiloka informed me that anyone who wishes to join the Sangha should first stay for a longer period of time in the Vihāro as a layman (Upāsako) and strictly observe the Buddhist precepts, and then stay for about a year as a novice. Only then, when the candidate is fully clear about his desire, can he be accepted as bhikkhu. That a bhikkhu can return anytime to the worldly life, and does not bind himself for life, should be well known...

(** The annual wage of a German elementary school teacher was about 2700 marks at the time.*)

Half a year later Zimmerman wrote in the same journal (*Die Buddhistischen Welt*, 4, 1911, p. 167) the following in an article called "A Touchstone":

...The result is deplorable, indeed downright shameful. Of the members of the DPG, of the members of Die Buddhistischen Welt, in short, of all the German followers, only nine have responded to the urgent request for donations; only nine have put their conviction into action. That the liberal daily press did not respond at all to our requests for support for our endeavours is unfortunate but understandable under the present conditions; but that they who profess to the Buddhist worldview failed completely for the most part is incomprehensible.

Some months later the following notice appeared in *The Buddhist Review*, Vol. II, Apr.-Jun. 1910, No. 2, p. 158:

The Bhikkhu Ñāṇatiloka, who was born at Wiesbaden, studied in a Catholic seminary, spent nine years in Ceylon and Burma, and became a Buddhist monk, will found, if the climate suits, the first European Buddhist colony at the mountain resort Noviaggio, overlooking Lugano, Italy. He has taken a house in the midst of a forest, commanding a view of Lake Maggiore, and will shortly be joined by our esteemed contributor the Bhikkhu Sīlācāra, together with some European converts. Around the house, permanent buildings may arise, and the missionaries will carry on their work by means of lectures and translations of the Sacred Books. Ñāṇatiloka is a philosopher and distinguished orientalist. His *Word of the Buddha* is much prized, and besides this work, he has published in German translations of many suttas. We owe to his pen the version of the *Puggala-Paññatti*, or *Book of Characters*, and at present he is engaged in a complete translation of the Aṅguttara Nikāya.

About the same time, in the journal *Coenobium*, 1910, Fasc. I, p. 150-151, the following notice appeared (in Italian):

FOR THE SAKE OF A BUDDHIST MONASTERY IN EUROPE—The Bhikkhu Ñāṇatiloka, about whom we talk also elsewhere in the present issue, has arrived from India and is a guest of ours. His mission—the readers of the *Coenobium* are already aware of it—is that of founding the first Buddhist vihāro in Europe. He is going to take up residence in a small house in the midst of a wood. A young Dutchman and a German man who were already ordained by him as sāmaṇeros three years ago, as well as the Bhikkhu Silācāra from Rangoon, are all due to join him. Seven German Buddhists have made a one-year-long commitment towards the support of the Bhikkhu, paying a small monthly instalment. Once the first nucleus is established, the small huts for the accommodation of the other monks will be erected. The architect Rutch from Breslau is currently preparing sketch drawings for these huts.

52. K. Gjellerup (1857–1919).

53. Published as *Wheel Publication* 152/154, Buddhist Publication Society, Kandy.

54. Stolz (1873–1960).

55. In *Coenobium* Fasc. II, 1910, pp. 145–147 the following article—called "Per Il Progettato Eremitaggio Buddhista"—by Ñāṇatiloka on the discipline in the monastery appeared (in Italian). Giuliana Martini kindly translated it into English.

For the Planned Buddhist Hermitage

Friends of the *Cœnobium*,

Time and again I was asked, and I am being asked, what the goal and the task of the life of us Buddhist monks truly is.

I regret the impossibility of offering a brief answer to those who are not familiar with the principles of Buddhist ethics; I shall however take advantage of the hospitality offered by the *Cœnobium* to provide them with some indication that could orientate them, and I also take this opportunity to refer them—in order to acquire a deeper understanding—to works on this subject written in a European language.

As far as the Bhikkhus (meaning *mendicants*) are concerned, I shall in the first place say that they form a community of men seeking the emancipation from all desires, from all egoistic appetites. Such is their intent, which is to be achieved through an intuitive knowledge of the transitory nature of all things, a knowledge that transforms the inner man and which intensive contemplation makes more and more refined, up to the point of certainty that the very self-styled "ego" is in reality nothing but a process of transitory and ever-changing physical and psychical phenomena (see my book *Wort des Buddha,* published by Grieben in Leipzig, or its English translation *The Word of the Buddha*, Rangoon, International Buddhist Society).

Thus, the Bhikkhu is not a priest and is not an intermediary between any superior intelligence whatsoever and the human being. He does not have anything to do with the actions, whichever they are, of the followers living the mundane life, for Buddhism is a purely ethical doctrine, and is not interested in the exterior life of its adherents. Thus in Buddhism there are no religious ceremonies on the occasion of weddings, baptisms, etc.; there are neither churches or absolution of sins. The "practice of ceremonies" (*silabbata-paramaso*) is in itself one of the major obstacles to inner light and purity.

As to the outward way of living, the Bhikkhu is to follow the rules of the order, as they were laid by the Buddha himself and as they are preserved in the Vinaya-pitaka and in the Patimokkha. These rules are more or less strict depending on the requirements of the climate where one lives. Those who wish to acquaint themselves more extensively on the subject may read the English translation *Vinaya Texts* by Rhys Davis and the German booklet *Sangha* by Tilbe (Leipzig).

The Bhikkhu, who struggles for detachment and renunciation, does not take a city, and not even a hamlet, as his domicile, and normally lives in solitude, far away from the world, and no mundane concern should distract him from his interior endeavour and divert him from his holy efforts. He lives alone in a separate hut, or in a cave in the forest. Even nowadays the Bhikkhus in Burma or in Siam often live in this way. And even though outward activity should not be compulsory for him, he can, from time to time, go among the people in order to enlighten them, occupy himself with the education of the youth, with the translation of ancient texts, the writing of Buddhist works on ethics, psychology, etc.

Amongst the Bhikkhus, as such, there is no distinction of rank, nor any difference in terms of rights and duties. Every hierarchy is excluded amongst them and nobody has the right to make any change to the rules of the order given by the Buddha. The Vinaya presumes and demands that the young Bhikkhu pays his respects and veneration to the elder Bhikkhu within the order's relationships. A non-religious person may believe that such a feeling is the result of coercion, but this is not the case; for the true Buddhist this is just the result of the confidence in the Buddha himself and in the community (*sangho*) instituted by him. This prescription is thus perfectly respected and obeyed in all Buddhist countries and is the only means to preserve the accord in the Bhikkhus' congregation. The true disciple and subordinate to the Bhikkhu is the Samanero, who obviously listens willingly to his master and advisor's instructions. The master has in turn the obligation to take care of his disciple as his own son. When his master reckons he is suitable and worthy, the Samanero can, if he so requires, be accepted into the Bhikkhus' congregation, upon a decision to be made by at least five of them.

Before gaining acceptance as a Samanero in our future and planned hermitage (whose founding will be possibly still postponed for another few months), the candidate is first required to live with the Bhikkhus as Brahmacari-Upasako (having devoted himself to chastity and poverty) for about two years. During this period—just as a Samanero—he will be doing some manual jobs, such as gardening, cooking, etc., besides the daily spiritual exercises and the study of Pali, which will be compulsory.

The attire of the Bhikkhu and of the Samanero is identical, according to the Vinayo. The Brahmacari Upasakos of our future hermitage will be distinguishable from Bhikkhus and Samaneros because of their grey colour clothing, while the formers' attire is yellow. They are free to extend their status as Upasako, and they are free to do so as long as they would wish.

Our rapports with the outside world will be conducted by a Brahmacari-Upasako, as Bhikkhus and Samaneros are not allowed to deal with pecuniary business. The Brahmacari-Upasako himself though, can not own anything, with the exception of that which is strictly necessary.

I shall assume, as you would expect, the duty of taking the physical well-being of all my disciples on board, as well as of taking care of their instruction in the Pali language and of their noviciate.

Young people could also be admitted as Brahmacari Upasakos and Samaneros; I shall entrust an Upasako or a Samanero of a mature age with their training.

The Bhikkhus, and if possible the Samaneros as well, will have to live each in his own hut located in a secluded place.

Neither the level of education, nor the social status or the fortune of the candidate will be taken into account as to the acceptance as Upasako, Samanero or Bhikkhu.

The doors of the Sangho are open to any serious aspirant, who—it is good to say this—is not required to take any oath which would bind him lifelong. Everyone is free according to the Vinaya and, without any bad reputation to be attached to his name, is free to leave the Sangho. Indeed, in Burma and in Siam each male, whether he be a prince or a farmer, follows the custom to live for a certain period of time the life of a Samanero or of a Bhikkhu.

No coercion will exercised on the individual, but we will endeavour that everyone will possess a real and full confidence in the Buddha, in his doctrine and in the mission of his disciples.

Thus, all discord will be banished from amongst the dwellers of the hermitage.

Lugano, 20th of April, 1910.

Nyanatiloka.

56. The Vihāra is mentioned in the novel *Die Intellektuellen* by Grete Meisel-Hess (1879–1922) Berlin, 1911, pp. 424–29:

You asked me once, when we met in Berlin, how and where you could join the European sect of new Buddhism, about which I told you. I could not give you an exact answer at the time, but today I can give the desired information. Three Germans, who have taken on the yellow robes in India, have founded the first European Buddhist monastery in Europe. Visit these men; you won't regret it if you join them...

The Lake of Lugano was near Werner's residence at the time, Ascona, on Lago Maggiore, and he did not delay visiting the settlement. A little distance from the radiant shores of the lake, hidden in the mountains, were some log cabins—the first settlement of European monks. He had been accepted, and in a few days he wanted to move there...

He reported about the keystones of the teaching explained to him by the German Buddhists. Above all, this teaching does not admit the existence of a personal god. There is hardly any basis for designating it as a religion, but it would be called a purely philosophical world-view if it were not for the fact that the mind that submerges itself in this teaching, full of religious devotion to existence, will emerge purified and elated from it.

The three German monks are colonists of a society which has its base in London and which calls itself "The Followers of the Buddha." No secret rituals are prescribed; debate of philosophical questions and moral self education are the most important principals of this society. This modern Buddhism has a scientific-rationalistic inclination with a strong social undercurrent. The translation of old, oriental texts, as well as religious-philosophical lectures, and certain exercises of immersion of the soul in itself are among the preoccupations of the colonists...

Originally only one German monk came to the shore of the Lake of Lugano. A small log cabin had been prepared for him; then he allowed two of his German disciples to come, and now some Dutchmen and Englishmen are expected. The log cabins are therefore enlarged. Thus this settlement appears to consolidate and spread itself in Central Europe. He himself is prepared to enter this community as a colonist. No vow will bind him. However, it is expected that he openly accepts Buddhism, but only after a preparatory period, which he will spend as a student in the community. In order to become a full monk, he will have to go to India later, to study Buddhism at its source in old monasteries. However, that time has not arrived yet.

The following article by the well-known Italian journalist Arnaldo Fraccaroli appeared in the Italian newspaper *Corriere della Sera,* March 1st, 1910, p.3 as "Un eremitaggio di buddhisti alle porte d'Italia." Translation by Giuliana Martini.

A Hermitage of Buddhists at the Gates of Italy

Lugano, Italy. February 28

Introduction

Enduring two hours of train travel, two more hours of carriage travel, and finally a small mountain-climb in the snow, does not seem like a waste when you realise that all this leads to the discovery of a Buddhist in the exercise of his functions—something that would usually call for a trip to Burma, at the least. Yet, even with all this, to find oneself before a German Buddhist who comes from the Orient is the truly unexpected thing!

But there he is—the Buddhist, perfect, and a *bhikkhu*. And when a Buddhist has become a bhikkhu, then nothing else is left to do. That means that once he has passed through the ranks of *upasaka* and *samanera*, he has reached the sublime state of Buddhism. The bhikkhu is the monk, the saint. Above the bhikkhus there are no other grades as Buddhism has no hierarchy. Higher up, higher than everybody, is the Buddha Gautama; he is the teacher or master, the blessed one, the omniscient lord.

Nyanatiloka in the Snow

Nyanatiloka, the bhikkhu whom I discovered yesterday in the Italian part of Switzerland, on the snow wrapped mountains of the Malcanton, in the clear solitude of a shepherd's summer refuge in the forest of Paz, above Novaggio, is a German who wonderfully plays the Indian. Wrapped in the yellow robe of Buddhist monks, his head bald, and the lean figure crushed under the weight of the fabric, the reverend—so they are called too—has a truly exotic and extravagant aspect. Seeing him in that deserted site, without the semblance of any other person—a bearded and Buddhist German companion of his went to hide in the refuge at my arrival—would give the illusion that one is lost in a far, far away land. Where is Europe?

Ah, here it is: Europe was being held in my hands, in the form of a package of books directed to Nyanatiloka in Lugano, courtesy of a good scholar friend, who had offered it to me as a way to approach the bhikkhu. The books are coming from Ceylon, from his far away fellow-brothers. Nyanatiloka welcomes them with a discreet joy; the joy a Buddhist can feel who has detached himself from worldly things. But such a detachment does not prevent him from thanking me, disclosing a mild smile with his thin lips, as red as a wound in the yellowish shade of the hair which gets winnowed on his cheeks and chin until the razor comes to stretch it to the ground. Nyanatiloka will allow it to grow to a certain point, but when it threatens to grow long and become an ornament, it will be gone! He disparages the vanity of beauty, without realising that such a disparagement is somehow wasted, as beauty does not seem inclined to afflict him!

"But aren't you cold?" I ask him, seeing that he is so little covered.

"No. It was a bit cold last night when the snow was falling. Now it has finished falling, and here is a sun that will soon dissolve it. But please, do make yourself comfortable. Take a seat and sit down!

He notices that I am standing, and offers me a chair, there on the snow, in the yard in front of the hut—one of those small houses the shepherds call "alpe." He takes a seat on a *scanno*, which is a three legged chair, and between the two of us stands a wooden table, old, and in bad shape indeed! Under our feet, a carpet of snow—the triumph of nature.

"What's the reason why you are here?" I ask him.

"Because it is solitary. I was offered another small house, further down, but it was too beautiful and too close to the village, while here nobody turns up."

I believe him straight away, without hesitation. But is this the place where he intends to establish the first *vihara*, the first Buddhist hermitage in Europe? Because this is the very reason why Nyanatiloka is here. After having spent nine years in Ceylon and Burma, encouraged by the experiences he had as a bhikkhu in the Singhalese and Burmese *viharas*, he feels prepared to introduce the Sangha in the West. "It seems to me," he wrote two years ago from Rangoon to the editors of the *Coenobium* of Lugano, the renowned international review of free studies, "that in the West Buddhism exists only in theory, lacking, for European Buddhists, in the absence of the Sangha, the possibility to live as a bhikkhu. With the establishment of a coenobium not only is such an impediment removed, but it also makes available the science of Pali and, by virtue of the latter, the real understanding of the doctrine is made available to European Buddhists." Now, he is here in order to put his purpose into operation. And he choose the Canton Ticino because of the freedom it offers, the favourable climate—when it does not snow, and when one does not have to be engaged in discussions outdoors!—and the affordable cost of living.

"The exact location has not been determined yet. Over the past few days the snow has prevented me from seeking the most suitable location."

"But are you going to do it soon?"

"Sure. Within a month's time the Buddhist colony will be a *fait accompli*. A German friend of mine is already here, and many others are expecting to be called and will come."

"And the women?"

"No. There cannot be women bhikkhus. Alas! Yet another source of sadness for the suffragettes!"

The location being found, the settlement of the colony will be an easy task. The forest will become populated with small stone huts for the Buddhist hermits. The architect Rutsch from Breslau has already drafted some sketches. Some *samaneras* (novices) consecrated by Nyanatiloka, as well bhikkhu Silacara from Rangoon, are preparing to settle in. But what will they be doing in the vihara? They will live in solitude and meditate. They will also prepare some translations of Buddhist texts and distribute them to further a knowledge of the true doctrine of the Buddha. Someone will also be in charge spreading Buddhism through public speeches and discussions, as in Europe it is either not understood or is misunderstood.

The Real Doctrine of the Buddha

It is a fact that all Buddhists moan about the way their religion is judged and commented upon in Europe. On the other hand, they do concede that the comprehension of Buddhism is a rather difficult affair. A Buddhist professor who had studied in Milan—and whom many can probably remember—Jinarâjadâsa, said, "It is impossible to the non-Buddhists, as erudite as they may be, to penetrate deep into the soul of Buddhism, unless they feel the affection, the veneration, and the gratitude, we feel towards the great Master in Buddhist countries."

Nyanatiloka is of precisely the same opinion, and it is for this reason that he has come back to Europe, aiming at the establishment of a Buddhist hermitage.

"But what is Buddhism?" I ask him.

"Buddhism cannot be explained by means of a few words. The spirit is required to have been introduced to it, and ready to receive its teaching and wisdom. Yet, in brief, it is the extinction of all desires in order to purge all pains. The Buddha taught that human life is full of suffering, which is born from the thirst for pleasures and from self-love. In order not to suffer, you shouldn't desire. Besides this truth, though, Buddhism also teaches the spiritual and essential unity of all beings. In the Buddhist religion everyone can reach the highest level: equality does not lower one to the common or ordinary level, but it exalts all to the highest peak or culmination. It teaches us to conquer ourselves, to face and appease restless desires, to order our soul in a peaceful and clear harmony in which our deepest intimate intuitions can then be reflected. 'Be a light onto yourself. Do not have recourse to any external refuge. As your own refuge, hold on to the truth. Do not seek refuge in anyone but yourselves.'"

Hence, in Buddhism, the intoxicating comfort of meditation. However, Nyanatiloka warns me that to even reach the latter there is much difficulty. But then, what a feeling of ineffable tranquillity and peace! I know that before becoming a bhikkhu Nyanatiloka could magnificently play the violin. Indeed it seems that he was an excellent concert artist. But now he cannot play, as the comfort of music is forbidden to because of his status as a bhikkhu.

"And haven't you suffered because of this?" I ask him.

"At first, yes, I did. But then I received my reward. Would you make a comparison between the comfort of music and what can ensue from a daily hour of meditation on death?"

The Perfect Life and Nirvâna

He speaks gently, with a meek demeanour—which is the only "meek" thing around there, though, as the climate is frigid—with the expression of a man who has known many things and who now appreciates the imperturbable serenity of his calm. Yet he is not old—quite the opposite. He is just thirty-two years old, and has been a Buddhist since nine. When he went to the Orient, his spirit had already turned towards Buddhism, giving up on his indigenous Catholicism. But because the bhikkhu had been a Catholic when he was young, he entered a monastery in Wiesbaden, his hometown. Obviously, he entered it driven by an insatiable and unappeased longing for peace, for solitude. Though he found that the monastery would almost keep out the external world, he was overcome by a strong spiritual crisis. He turned to Buddhism, went to Ceylon as a layman, was accepted before long as a novice, and, finally, became a bhikkhu. He then adopted a new name—his other name is not widely known—and called himself "Nyanatiloka," that is "Man who possesses the science of the three worlds." The three worlds would be the material world, the world of forms, and the spiritual world.

He must now live the perfect life, and every effort of his stretches towards that goal. Buddhism teaches "four efforts" that we need to pursue: not to do new evil, to become free of the evil that has already been done, to generate the good that does still not exist, and to increase the existing good. Furthermore, there are ten meritorious deeds. Thus, living the perfect life, one reaches Nirvâna.

"And what would Nirvâna be like?"

"Liberation. Nobody can know it directly if he does not live the perfect life. It is not merely the cessation of every desire, the annihilation of every craving. It teaches us to win ourselves, to face and appease restless desires." Gautama Buddha, talking about the perfect life, said that it is an immutable dwelling, beyond the objects of the senses: "Truly this is the end of grief." The matter of Nirvâna has always been one of the points on which scholars and philosophers have doggedly persisted, precisely because it cannot be exactly defined. Professor Höffding said it is "the liberation from all needs, from all pains, from hatred and from passion, from birth and from death," and said that it is only possible by virtue of the highest concentration of one's thought and will. Conversely, in an old installment of that same *Coenobium* in which Nyanatiloka had written in order to express his purpose, the Hindu professor Jinarâjadâsa states that, whatever Nirvâna is, the following can be said for certain: it is not annihilation. It seems, therefore, that agreement is not easy to reach. In any case, this also represents an element of freedom: freedom of interpretation.

Will Nyanatiloka, the very learned one, possessing the science of the three worlds, be able to define it in a definitive way? If Nirvâna is the liberation from all desires, the Buddhists of Europe—and there are many—will not be able to enjoy it for some time. They have one desire at the bottom of their hearts, though: to see this first *coenobium* of Buddhists flourish in the mountains that overlap one another, to look down towards the lake of Lugano with the vanity of seeing themselves there.

57. Monte Verità, near Ascona and not far from Lugano, was a haven for spiritual seekers and freethinkers of all sorts such as mystics, anarchists, hermits, etc. See Landmann, Robert: *Ascona, Monte Verità: auf d. Suche nach d. Paradies,* Ulstein, 1979, p. 70 & 106; quoted in the Neobuddhismus webpage mentioned in note 46.

58. H. P. Blavatsky (1831-1891).

59. Because Ñāṇatiloka had been for several years in the tropics, his body would have gotten used to a hot climate, and therefore it would have been quite a physical shock to go in a short time from the warm tropics to a cold alpine hut in mid-winter.

60. A. Costa (1857-1943) published his first Buddhist book, *Il Buddha e la Sua Dottrina,* in 1903 in Torino and his second book, *Filosofia e Buddhismo,* also in Torino in 1913. He was professor at Music Academy of Santa Cecillia but retired early to devote himself to religious studies.

61. A. David-Néel (1868-1969), was a well-known Buddhist adventurer and author who wrote several books on Tibetan Buddhism, which were translated into many languages. Earlier she was a Theosophist and anarchist. According to Ankenbrand, *Indische Welt,* February 1953, p. 24, Ñāṇatiloka had already met her during his concert tour in Algeria in 1901. Although this probably is an error, it could have been possible as she was a light opera singer at that time and could have sung in Algeria. She married in Tunis in 1904.

62. Stephen Batchelor, *Awakening of the West* p. 308, mentions that Ñāṇatiloka had been guest at her house in May-June 1910.

63. Rodolphe-Adrien Bergier. Dr Martin Baumann writes the following about him in "Buddhism in Switzerland" (ISSN 1527-6457 at http://www.globalbuddhism.org/1/baumann001.html):

> The local archives in Lausanne hold a few records of Bergier, as he belonged to a wealthy bourgeois family in Lausanne. Born in 1852, Bergier worked in the USA as a miner during the 1880s. It seems that he was able to make a fortune, and, after having returned to Lausanne

in 1901 as a well-to-do engineer, he sooner or later must have come into contact with Buddhism. The records contain an index card stating that he became a member of the German Pāli Society (based in Breslau/Warsaw) on July 1, 1911. Bergier seems to have been the first Swiss lay Buddhist (*upāsaka*), supporting Ñāṇatiloka and his three disciples generously for months.

64. Bartel Bauer (1887–1940). His twin brother Franz J. Bauer (1887–1956) became a novice on the Island Hermitage on 14 February 1914.

65. He was accepted as a novice on 23 October 1910 in the Caritas Vihara in Lausanne and left for Colombo on 6 December 1910. According to Bhaddiya (see note 70) Bauer was accepted as novice so quickly because he had a very good character and made quick progress in Pali studies, etc. He became a Bhikkhu in Burma in the spring of 1912 and returned to Polgasduva on 3 June 1913. He, along with the other German Buddhists, was interned by the British. Together with his brother he disrobed in the internment camp near Sydney in order to earn money. In November 1916, when the German monks were allowed to leave Australia, he and his brother went to the USA. In 1919 he was again in Germany and remained a lay follower.

66. H. Spannring had heard of Ñāṇatiloka's monastery plan through the news and thereupon had written to him. He visited Ñāṇatiloka in Lausanne during Easter 1911 and then went to Ceylon with him.

67. Bhaddiya (see note 70) wrote that the hermitage was at Galvaddagoda.

68. A postcard sent from here to F.C. Beck by Ñāṇatiloka is dated 25 February 1911.

69. This was around the middle of 1911.

70. Friedrich C. Beck. Although he was born in Breslau, Germany, he had an American passport. He was a friend of Markgraf and the librarian of the Deutsche Pali Gesellschaft. *Pabbajjā*: 9 August 1912 Polgasduva; *upasampadā* 14 February 1913; died Dec. 1914 in the Gonamātara monastery. Bhaddiya's account of the founding of Polgasduva, written as a letter, was translated into French and was published in *Coenobium*, Fasc. X, October 1913, pp. 43–51 as "Sur les silencieux efforts faits au XXme siècle pour metre en lumière la Doctrine du Bouddha." Bhaddiya mentions that he was about 40 years old and that Spannring was 20.

71. In the postcard send to Beck, Ñāṇatiloka writes that he booked places on the Gneisenau (Australian line, 3d class, Naples–Colombo, 240 mark) on the 26th of April.

In *Coenobium* V Fasc. VI, June 1911, pp. 85–86, a letter by Alexandra David-Néel (dated 20 May 1911) was published in which she mentions the return of Ñāṇatiloka:

... my first destination will be Ceylon... where I will meet our friend Ñāṇatiloka, who as you will know, has returned to the Orient. I think that he did well to do so. The life that he wants to lead doesn't fit the European milieu. I told him this in Tunis, and he experienced it for himself...

72. According to Bhaddiya (see the article mentioned in note 70 above), Spannring got homesick, went to the Jesuits (as a pretence to get money for his ticket back), and was repatriated. Back in Europe he regretted his decision and soon wanted to return.

73. On 11 August 1912 at Polgasduva. Bhaddiya writes that about one thousand people came to the island for the ceremony. Preparations took place for days to receive them. Villagers came and made a large clearing, paths, and landing places for the boats.

74. Bhaddiya mentions that the hermitage was built close to the railway line and village-houses and therefore lacked tranquillity and solitude.

75. Polgasduva ("Coconut-tree Island"), situated in Ratgama Lake, is one of three small islands in a brackish lake. Dodanduva is not an island but a village with a train station situated in the thin strip of land between the sea and the lake.

76. Hilliges was a Theosophist and came from Dortmund. He was a member of the German Pali Society.

77. Stomps (1864–1939) arrived on 8 October 1911 at Polgasduva.

78. There were two monks with the name Mahānāmo. Hilliges was Sāmaṇera Mahānāmo (I) for a short time from 4 November 1911 to 21 or 22 December 1911. Stomps became Sāmaṇera Mahānāmo (II) on 24 May 1913 and Bhikkhu on 14 February 1914. He disrobed in 1915, but became a monk again in 1928 until 1939.

79. This should be 1911. According to the biographer Jean Chalon (*Le Lumineux destin d'Alexandra David-Néel,* p. 196), David-Néel "...perfected her knowledge of Pali with as teacher Ñāṇatiloka, a friend. She presided over a meeting of the Buddhist Theosophical Society. Then she alternated Pali lessons with photo sessions." Stephen Batchelor (*Awakening of the West,* 1994, p. 308) adds (without giving his source) that the meeting was at the Island Hermitage on the 9th of September 1911, ten days after her arrival in Ceylon and exactly two months after the founding of the Island Hermitage. David-Néel had established contact with Ñāṇatiloka when he was staying in Switzerland (supposedly at the Caritas Vihāra) in 1910 and he then stayed with her in Tunis from May to June 1910.

80. Carl Theodor Strauss (1852–1937). This German became interested in Buddhism after his wife read out Edwin Arnold's poem *The Light of Asia* to him. He became active in many Buddhist organisations such as the Maha

Bodhi Society, and translated Subhadra Bhikshu's *Buddhist Catechism* into English, the work which inspired Ñāṇatiloka to become a Buddhist. In 1893 he participated at the Parliament of Religions in Chicago and publicly converted to Buddhism there, which caused a great sensation because he was the first German, and perhaps even the first European, to do so.

81. Anāgārika Dhammapāla (a.k.a. Dharmapāla), formerly David Hewavitarne (1864–1933). He was an internationally well-known and influential Sinhalese Buddhist reformer and preacher. He founded the Mahābodhi Society. See *Anagarika Dharmapala* by Bhikshu Sangharakshita, 1964, *Wheel* 70–72, BPS, Kandy).

82. The manuscript has an incomplete passage which starts with: "19th of January: Vappo and Vipulañāṇa (the later Nyānavipula)...". Possibly it is referring to the novice acceptance of Ludwig Stolz and the Burgher (someone of Dutch-Sinhalese descent) named Ferdinand.

83. There is the following appeal in the notice section of *Maha-Bodhi and the United Buddhist World,* Vol. XXI. July & August, 1913, Nos. 7–8, Colombo:

THE EDUCATION OF THE RODIYAS

The Rodiyas are the outcasts of Ceylon. Through the evil actions of their forbears they have been degraded to the lowest class of human beings whose touch is a pollution and whose life is a misery. Forced by public opinion to the lowest and most despicable means of livelihood they live and die amidst indescribable squalor and ignorance and viciousness. No ray of light has come to illumine their sad life, and through evil Karma they are born outside the pale and live to be the most despised. In spite of all adverse circumstances however they have continued to increase and form settlements in different parts of the Kandyan districts. Many attempts have been made to educate them, but so far with little success.

We are glad to hear, however, that Revd. Bhikkhu Ñāṇatiloka, has started a Buddhist School to educate the Rodiya children at Kadugannawa where there is a large settlement. The Reverend Bhikkhu is in need of funds for the maintenance of the school and the building of an Avasa; the education and the moral welfare of this poor despised community is looked after by the Bhikkhu. A fund has been started known as the "Bhikkhu Ñāṇatiloka Rodiya Mission Fund," and contributions may be sent to E.A.L. Wijewardene Esq. Advocate the Secretary of the Buddhist Brotherhood, 4, Hultsdorf, Colombo.

84. Ñāṇāloka (1900–1976) was abbot of Polgasduva from 1957 to 1976. He got his novice acceptance in 1914 at the Island Hermitage under the Ñāṇatiloka and his upasampadā in 1920 in Burma. After the passing

away of Ñāṇatiloka he became the abbot of the Island Hermitage until his own death. He guided many Western candidates and young monks.

85. Dr. Arthur Fitz. He said that he came from Graz, Austria, and was the illegitimate son of an Austrian prince. The following notice appeared in the *Buddhist Review* (1914, p. 317)

> THE GRANDSON OF THE EMPEROR OF AUSTRIA AS A BUDDHIST MONK.—It will be of interest to our readers to know that there in Ceylon at the present time a Buddhist monk who is a grandson of the Emperor Francis Joseph of Austria, his mother having been a daughter of Austria's reigning monarch. The young *bhikkhu* is very reticent about his parentage. Having taken leave of the world, having donned the yellow robe, he has cut himself adrift from all human ties. A university professor, popular among his co-religionists, he was but recently admitted to the Order of the Yellow Robe. Together with several other European *bhikkhus* he lives in an ideal spot near Dodanduwa known as Polgasduwa, an island in the centre of a beautiful lake.

This notice was refuted by Ñāṇatiloka in the next issue of *The Buddhist Review*:

> AN ERROR.—Our colleague, the Very Rev. Nyanatiloka is, as we have seen before stated, now a civil prisoner of war at Diyatalawa, Ceylon. We feel sure that our good Sinhalese friends are mitigating as far as possible the unavoidable hardships of his internment. Nyanatiloka asked us to state that the paragraph on p. 317 of our issue of October last is without foundation. The information reached us in a cutting from the *Ceylon Morning Leader* of July 1st, 1914.

As mentioned by Ñāṇatiloka, he became Sāmaṇera Soṇo and suffered from episodes of mental derangement. Dr. Hecker (*Lebensbilder Deutscher Buddhisten, Band II, Die Nachfolger,* Konstanz, 1997, pp. 93–94) mentions that he went with Ñāṇatiloka to the camp in Australia and after WW I went to Java. In Chapter 14, Ñāṇatiloka mentions that in 1921 he stayed with Dr. Fitz for a few days in Java. Hecker mentions that, as an Austrian, he was arrested again in Java at the outbreak of WW II and ended up with Ñāṇatiloka at the camp in Dehra Dun in 1943. After WW II was over, he was about to be repatriated to Germany. However, because he feared going back to Germany, he escaped from the train bringing him to the ship and fled to the Portuguese colony of Goa. The Portuguese handed him over to the British, and, because of his pleading, he got permission to go to Ceylon. Thus, in March 1947, he came again to the Island Hermitage after 33 years, where he lived for a short time as an *upāsaka*. Then he taught English at a nearby school until he was allowed to return to Java, where he died in the 1950s.

86. According to Ankenbrand, *Indische Welt*, February 1953, p. 25, Freudenberg was a schoolmate of Ñāṇatiloka at the Gymnasium. Ankenbrand relates that Freudenberg and his brother, the consul of Austria, were present at the ordination of Vimalo and Yaso, and that many Burmese monks came for this occasion.

87. H.H. Sri Maharaja Sidkeong Tulku Namgyal (1879–1914). The old Maharaja Thuthob had died in February. His son, the new Maharaja, Sikyong (or Sidkeong), who had studied at Oxford, intended, on advice of Alexandra David-Néel, to reform the "degenerated Buddhism" of Sikkim. Thus he had turned to Theravāda Buddhism and Ñāṇatiloka was welcome to him. However, in December that year (5 December 1914), after Ñāṇatiloka had returned to Ceylon, Sikyong was found dead, perhaps murdered with poison by enemies. His successor Tashi (1914–1963) later became friendly with Govinda.

88. Lama Yongden from Sikkim. He stayed on with David-Néel and died in France in 1955.

89. Perhaps the Ven. Samana Puññananda M.R.A.S. who was the editor of the Chittagong Buddhist magazine *The Bauddha Bandhu* published in Calcutta. He is mentioned in *The Buddhist Review* Vol. VIII, 1916, No. 1, p. 55.

90. In Sri Lanka still famous as (Tibetjātika) S. Mahinda. In 1930 he became a novice, and in 1931 a bhikkhu under Siridhamma Thera at the Sailabimbārāma temple in Dodanduwa. He studied at the Mahabodhi College and the Vidyodaya Pirivena. He is especially known for his children's poems and patriotic poems. See "Tibet and Sri Lanka," S. Venerable Dhammika, *The Middle Way,* May 2001, p. 19.

91. From the "Notes and News" section of *The Buddhist Review,* October-December 1914, VI (No.4), p. 318:

> AT DODANDUWA.—On June 13th two Sāmanera monks, German by nationality, were ordained, and the same occasion two young men from Tibet donned the yellow robe of the order of the Buddha. Two wealthy Germans also, by taking *Pansil* (the precepts) became converts to Buddhism. *Bhikkhu Ñāṇatiloka* is most energetic in carrying on the work of educating the Rodiyas, the despised class in Ceylon.

92. The centre of Colombo, where previously the Dutch Fort was located.

93. That is, the German ambassador Freudenberg, note 86 above.

94. A town and railway junction north of Colombo.

95. Sir Robert Chalmers, born 1858, was an Indologist and the governor of Ceylon from 1913–1916. He edited volumes II and III of the *Majjhima Nikāya* and volume II of the *Dīgha Nikāya* for the Pali Text

Society, and made an edition and translation of the Suttanipāta (Harvard Oriental Classics series).

96. Ludwig Ankenbrand (1888–1971). A German Buddhist layman who had come to live with his wife Elise Symanzich at the Island Hermitage from 18 September 1913 until the start of WWI, when they, together with the monks, were interned.

97. The Lepcha are the aboriginal inhabitants of the Kingdom of Sikkim.

98. The following notice was found in *The Ceylon Morning Leader,* Wednesday, 4 November 1914.

> **More Germans and Austrians for Ragama**
>
> Prince priest and monks removed
>
> Seven German Buddhist monks who were at the Island Monastery in Dodanduwa were brought down to Colombo on Monday and removed by the 2.15 p.m. train from Maradana to Ragama, the party including one female priest.
>
> Yesterday the Austrian prince priest was brought down and removed to Ragama under police escort by the 1 p.m. train from Maradana. The priest appeared to be unwell and was lying down in the compartment closely wrapped up.

The "Austrian prince priest" was Soṇo, apparently held in a straitjacket, see note 85. The "female priest" referred to would have been the wife of Ludwig Ankenbrand; see note 96.

99. In the "Notes and News" section of *The Buddhist Review,* 1915, p. 157–158, the following notices are found:

> German Bhikshus at Diyatalawa.—A number of Bhikshus—German monks of the Island Hermitage at Dodanduwa—have been removed to the Diyatalawa camp as prisoners of war with other German and Austrian subjects. Through no fault of their own these Bhikshus find themselves in an unfortunate predicament. While we sympathise with them most sincerely we must at the same time try to understand the position of the Government and remember that it is not Buddhist Bhikshus of German birth alone who are detained at Diyatalawa. A number of Catholic priests are in the same position. In these circumstances it is perhaps impossible for the Government to discriminate in favour of one religious denomination. Undoubtedly hard as it is that the Bhikshus should be confined in a prison camp, it is but one of the many hundred instances in which this cruel war has inflicted undeserved suffering upon harmless and innocent people.
>
> * * *

The Truth Spreader.—The Daily Mirror has published a picture of the Buddhist preacher Ledi Sayadaw, who is now touring Indian villages explaining, as far as possible, the causes of the dreadful conflict into which the demon of German militarism plunged Europe seven months ago. He counteracts the German lies and tells his listeners how the fair land of Belgium has been rendered a desolate waste, while her people, including thousands of helpless women and children, have fallen, become beggars, or have fled to other lands, where they are living upon the charity of their kindly hosts.

100. The famous German battleship SMS Emden, under the command of Captain von Müller, had destroyed 51 commercial ships and two warships within four months in the Indian Ocean. This threat to the British naval supremacy made the British so paranoid that they suspected that every German in Ceylon could be a supporter of the Emden and could have been the real reason why the German monks had to leave Polgasduva. The Emden was sunk by SMS Sydney in November 1914 off the coast of West Australia. Part of the crew managed to escape with a schooner to Turkish Arabia, the rest was captured by the British.

101. The Kursk was a troop transporter that had brought Australian troops to the frontline in France and was coming back empty.

102. The German internment camp was located in an old prison called Holdsworthy, which was located about 5 km south of Liverpool, a town in New South Wales, north of Sydney. For more on this camp see "Objects Through Time", Steve Thomson, 2007: http://museumsaustralia.org.au/ UserFiles/File/National%20Conference/2007/ StephenThompson_ConferencePaper07.pdf

103. Inglorious as it was, this was the first visit of Western Buddhist monks to Australian shores; nonetheless, given Australia's origins as a penal settlement, there is perhaps an ironic appropriateness here.

104. Although even Australians whose grandfathers were German or Austrian were classified as "alien enemies" by the Australian government, it turned out to be impractical to intern them all due to their great number. Thus, a selective policy of internment was implemented. German Australian community leaders—such as Lutheran pastors and businessmen—criminals, and the destitute were selected for internment.

105. Trial Bay is situated on the coast about 500 km north of Sydney. The ruins of the jail are still there and it is now an Australian heritage site. Only the elite of the German prisoners, that is, scientists, diplomats, officers, missionaries, and so on, was interned here. For more information about the gaol in WWI see http://www.migrationheritage.nsw.gov.au/

exhibitions/zivillager/history.html and "Objects Through Time", Steve Thomson, 2007: http://museumsaustralia.org.au/UserFiles/File/National%20 Conference/2007/StephenThompson_ConferencePaper07.pdf.

The following information is from *Trial Bay Gaol,* a historical booklet by M. H. Neil:

> Their number grew to over five hundred and included men who had come from Ceylon, Hong Kong and the British and German Islands in the Pacific. The gaol accommodated rubber planters, ship officers, military officers and even some Buddhist priests from Ceylon who wore yellow and brown robes and took little part in the activities shared by the other internees.

Another brief, but more interesting reference is found in Ernest Scott's *Official History of Australia in War 1914–18,* Volume XI: *Enemy within the Gates.* It speaks of the guards nicknaming the Buddhist monks "canaries" (due to their yellow robes), their philosophical manner and refusal of requisition supplies, a request to get stones to use as pillows—and finally that most forsook their religion, wore ordinary clothes, and took three meals under the pressure of their countrymen.

106. Reichsgraf Carl von Cosel, a.k.a. Georg Carl Tänzler, a.k.a. Count Carl Tanzler von Cosel (1877–1952). In 1926 this eccentric German emigrated to Florida, USA, where he became a radiologist and bacteriologist. In 1940 he became infamous as the romantic necrophiliac of Key West. See http://en.wikipedia.org/wiki/Carl_Tanzler.

107. Until 1917 the USA acted as a protecting power for Germany.

108. M. E. Foster (1844–1930) was a descendent of King Kamehameha of Hawai. She had met Dhammapāla in September 1893, when he was returning from Chicago to Sri Lanka by way of Honolulu. He had given her advice on how to control her temper and from then on she was fond of Buddhism and of Dhammapāla, greatly supporting him financially. See p. 65 of *Anagarika Dharmapala* by Bhikshu Sangharakshita, 1964. (Wheel 70–72, B.P.S., Kandy.)

109. Graf J. H. von Bernstorff (1862–1939), German ambassador to the USA since 1908.

110. A. K. Reisschauer was a missionary to Japan. He published seven books on Japan.

111. Hankow is nowadays part of the city of Wuhan. There was a small German Concession in Hankow from 1895 until 1917. It had been taken over from Japan and was administered by the German Consul General.

112. Ed. Val Clément.

113. Sumano was the monastic name for Stange.

114. This was on 14.3.1917. See note 119.

115. These Jews have been in China for centuries and are physically indistinguishable from other Chinese. Because their lineage has been carried on patriarchally in defiance of the Jewish tradition, they are not recognised as Jews by the Israel government. On their history, see the Wikipedia page on http://en.wikipedia.org/wiki/History_of_the_Jews_in_China.

116. The following information on these porters is found at http://www.discoveryangtze.com/Yangtzediscovery/history_of_chongqing.htm: "Visitors to the city in the 1920s and '30s commented on its 30-metre (100-foot) high city wall and the rough steps from the river up to the city gates 'dripping with slime from the endless procession of water carriers.' At that time, Chongqing, with a population of over 600,000, had no other water supply. Between 10,000 and 20,000 coolies carried water daily to shops and houses through the steep and narrow lanes of the city. All porterage was done by coolies as there were no wheeled vehicles in the city, only sedan chairs. The staircase streets are still there, but all that remains of the city wall today is the odd outcrop of masonry that props up a house here, or abuts a path there."

117. At present there is no monastery with this name Hsiang Kuo Ssu in or near Chungking (or Chongging). Perhaps it is the Huayan monastery which is situated at the bottom of the Dalaoshan mountain in west Chungking and is renowned for its beautiful views. The population of Chungking municipality has grown more than fiftyfold—to 31 million people, being the most populated municipality of China—since Ñāṇatiloka was there and probably the temple he stayed in is now within the city.

118. See the correspondence in the next note.

119. This was on 14 August 1917. See Ch. V of W. Reginald Wheeler, *China and the World War*, New York, 1919 (Online at http://net.lib.byu.edu/~rdh7/wwi/comment/chinawwi/ChinaTC.htm). The decision by the Chinese republican government was a cause of great discord—in fact it caused a rebellion—because amongst others, there was great uncertainty about who was going to win the war. The Germans were quite influential in China and German propaganda made the Chinese believe that Germany was winning.

120. In an appendix to the edition of the original German autobiography by Hellmuth Hecker, the correspondence is reproduced of the British Foreign Police Department (from the National Archives, New Delhi). The British Foreign Police in Asia were on the lookout for a Norwegian called Sven Hedin (i.e. the famous Central Asia explorer, geographer, and Germanophile) who was travelling to Tibet disguised as a native. He was reportedly sent by the German emperor to create rebellions in Asia. When Ñāṇatiloka and Sobczak were detected by the

British in Hankow, they were watched as they were suspected to be spies and agitators.

The major reason for their imprisonment in Hankow was that Ñāṇatiloka and Sobczak had been given special permission to leave their imprisonment in Australia on the condition that they would return to Germany by way of America within three months. This however they did not do, even though the special passes that had been granted to them stated that if they failed to do so they would be liable to re-arrest and internment. The British suspected that it was on the orders, or at least with the consent, of Count von Bernstorff that they came to China. Von Bernstorff was a nuisance to the British as he tried to prevent America from declaring war on Germany. Ñāṇatiloka had received financial support to go to China through von Bernstorff, as can be read in the account of his stay in Honolulu. Ñāṇatiloka's contact with two German "intriguers" in Hankow (presumably, these were the two young Germans at the German Consulate who helped Ñāṇatiloka) also aroused suspicions that he and Sobczak were German agents in disguise. The British Foreign Police asked the Chinese government to hand over Ñāṇatiloka and his companion as escaped prisoners of war, but they were instead interned in a prison in Hankow.

The following is a letter to Bhikkhu Sīlācāra that had been intercepted by the British government in Burma, followed by some of the secret correspondence of the British Foreign Affairs about the "German spies." The complete correspondence is reproduced in EDB, pp. 293–311:

10th February, 1917.
Dear Silacara,

You may have heard already that I have been released from the camp at Australia. I went to Honolulu with the hope of being able to stay there in some Japanese monastery; but I found that there is none. I therefore hoped to find in China (Japan was forbidden to me as a German) some place where I could stay and eventually try to go to Yunnan, North of Burma or Siam where I am told that there are monks and monasteries our Buddhist Order (Southern Pali Buddhism) I assure you I suffered much and if not for an America lady at Honolulu I would have had to starve. But she saved me. Moreover I sent a petition to Washington (German Ambassador) asking to pay mine and the other 8 Buddhists passage to China (and 5 also to Germany) and this was granted. But the same time it seemed to have

raised the English Consuls suspicion so that finally I am regarded as a spy (Only this morning I got this news). What do you say about such folly? I think there is nobody who hates everything which is connected with war, militarism, patriotism etc., more than myself. You yourself know too well that I stand above all nationality and that being a Buddhist I do not make any difference between the nations. I hope to be able to proceed soon on my way to Talifu and Momein and near the latter place I may find some suitable monastery to stay but in no case I shall try to enter English territory.
I beg you kindly if necessity arises to point out to the English Government that I have nothing to do with the German Government. I am now a hermit for 14 years and my sole occupation was concerned with religions and translations into the German language.
What I want now is to find a solitary place in order to continue my religious duties and my literary work. Truly I had to suffer long enough. Further I hope you will kindly pay me a visit when at or near Momein. After my arrival I shall send you a post-card.
Two pupils from Ceylon will come to Burma and I kindly ask you to take care of them and bring them to the Kyemdaw Kyaung and later perhaps along with you to Bamo.
With my best wishes for your weal and welfare and longing for peace and the end of all this trouble.
Yours affectionately,
NYANATILOKA
(Sd) (A. GUETH)
Address.
Nyanatiloka
C/o. Mrs. Ed. Val Clement, French Concession
Hankow, (China)

BRITISH LEGATION
PEKING
To Wai Chiao Pu. May, 3d, 1917
Sir,

I have the honour to inform Your Excellency that I learn from his Majesty's Consul-General at Hankow that two Germans named Sobezak and Gueth have recently left that port for Chungking disguised as Buddhist priests...

I can only assume that the passports under which they are traveling were probably issued before the rupture of relations with Germany and if so how are they valid under the present regulations governing the residence of Germans in China? Moreover, it is obviously not in China's own interests to allow German Agents to visit the frontier provinces in disguise and I would urge upon Your Excellency the necessity of having these two men sent back to Shanghai and kept under close supervision...

Translation WAICHIAPU TO H.M. CHARGE D'AFFAIRES.

May 16th, 1917
Sir,

I have the honour to acknowledge the receipt of your letter... I immediately telegraphed the Commissioner of Foreign Affairs at Chungking to deal with the matter and have now received the following reply:

The passports held by the Germans in question were issued by the Shanghai Procurator and the Hankow Customs and bear the photographs of the bearers. The Occupation Commissioner's Office has been notified and has ascertained after examination that they have no prohibited articles with them. Their request to be allowed to move to Tengyuen has been refused and they are now living in the Hsiang Kuo ssu temple outside the city, where the local authorities have sent soldiers for their protection and supervision.

As the Ssuchuan Provincial Authorities have sent soldiers to supervise the Germans there need be no fear of their stirring up trouble. I have the honour to inform you of the above and avail etc.,

(Signed) Wu Ting Fang.

FILES ONLY. (17454/17)
Cypher telegram to Mr Alston (Peking)
Foreign Office, September 13th 1917 5.30 p.m.
No. 340.

....
Your despatch no 210 (16th July).

Gueth and Sobezak were only released from internment by Military Authorities in Australia on condition that they returned straight to Germany via America and in November 1916 were given passes for repatriated alien enemies available for three months only. By returning to China from Honolulu and San Francisco respectively they

broke the conditions of their release, which is proof of their mala fides, and it was on orders or at least with the consent of von Bernstorff that they returned.
They were at Hankow with von Hentig and Dr Veretzsch before these intriguers returned to Germany.
You should, therefore, unless you see objection renew representations to Chinese Government asking that these two men should either be handed over to us as escaped prisoners of war or placed under proper control.

Copy. No. 320 (230549/45a

British Legation.
Peking.
October 5th, 1917.

Sir:-

I have the honour to report that on receipt of your telegram no. 34 of September 18th, I communicated to the Wai Chiao Pu the information contained therein respecting the two Germans Soboczac and Gueth, and requested that they should be handed over to the British authorities as escaped prisoners of war, or interned in China until the end of the war.

Telegraphic instructions were at once sent to the Military Governor of Rupoh to intern these men and the Wai Chiao Pu informed me on September 24th, that this had been done and that the men would only be released on the termination of the war. His Majesty's Consul-General at Hankow reports that Sobczac and Gueth have been placed in the German Municipal Gaol, with only the yard space allowed them for exercise.

The men vigorously protested to the Delegate for Foreign Affairs, saying that they had not been formally tried in court. To this protest 2r su [? illegible] had replied that what has been done is within the legitimate authority of the Chinese Government in regard to alien enemies.

I have,
(Signed) B. Alston.
The Right Honourable
A.J. Balfour, G.M., M..,
sc. sc., sc.
Secretary of State for Foreign Affairs

There was widespread hatred and suspicion against Germans at this time, even in Buddhist circles. In a letter of Alexandra David-Néel from

India to her husband in Tunisia, dated 12 October 1915 (published in A. David-Néel, *Correspondence avec son mari, Editions intégrale (1904–1941)*, pp. 395–96), the following mention is made about Ñāṇatiloka and his disciples:

> In the newspapers in Calcutta I saw that we seem to have continued to progress slowly but surely. The Germans seem incapable to breach our front and are recoiling little by little. In Russia they haven't been any more victorious... Do you remember Ñāṇatiloka, the German monk? I don't belief that he is a spy, although one can never be sure. However, what is surprising is that since he has set himself up in Ceylon, a certain number of Germans immediately found a vocation in Buddhism and the state of being Bhikkhu, and arrived from the heart of Germany to live in the Eden of Ñāṇatiloka in a state of semi-nudity*. I have always found this strange and have even talked about it to some friends. But now it appears very clear that among the above mentioned bhikkhus are found a few German secret agents, who are on a mission to stir up agitation among the natives against the English under the guise of the yellow robe.

* David Néel probably refers to the monks going bare-chested because of the humid heat at the Island Hermitage. There are some pictures from the 1930s with bare-chested Western monks.

Next year, 28 April 1916, she wrote:

> I got some news of Ñāṇatiloka the last few days. You remember this German monk, don't you? He is in a camp in Australia along with other Boches who have been picked up in India. He has enough tact not to write me on the subject of the war. I don't know what is at the bottom of his Teutonic mind, but he is an erudite one.

The suspicions kept surfacing again and again in Ñāṇatiloka's life, for example when he went to Thailand, and before WWII, see the letter by Govinda dated 22 May 1939, in note 185.

121. Published in 1922–23 by Oskar Schloss.

122. By E. F. von Fuechtersleben.

123. Prince Damrong was the brother and chief minister of King Chulalonkorn. He was also the brother and advisor of the Sangharāja Vajirañāṇakosa. Damrong was, among others, in charge of the education reforms in Thailand.

124. Perhaps: Haupt Graf von Pappenheim (1869–1954). See http://www.thepeerage.com/p6519.htm.

125. From 11 to 16 November 1918 the Communist Labourer and Soldier Council governed at the Senate of Hamburg.

126. Dr George Grimm (1868–1945), a judge, author of books such as

The Buddha's Doctrine and *Buddhist Wisdom—The Mystery of the Self,* and founder of the *Altbuddhistische Gemeinde* (Old-Buddhist Community). He expounded a controversial Vedantic, eternalist interpretation of Buddhism, which did not agree with many other German Buddhists.

127. Else Buchholz (1888–1982), later Sister Uppalavaṇṇā. She was born in Hamburg. When both her parents died during a cholera epidemy in 1892, she was adopted by a rich English foster mother in Berlin. When her foster mother died in 1912, she inherited a large fortune. Her engagement to an attaché of the British consulate ended when WWI broke out. She then broke off her music studies and went to Odenwald. With her fortune she wanted to help gifted and unfortunate young people, but encountered a lot of ingratitude and misunderstanding. Disenchanted, she came across the saying "No one can pull someone else out of the quagmire, except when standing on firm bottom" in a book. Searching for its origin, she read Neumann's translation of the Majjhima Nikāya and found the saying in the eighth discourse. She stopped reading after the tenth discourse, the famous Satipaṭṭhāna Sutta, and for the rest of her life practised the meditation of mindfulness of breathing.

128. P. Geheeb (1870–1961) founded the Free School Community in 1906 and the Odenwald School in 1910.

129. On January 1st, 1919, members of the communist Spartacusbund rose in an attempted revolution. The newly formed Weimar Government reacted promptly, and brutally. On January 10 the army, aided by the Frei Corps, a paramilitary group consisting of former servicemen, was deployed to bring the revolution to an end. Order had been restored to the streets of Berlin by the 13th of January.

130. O. Schloss (1881–1945) published Ñāṇatiloka's translation of the *Aṅguttara Nikāya* and other Buddhist works.

131. W. Geiger (1856–1943) translated *Saṃyutta Nikāya* I and II, and the *Mahāvaṃsa.* He also wrote a Pali grammar.

132. W. H. Mannis, governor of Ceylon from 1918–1925. Only under his successor was Ñāṇatiloka allowed to return to Ceylon.

133. K. Watanabe (1872–1933).

134. E. Leumann (1859–1931).

135. W. Solf (1862–1936) was the first German governor of West Samoa in 1900; in October-December 1918 the German foreign secretary, and in 1920–28 German ambassador in Tokyo. His wife Hanna had been at the same boarding school with Uppalavaṇṇā .

136. This was a lecture in German called "Quintessenz des Buddhismus." It was later published; see Bibliography section.

137. Probably Sir Ernest Mason Satow (1843–1929) who wrote books about Buddhism in Japan.

138. The Dutch capital of the Dutch East Indies. It is now called Jakarta, the capital of Indonesia.

139. See note 35.

140. Khrom Phra Vajirañāṇavarorasa, Vajirañāṇa in short. 1860–1921.

Vajirañāṇa was the *saṅgharāja* or Patriarch of the Sangha of Thailand. He was a son of King Rāma IV and a brother of King Rāma V Chulalongkorn. Being a prolific writer, he wrote an influential Thai Vinaya commentary called *Vinayamukha,* which was first published in 1916. This work was part of his failed attempt to bring the two great sects of the Thai Saṅgha together. The English translation, published in 1969, is called *The Entrance to the Vinaya.* His autobiography was translated by C. J. Reynolds and published as *The Life of Prince Patriarch Vajiranana of Siam, 1860–1921,* Ohio University Press, 1980.

Vajirañāṇa was, in line with his tradition, a strict disciplinarian. According to a first-hand account from a Western Buddhist monk, even in the 1970s senior monks occasionally walked around with sticks in Wat Bovorn, the head monastery of the Dhammayuttika Nikāya, where Vajirañāṇa lived. They were doing so to discipline any misbehaving young novices and schoolboys who were living at the monastery.

Taking the perspective of Vajirañāṇa, it is not surprising that he did not help Ñāṇatiloka. Like other Thai royals at the time, he had received a British education and was pro-British. In 1918 and 1919 he even wrote two allocutions, "Right is Right" and "The Triumph of Right," praising King Vajiravudh for defending "Right" by making Siam join the Allied Powers against the unjust Germans. (See *Visakha Puja B.E. 2519,* Bangkok, 1976.) Ñāṇatiloka's association with the "disloyal" Prince Prisdang also would not have stood in his favour.

141. Ñāṇatiloka uses the term *"Einjähriger",* "one-yearer", which supposedly refers to the one year of obligatory military service of the young military doctor mentioned below.

142. King Vajiravudh, or Rāma VI, ruled from 1910 till 1925 and tried to continue the great modernizations his father, King Chulalonkorn, had initiated. However he was not able to undo the trade-deficit and other serious problems plaguing the country, many of which were due to the modernizations. Some of his people were disappointed with him because, although he himself was living a luxurious Western lifestyle, he was preaching his people to be austere. They also felt he spent too much time on the arts—the Oxford-educated Vajiravudh was a prolific writer and artist—and not enough time on ruling the country. In 1911 there was a coup d'état by young soldiers, but it failed to overthrow him.

143. Due to pressure by the Allied Forces, Thailand had to declare war on Germany in 1917. A German representation did not exist yet. H. J. W.

Huber had been the Dutch envoy since 1919.

144. Kawaguchi (1866–1945) had published his book in Benares in 1909. He taught Tibetan at a university and also published a grammar of the Tibetan language, having brought the Tibetan Canon to Japan with him.

145. Takehiko Yamashina (1898–1987), was the chief of a collateral line of the Japanese imperial dynasty.

146. *Laṅkā* is the traditional Sinhalese name for Ceylon. The modern official name *Sri Lanka* was first used in 1972.

147. Sir C. Eliot was British ambassador in Tokyo since 1919.

148. S. Tachibana (1877–1955) did his doctorate in 1923 in Oxford with the well-known dissertation *The Ethics of Buddhism,* which was published in London in 1926.

149. B. Petzold (1873–1949).

150. Tokumei Matsumoto (1898–1981) visited Ñāṇatiloka at the Island Hermitage after 1926 and stayed there for eight months studying Pali. After that, he went to Germany and did a doctorate at the University of Bonn in 1932 on the *Prajñāpāramitā* literature.

151. J. Takakusu (1866–1945) was a famous and prolific Buddhist scholar and author.

152. H. Driesch (1867–1941) was a philosopher and since 1924 was especially interested in parapsychology.

153. R. B. Bose (1886–1945) had written a book in Bengali which was translated into English as *British Misdeeds in India* (Tokyo, 1942). He fought on the side of Japan and Germany against England during the Second World War.

154. Raja Mahendra Pratap (1886–1979) was a freedom fighter, journalist, writer and revolutionary social reformist of India. Trying to liberate India from the British colonial rule, he made contacts with anti-British forces such as the German Kaiser and Enver Pasha, the son-in-law of the Turkish Sultan. After setting up a government-in-exile of Free Hindustan in Kabul, the British put a price on his head. In 1925 he went to Japan, where he set up the idealistic World-Federation, treating the world as one family. See http://en.wikipedia.org/wiki/Raja_Mahendra_Pratap.

155. This earthquake is known as the "Great Kanto Earthquake". Having a magnitude (Ms) of 8.19, the earthquake and the no less ferocious conflagration that followed devastated southeastern Japan including the cities of Tokyo (population of about 3 million) and Yokohama (population of about 423,000). The loss of life exceeded 140,000 lives. At least 80% of the total destruction in Yokohama was due to fire. More than 694,000 houses were partially or completely destroyed. Of these, some 381,000 were burned, 83,000 collapsed, and 91,000 partially collapsed. See *The 1923 Tokyo Earthquake and Fire* by

Charles D. James, Berkeley, 2002.

156. More than 200 aftershocks followed the main earthquake of 1 Sept. On 2 Sept., more than 300 shocks were felt. More than 300 additional shocks would follow from 3-5 September.

157. *Der Pfad*, 1923/1924, first volume.

158. This is probably the disaster at the Military Clothing Depot in Honjo Ward. Most refugees carried their belongings such as furniture with them and these materials served as a ready fuel source. The firestorm incinerated and suffocated an estimated 40,000 people on this field.

159. There was no large tidal wave inside Tokyo Bay, but a substantial 12 meter tsunami did strike along the north shore of Oshima Island but did comparatively little damage.

160. Kenkichi Okiyama.

161. The Ogasawara or Bonin islands became an American colony in 1830 and the two inhabitable islands were, among others, settled by Westerners. In 1870 Japan claimed the islands. They are located about 1000 km south of Tokyo.

162. H. Clifford, who was Governor of Ceylon from 1925-1927.

163. *Der Erste Deutsche Bhikkhu: Das bewegte Leben des Ehrwürdigen Nyānatiloka (1878-1957) und seine Schüler*; edited by Hellmuth Hecker, Konstanz, 1995. *Nyānatiloka Centenary Volume*, edited by Nyānaponika Thera, Kandy, 1978.

164. Ernst Lothar Hofmann (1898-1985).

165. Tomo Geshe Rimpoche (1864-1936).

166. Paul Debes (1906-2004).

167. This is the spelling which Ñāṇatiloka himself gives in his brief notes for his biography after 1926. Another spelling is Ñāṇadhara. *Dhara* means "holding" while *ādhāra* means "holder," or "one who holds."

(The notes, a few small scraps of paper, are in the Forest Hermitage archives.)

168. In a letter of Govinda to Ñāṇatiloka dated 6 June 1935 (quoted in H. Hecker, EDB, p.171), the following passage is found about the death of Ñāṇādhāra:

> You must have gone through a difficult and sad time. Vappo wrote to us already about your self-sacrificing nursing, which lasted for months. Didn't the Buddhists of Burma do anything for Ñāṇādhāra? You wrote that there were no nurses and food in the hospital. This is unbelievable and needs to be pilloried. I am also convinced that Ñāṇādhāra would not have been killed by his disease if he hadn't undermined his health by the insufficient, at least for Europeans, disagreeable Ceylonese food. I am sure that I

too, if I had entered the Sangha in Ceylon, would have awaited the same fate. As the Ceylonese are not really willing to care for European bhikkhus, one should warn every European Buddhist against entering the Order there. Please do write an obituary. The people here should at least know what sacrifices European Buddhists make for the realization of their ideals."

169. Peter Joachim Schönfeldt (1906–1984). He was working as an apprentice bookbinder at a small printing press in Berlin where poets had their works privately printed and bound. Through meeting them and reading their poems, Schönfeldt entered the esoteric circle of young intellectuals and artists around the Nietzschean, symbolist and homosexual poet Stefan George. Schönfeldt later became the Swami Gauribala, see note 182 below.

170. That Feniger was from a Jewish background is well known. According to Bhikkhu Bodhi, a long term pupil of Ven. Nyanaponika, and Dr. Patrick Harriger (a disciple of Swami Gauribala), Peter Schönfeldt and his brother Malte were Jews too. Although Peter and Malte are not Jewish names, it is possible that they were half Jews (i.e., that only their father or mother was Jewish) or that their parents had denounced Judaism.

171. *Pali-Anthology und Wörterbuch,* published in Munchen-Neubiberg in 1928.

172. Otto Krauskopf, 1884–1950. He had been a Prussian photographer who came to Buddhism through Dahlke. Together with Feniger (the later Ñāṇaponika) and his brother Georg, he founded a Buddhist group connected to Dahlke in Köningsberg. In Dehra Dun he stayed in a barrack with Eidlitz, see below, who mentions that Ñāṇasīsi always carried a skull and used it to contemplate impermanence. He remained a monk for the rest of his life and died in Colombo.

173. Joseph Pistor (1895–1976). He was first a Trappist monk, then was a Buddhist monk from 1936 until 1939, and was again a Buddhist monk, named Vajirabodhi, from 1951 until his death in 1976. Because of previous problems (see the description of Wirtz at p. 129), Ñāṇatiloka did not accept him back at Polgasduva in 1951 and instead he stayed at Sailabimbārāma in Dodanduva.

174. Max Bruno, 1895–1951.

175. Ñāṇaponika was accepted as bhikkhu in a Siam Nikāya monastery in Ovakanda on 29 June 1937. The others became monks at the Island Hermitage in July. It is not completely clear why Ñāṇaponika was accepted separately. According to one report given in EDB 188, Ñāṇatiloka had been called for by the German consulate in Colombo and was admonished because he had ordained Jews. So Ñāṇaponika might have

been ordained separately because he was Jewish and Ñāṇatiloka wanted to avoid problems with the Nazis. (See Govinda's letter at note 185.)

In any case, it seems that there was no publicity about the *upasampadā* on Polgasduva in July 1937, unlike the novice acceptance in 1937, which was reported in the *Ceylon Daily News* together with pictures. The exact date of the ceremony is unknown.

Further, unlike before, when Ñāṇatiloka had friendly relations with the German diplomats in Ceylon, no visits of German diplomats are mentioned in the Island Hermitage's *Visitors Book* during the Nazi period.

Hecker writes (EDB 189 n. 12) that this separate ordination of Ñāṇaponika explains the reason why Ñāṇasatta, a direct disciple of Ñāṇatiloka, and not Ñāṇaponika, spoke at the funeral ceremony of Ñāṇatiloka. This is unlikely. The reason probably is that Ñāṇasatta regularly gave public Dhamma speeches in Sinhala as well as in English and was an experienced speaker. On the other hand, Ñāṇaponika never learnt Sinhalese well and never gave formal public speeches to large audiences. (This is the reason why he wasn't, and isn't, well-known amongst the Sinhalese. According to Dr. Hecker, he did give Dhamma-talks to small groups in Germany during his visits.) Ñāṇaponika would have been reluctant to give a speech in front of thousands of people. Vappo would have been the most senior disciple of Ñāṇatiloka at the funeral.

Ñāṇaponika mentions in the *Nyanatiloka Centenary Volume* p. 7 that he became a bhikkhu together with Ñāṇasīsi. Hecker also mentions, or repeats, this in Ñāṇasīsi's biography in *Lebensbilder Deutscher Buddhisten, Band II, Die Nachfolger,* Konstanz, 1997, pp.162–163.

176. Malte Schönfeldt (1917–1989).

177. Nyanasatta (1908–1984). Born in Moravia. Layname: M. Novosad. Received *pabbajjā* on 20 August 1939 and the *upasampadā* on 20 August 1939, both at the Island Hermitage. In 1940 he moved to Bandāravela where he founded the Verdant Hermitage, Kolatenna, where he lived until 1982. He died at the Island Hermitage. He was well versed in Pali, German, English, Sinhala and Esperanto and wrote *Basic Tenents of Buddhism* (1964). He also wrote Buddhist works in Esperanto.

178. Bern, 1942. The Swiss ethnologist and researcher Paul Wirz (1892–1955) is known for his thorough scientific studies of tribal cultures in New Guinea and elsewhere, and his extensive ethnographic collections. On 14 December 1934 he and his wife are first listed in the visitors' book of the Island Hermitage. Wirz came to Dodanduva to do research for his study on exorcism and healing. Around this time he bought the Parappaduva Island (meaning "Cuckoo-island") island and built a house

on it. In between travels he worked here on his publications.

179. Bern, 1942.

180. Before he died, Ñāṇatiloka made a similar remark in a handwritten note (found in the Forest Hermitage archives) intended as a guideline for the intended but never commenced autobiography of the latter years of his life: "Many of the monks I ordained went away... many died. Only very few remained, such as Vappa Mahāthera and Ñāṇāloka. Especially literary inclined types are to be mentioned such as Nyanaponika and to a lesser degree Vappa Mahāthera."

181. This was Ñāṇapiya, a.k.a Joseph Pistor. See note 173.

182. A long bibliography is given in *Lebensbilder Deutscher Buddhisten, Band II, Die Nachfolger,* Konstanz, 1997, pp. 262–265.

183. A German bookseller called Walter Mangelsdorf visited the Island Hermitage for a few hours in 1929 and gave a somewhat similar description of his meeting with Ñāṇatiloka:

> Out of the doorway stepped a monk with a faded yellow robe who reached us his hand. Ñāṇatiloka is in his fifties, stately, pale, and shaven... He does not have anything priestly to him, and in the civil world one would take him to be an academic scholar, which in fact he is. His glance and speech are tempered; one sees in him the complete absence of suffering, "like the earth that is not affected by anything done to it."

184. Ñāṇagutta (Alfred Günther). According to the Island Hermitage visitors' book, he arrived on 15 June 1937 and his parents and siblings on 05 January 1938.

185. On 22 May 1939, Govinda wrote the following to Ñāṇatiloka:

> When Mrs. Lounsbery was in Calcutta in December she took me aside one day and asked if she could speak confidentially with me. She told me that she had heard rumours from various sides in Ceylon that the German monks were working for the Nazis under the disguise of the yellow robes and that they would be arrested as the first ones in the case of a conflict. She believes that such a conflict will be unavoidable in the near future and sincerely requested me to inform you about the impending danger and to encourage you to naturalize as soon as possible to pinch all misunderstandings in the bud. Because you don't receive any money anymore from Germany you have nothing to lose. I am wondering why you have not done so long before as you have been thinking for years of the thought of naturalizing in Ceylon.
>
> I am happy that Nyānakhetto and Nyānamalito are with you again and also that you got rid of the Nazis who disturbed the peace at

Dodanduwa and apparently are discrediting you everywhere. In any case, I wouldn't ordain people whose political orientation is not compatible with the Teaching of the Buddha, because one can't serve two masters.

(H. Hecker, *Der Erste Deutsche Bhikkhu*, p. 173–174)

186. Vappo, Ñāṇasisi, Ñāṇaponika, Ñāṇakhetta, Ñāṇasīsi, Ñāṇamālita, and Ñāṇabrūhana.

187. Jawaharlal Nehru and his father were prominent in the Indian Independence Movement. Jawaharlal, as the head of the Indian National Congress, became the first Prime Minister of India when India won its independence.

188. See note 167 above.

189. EDB p. 242. This is in contradiction with Dr. Hecker's statement one page earlier (EDB 241) that Govinda's and Ñāṇatiloka's ways separated after Ñāṇatiloka stayed on in the Nazi side of the camp. Hecker also mentions that after WW II there was no correspondence between the two. There might have been no regular correspondence, but it seems that they did not lose complete contact because at the Forest Hermitage archives there is a cordial letter from Govinda to Ñāṇatiloka dated 25 February 1953 in which he wishes Ñāṇatiloka a happy 75th birthday and expresses his appreciation for Ñāṇatiloka's literary works, etc.

190. Dutton, 1955.

191. Gütersloh, 1959.

192. There is a bit of a mystery here. Patrick Harrigan, a disciple of Gauribala, and Ñāṇaramita Thera, a German monk who knew Gauribala, were under the impression that Gauribala escaped with Heinrich Harrer's group to Tibet. However, this seems unlikely because he is not among the names of Harrer's group of seven which are given in *Seven Years in Tibet*. Harrer, a nazi-sympathiser, would have been staying in Wing One, while Schönfeldt was in the Anti-Nazi wing. Ñāṇaramita Thera further said that during the inmates' weekly outings Ñāṇaponika also met the yogi who taught meditation to Ñāṇakhetta. So the yogi would have been staying within walking-distance from the camp. This is also implied in Hecker's account of Ñāṇatiloka in Dehra Dun (EDB p. 243) where it is mentioned that Gauribala/Ñāṇakhetta met his teacher during one of the allowed outings from the camp. This seems to be in contradiction with the escape account Hecker gives earlier (EDB 216). According to Ñāṇaramita, the yogi could do feats such as stopping breathing and being buried alive for days.

193. Walther Eidlitz (1892–1976). Jewish Austrian lyricist, novel-writer, playwright. Before WWII he lived in Vienna. After WWII he moved to

Sweden, where he died.

194. *Bhakta, Eine indische Odyssee,* Eidlitz, Walther; Hamburg, 1951, pp. 107–125. (The book can be downloaded from: http://www.bhakti-yoga.ch/Buch/BhaktaEineIndische.html .) The English translation was published as *Journey to Unknown India,* California, 1999. The present translation was made by Bhikkhu Nyanatusita without having been able to see the published translation.

195. Like his brother, he continued to live in Ceylon. He worked for the German consulate and married a Sinhalese.

196. 1920–1965.

197. Ñāṇamoli/Osbert Moore (1905–1960).

198. *The Doctrine of Awakening: A Study on the Buddhist Ascesis,* Julius Evola, Tr. Harold Musson. London: Luzac, 1951.

199. Quoted in "Existence, Enlightenment and Suicide" Stephen Batchelor http://www.stephenbatchelor.org/existence1.html. Published in Tadeusz Skorupski (ed.) The Buddhist Forum. Volume 4. London: School of Oriental and African Studies, 1996.

200. These are the sounds of drums used during exorcisms, which are popular in Southwest Sri Lanka.

201. Quoted in the chapter "A Sketch of the Life of Ñanamoli Thera (Osbert Moore)" in *From Tresco to Dodanduwa* by Maurice Cardiff, 1996. See http://www.geocities.com/Athens/9366/Nanamoli_bio_sketch.htm [URL functional 1Dec2007]

202. *Notes on Dhamma,* Colombo, 1963, republished together with Ñāṇavira's letters as *Clearing the Path,* Colombo, 1987, and in separate volumes as *Notes on Dhamma* (Dehiwela, 2001) and *Letters of Ñāṇavīra* (Dehiwela, 2002). See online edition at www.nanavira.org.

203. Dhammadinnā, lay-name Pearce or Van Stemm (1881–1967), was born in San Francisco. She became a Buddhist in the late 1920s after having heard some speeches. In 1931 she became a Buddhist nun in China and in 1933 went to Sārnāth where she wrote many articles for the *Mahā Bodhi* journal. After a failed attempt to found a Buddhist monastery in San Francisco, she went to Ceylon and lived at the Forest Hermitage for some years. In 1953 she moved to Sydney, Australia, where her visit resulted in the founding of the Buddhist Society of New South-Wales. A year later she moved to Hawaii, where she died.

204. U Nu (1907–1995).

205. The following article on the Council, written by the Buddhist writer Edward Conze, appeared in the *The Manchester Guardian* on 11th May 1954:

Sixth Buddhist Council

A Two-year Session in Burma

On 17th May, the day of the full moon, the Sixth Buddhist Council is due to begin in Rangoon. It will remain in session for two years, to be concluded on the full-moon day of May, 1956, which, on the chronology adopted in Burma, coincides with the two-thousand-five-hundredth anniversary of the Great Decease of the Lord Buddha. A Buddhist "Council", of course, differs widely from what Christians understand by that term. Christian councils were usually devoted to the discussion of definite controversial items, and they resulted in new definitions of the doctrine in the form of creeds, catechisms, and such like documents. Buddhists have generally believed that the peace of the world is not promoted by narrowing down the limits of orthodoxy, and the main concern of a Buddhist "council" is the collective recital of the scriptures. A meeting of the monks for that purpose is called a *saṃ-gāyana*, a word composed of the prefix "*saṃ-*," which moans "together", and the noun "*gāyana*", which means "chanting".

We must further bear in mind that Buddhism is divided into a great variety of schools or sects, which each have their own organization, traditions and scriptures. Perhaps the oldest of these are the Theravadins ("Those who teach what the Elders taught"), who dominate the religious life of Burma, Ceylon, Thailand, Cambodia and Laos. Pali is their holy language, and the Pali scriptures will be recited at this Saṅgāyana. According to the reckoning of the Theravadins, five councils have taken place up to now, the first three in India, the fourth in Ceylon, and the fifth in Burma. At the first, immediately after the Buddha's death, his teachings were recited and codified, although for more than four hundred years they continued to be transmitted orally. At the fourth, circa 20 B.C., they were for the first time written down on palm leaves, and at the fifth council, in 1871, they were recorded on 729 marble slabs at Mandalay.

Authorised Text

The text incised on the marble slabs will now be collaged with other editions made in Ceylon, Thailand, Cambodia and England. Errors will be removed, the text will be thoroughly "purified", and an authoritative printed edition will be issued, as a result of the council's deliberations, in 50 volumes of four hundred to five hundred pages each, to be issued in five thousand copies. A huge printing press for this purpose has already been opened at Rangoon, in October 1953, and some of the machines have been donated by the "Committee for a Free Asia", an organization not unconnected with the United States. The first volume of the scriptures has already been printed, and once the new edition has appeared it will be the official one in Burma and the sale of all other editions will be forbidden.

The council will also prepare an abridged edition of the scriptures, in two to three volumes of 500 pages each. A special bureau is charged with the translation of the canon into modern and understandable Burmese, a task of quite exceptional difficulty in view of the nature of the Burmese language. The translation, the work of Burmese laymen, is already for advanced and awaits final approval by groups of learned monks. In an endeavour to reawaken the interest of India in the Buddhist religion, which she discarded seven hundred years ago, a translation into Hindi has also been contemplated, but it is not likely to get under way before the council is over. An English translation was also originally planned, but for the time being the plan seems to have been dropped, very largely owing to the dearth of scholars qualified for this task.

The council is not merely an affair of a few monks, but the whole Burmese nation is concerned with it. It is the result of a resolution by the Burmese Parliament in 1951, which stated that material improvements are not sufficient to solve the problems of society and that "measures for the spiritual and moral well being of man" could alone be effective. A hundred acres of land have been set apart for the council, and Pounds one million is being spent on buildings which are grouped round the new "World Peace Pagoda", which was built in 1952 and which contains portions of the relies of Sāriputta and Moggallāna, two direct disciples of the Buddha. It will be remembered that these relics were housed for forty years in the Victoria and Albert Museum and that their transfer to Asia a few years ago everywhere greatly stirred the people and roused their faith in Buddhism. Relics of some kind or other are essential to all pagodas. Formerly they were buried underground, but nowadays a modern pagoda is build like a museum, with everything exposed in showcases all round.

A Miracle

Then there is to be an assembly hall for 2,500 people, hostels, a library, a hospital and the printing works mentioned above. The assembly hall is called the "World Peace Cave", because it is built on the model of the cave of Rājagaha, famous in Buddhist history. The hall was built in this form as a result of a vision which U Nu, the Prime Minister, had, and its consecration is said to have been hallowed by a miracle, the fall of rain in the dry season at just that spot and place only. After the conclusion of the council these building are intended to form the foundation for an International Buddhist University. The money is raised by Government grants and donations from the public, and tens of thousands of Burmese have done voluntary labour on the site. The thousand monks responsible for the new edition of the scriptures have been divided into a hundred groups, each responsible for a particular portion of the sacred texts. The final decision in cases of doubt and difficulty will be in the hands of an editorial board composed of monks from Burma, Ceylon and Thailand.

Although chiefly devoted to the preservation and purification of the scriptures, the meeting of so many scholarly monks will also be used for the propagation of their message. "Observers" have been invited from Nepal, Japan, China and Tibet – countries which lie outside the Theravada sphere. They are not expected to take part in the work of the council, but only to hear the recitations, to acknowledge the solidarity of Buddhism, and to give their blessing to the proceedings. Missionaries are being trained to go abroad, and a college for their training was opened on the site of the council in January 1953.

Another concern of the council is the spread of Buddhism among the hill tribes of Burma itself. For the faithful it organizes examination in a special branch of the scriptures, known as the Abhidhamma – twelve thousand of them in 1953. In an endeavour to reduce criminality the council has also arranged such examinations in the goals, and prisoners can earn a remission of their sentences by showing that they have studied the scriptures with some care and attention. Finally, considering that Buddhism is not so much a set doctrine as a method of meditation, the council subsidizes "meditation centres" throughout Burma, where people are led to a direct realization of the truths proclaimed in the sacred texts.

It will be seen from this brief outline that no effort is spared to promote the spiritual well being of South-east Asia, and that, unattracted by either communism or the American way of life, the Union of Burma shows that there is still plenty of vitality in the old ideals of the religion of the Buddha which have guided her people for the last 1,500 years.

206. The following address was found in the Forest Hermitage archives. Presumably, it was read out during this visit.

Ven. Monks and Dear Friends of the Dhamma,

May I be permitted to express my profoundest thanks for the great honour bestowed upon me and my pupil of inviting us to your country, for the purpose of considering and finding out the best ways and means how to spread our peaceful Dhamma all over the world. The Hon. U. Thaki Nu, Sir U. Thwin and other wise leaders of your country are to be thanked for having taken the first steps to realize this noble object. Such a gigantic undertaking planned by you, was hardly ever witnessed in the long history of any country. But the taking of such steps was absolutely necessary under the present condition of the world. For the Buddha's doctrine forms the only safe and firm road that will keep mankind away from those crude materialistic notions which are the root-causes of all selfishness, greed, hate and therefore of war and cruelty, and of all misery in the world. Let us hope that we shall meet success and that the 2500th anniversary of the Buddha's Passing away will bring peace to the world.

This is not the first time that I have come to this once so happy country. Forty-nine years have passed since I, as a young man of 25, arrived to this country and was ordained a Sāmaṇera and a Bhikkhu. Now you see me as an old man of 74. But, still, I am not too old to work from morning till evening for the spread of the genuine Dhamma in the world, esp. Germany where I was born.

Now, let me introduce to you our pupil U. Nyanaponika, who has already proved by his numerous writings and translations his great abilities as a Pali and Abhidhamma scholar. I am fully convinced that he will also be of great help and play an active part in the planning and carrying out of a methodical propagation of the Dhamma in the West. He has brought along with him a very ably drafted memorandum for the intended Buddhist Mission Program, which he wishes to submit to the Buddha Sasana-Council of Burma.

Supposedly the memorandum Ñāṇatiloka refers to is the following memorandum which was found in the Forest Hermitage archives:

Memorandum A
Mission Work in General

Drafted by Nyanaponika Thera
Recommended by Nyanatiloka Maha Thera

NOTE : The following pages (1–5) deal mainly with long-view plans, with the first steps to be taken for their implementation.

Some suggestions are added, on p.6, providing for the case that missionaries are sent out previous to the implementation of the systematic Mission Plan.

Methodical procedure, i.e. to do first things first and in an efficient way, is an important factor of success in mission work too. Such methodical endeavour was up to now not possible as just the basic needs of mission work require expenditure beyond the means of the organizations and individuals engaged in that work.

Thanks to the initiative of the Union of Burma Government in establishing and supporting the Buddha Sasana Council, it is to be hoped that other Buddhist nations too will follow suit in preparing for the year 2500 B.E. Some *constructive* work that serves to strengthen the Sasana, and thereby the peace and spiritual welfare in their own countries and in the world at large.

To that purpose, it may be considered to make an appeal to all Buddhist nations, larger Buddhist communities and organizations, and it should be suggested to them to *co-ordinate* efforts, as far as possible.

If these expectations materialize even partly, it will be possible to plan mission work in a systematic and efficient way.

Before entering into detailed proposals, one fundamental Basis of the mission principle has to be stressed: *all missionary activity should be based on the original and genuine tradition of the Buddha-Dhamma, known as Theravada.*

Only if the exposition of the Dhamma, in books or by the spoken world, is consistent, straightforward and definite, it will carry conviction. But if, in the exposition, consideration is given to divergent Mahayana views, the statement will become ambiguous, Vague or evasive, by trying to include those views or not to contradict them.

As we do not regard Theravada as a "sect" or a "school", but as the faithful presentation of the genuine Buddha word, the term "Theravada" need not be used except in historical context.

Mission work is mainly of two kinds; by the spoken, and by the printed word, i.e. by preaching or lecturing, and by literature.

The basic requirement for mission by the spoken word is a central *Missionary College* of a high standard; for mission through the sprinted word, it is a financially well endowed central *Publishing House* and a *Distributing and Propaganda Center for Buddhist Literature.*

I. Mission through the Spoken Word (through Dhammadutas)

The Central Missionary (or Dhammaduta) College should have a high standard approximating that of a university. It will therefore be advantageous to attach it to a Buddhist University. In that way, duplicating of efforts and unnecessary expenditure will be avoided, since many lectures held at a Buddhist University, will likewise be required for a Missionary College. The latter will have to provide only such special subjects which are needed for the training of missionaries.

Only a *Buddhist* University will serve the afore-mentioned purpose. A State University of general scope would have to observe neutrality in religious matters, even in its Buddhist Department; there the lecturers in many of the required subjects might be non-Buddhists with attitudes entirely alien to the Dhamma; and last but not least, the entire atmosphere of a general university would not be congenial to the Dhammaduta students, be they monks or laymen.

As the buildings to be erected for the Sixth council are already earmarked for a Buddhist University, and on other reasons too, it will be the best choice that the Central Missionary College should likewise be established in *Burma*, be attached to that University, and planned together with it.

The medium of teaching in both institutions should be English, as they should have an international character. Students and lecturers may be both monks or laymen, from Eastern or Western countries.

Monks, lecturers and students, should pledge themselves to the observance of the Vinaya. Laymen should keep to a high standard of Buddhist lay morality. Only if linked with exemplary conduct, the activity of missionaries will carry conviction, and command respect.

The College should aim at producing missionaries who are models with regard to knowledge, ability and conduct. "Character building", by direct and indirect methods, should therefore form an important part of college life.

The College should also have in view the training of teachers for smaller, regional mission schools in the various Buddhist countries.

The University will provide for an advanced study of Pali and the Dhamma; lectures on the history and culture of Buddhism, on Eastern religions, philosophy, and history; perhaps also on Western philosophy and psychology, etc. The missionary College will provide for such auxiliary subjects as are required for its purpose, e.g. elocution, apologetics (defence of the Dhamma against criticism); specialized instruction for mission in single countries or regions: social customs, language, etc., of those countries, fundamentals of their religion, e.g. Christianity. There should also be study groups, at the Mission College, where the material provided in the University lectures, is applied to the tasks of mission work.

No expenses should be spared to have really capable lecturers in both institutions. If in certain subjects suitable Buddhist lecturers are not available, sympathizing non-Buddhists who are capable, should be preferred. Their lecturers may, if necessary, be supplemented by the afore-mentioned study groups which will the Buddhist back ground.

As soon as the curriculum for both institutions has been drafter, with the help of expert advice, systematic search for suitable lecturers should be undertaken at once. This is particularly urgent as it is very probable persons will first have to train themselves for a few years, well ahead of the actual establishment of the institutions.

II. Mission Through the Printed Word (Propaganda through literature)

i. Publishing House and Distributing Center

There are a number of facts making it urgent to establish a publishing and distributing center:

- i. Many books, important for study, research, and propaganda remain unpublished as private firms are not willing to take the risk.
- ii. Private publishers will not be interested in systematic distribution and publicity, under the view point of propaganda the Dhamma.
- iii. Many books on important subjects remain unwritten as authors have little hope that their books will find a publisher. But a Buddhist Publishing House may even take the initiative by commissioning the writing of books on vital subjects, as e.g. Modern Buddhist Education, etc.
- iv. Many of the existing Buddhist publications are distributed very insufficiently and inefficiently and do not reach the proper channels of the book trade, etc.; therefore even small editions are partly left unsold though, with a little skilled organisatory effort, the sale could easily and considerably be increased.

The enterprise should be managed by an expert in publishing, book-selling and printing. It should be furnished as soon as possible with a modern printing press.

In view of the great demand for Buddhist literature all over the world, this enterprise would soon become a paying concern in many of its department. As an extension of its activity, the establishing of Buddhist book shops in major cities could be considered for the future.

The Distributing Department may also act as agent for other publishers of Buddhist books. It should undertake systematic propaganda for the Buddhist book, by advertisements, etc.

A separate department should be in charge of free distribution of literature to libraries, schools, universities, hospitals, etc.; it could be subsidized by private donations.

As the Buddha Sasana Council intends to undertake the printing of the Tipitaka text in two scripts, and of Burmese and English translations, the proposed Central Publishing House could well act as the publisher and distributor, at least of the editions in Roman script. This would give to the enterprise a certain status and international reputation.

On various reasons, Ceylon would be a suitable domicile for that enterprise. It might, e.g., not be advisable that all those Buddhist institutions of key importance which are to be established, are concentrated in a single country.

II.2 "The Word of the Buddha"

As a nucleus for a Buddhist counterpart of the "Bible Societies" it is suggested that first full support is given to the systematic and world-wide distribution of the "Word of the Buddha", being a small-sized, popular publication, suitable for that purpose.

The "Sasanadhara Kantha Samitiya" at Colombo has established a "WORD OF THE BUDDHA" Publishing Committee" which has undertaken to print, as a beginning,
5 -10,000 copies from funds raised in Ceylon.

This will prepare the ground and provide an organizational network for the planned central Publishing House with which the said Committee may later be amalgamated if both parties agree.

It is suggested that the Buddha Sasana Council, or any other Buddhist organization of Burma, takes over, for distribution in Burma, a number of copies of the new, revised edition which is to appear in the beginning of 1952, and supports as much as feasible the work of the aforementioned Committee.

For details, see Appendix

II.3 Leaflets (tracts)

A primary requisite of literary propagation is a Comprehensive Series of Leaflets (tracts, folders) of 2–4 pages, first in the English language. They should be well written, with psychological understanding, and furnish reliable information.

The following four series of leaflets are suggested:

A. General *introductions* to the Dhamma, adapted to various view points, partly with a specialized approach to various classes, professions, etc.
B. *Instructive* leaflets, covering systematically all important parts of the Dhamma, suitable for popular exposition.
C. *Topical* subjects, seen form the Buddhist point of view (ethical, social and other problems).
D. *Translations* of short and popular scriptural texts (abridged Suttas, Dhammapada verses, devotional texts, etc.)

A separate committee may be formed for editing such leaflets, and financing their distribution.

III. Mission in Germany

It is suggested that, for mission work in the West Germany be selected as a Starting- and testing-ground.

For details, see Memorandum B. There is an initial amount of Rs. 15,000 was suggested. But if systematic work is to be done, i.e. if all fields of missionary activity are to be covered efficiently, an allocation of one lakh of rupees is recommended which is to be spent gradually for specified items.

But also in case that activity is started in a smaller scale, the following items are recommended for gradual implementations:

Proposals, made in Memorandum B:

1. Lending libraries with Reading Rooms;
2. Leaflets;
3. Special allocation for Berlin;
4. Refundable subsidies, or donations, for German publications.

Additional proposals:

5. Maintenance of two itinerant lay preachers;
6. Furnishing them with short documentary films from Buddhist countries, dealing with their religious life, Buddhist art, etc.

IV. First Steps for the Implementation of the Systematic Mission Plan

1. Missionary College

1. Drafting of a provisional curriculum for the Buddhist University, and a supplementary one for the Missionary College;

2. Search for, or training of the required lecturers. It may be considered to grant stipendia, for training in required subjects, to promising and recommended students or young scholars at universities, monastic colleges, etc.

3. Collecting of books for a Reference Library.

2. Publishing House

It may be ascertained whether the Buddhists of Lanka would undertake to finance a Buddhist Publishing House and Distributing Center, to be domiciled in Lanka.

3. Mission in Germany

If this project, in smaller or larger scale, is not taken over by Burma, the help of other Buddhist governments, organizations, etc. may be solicited, for providing for any of the six items required (see above). Alternatively, a single Buddhist country may act as the patron of Buddhist mission in Germany, while others may sponsor work in different countries.

4. Various Items

The help of other Buddhist governments, organizations, etc., may be solicited for taking over work on

(a).Tracts in English
(b).Printing and distributing of the "Word of the Buddha"
(c).Maintenance of missionaries abroad
(d).Establishing the planned London Vihara

5. Sending Out of Missionaries

If missionaries are sent abroad, previous to the implementation of the Mission Plan, the following recommendations are made:

1. Personal pledge by the missionary monk to observe the Vinaya. His conduct should be dignified and self-controlled.
2. For missionary monks in non-Buddhist countries arrangements should be made beforehand enabling them to dispense entirely with the use of money. Suitable provisions to be made either be the country of destination, or by the home country (traveling together with a layman who may also serve as an assistant lecturer, or as secretary to the monk).
3. Meals must be served to the monk at the proper time, and the quality and quantity of the diet should enable him to dispense with the evening meal, also in cold countries.
4. Monks in cold countries should be supplied with supplementary clothing, in accordance with Vinaya rules providing for such cases. A certain uniformity of that equipment is desirable.
5. Accommodation should be befitting for a monk, i.e. not together with families or ladies; if possible he should be housed outside of the town.
6. The activity of the missionary should be backed by simultaneous literary propaganda in the respective country. He should be furnished with tracts and other literature.

APPENDIX

A Plan of Worldwide Distribution of "The Word of the Buddha"

(see p.4)

The English version of "The Word of the Buddha" by the Ven. Nyanatiloka Mahathera was first published in 1967, at Rangoon. It has since run to ten editions, and translations into six languages have been published.

This little book has proved to be one or the most important small-size publications, giving a systematic presentation of the Dhamma in the Master's own words. Many have made their first acquaintance with the Dhamma through that book.

Yet, only a small fraction of potential readers has been reached, as no systematic distribution has been undertaken so far. Since several editions of the English version were printed for free distribution, the book was for a long time not available through the book trade, and, generally, very few copies have reached the West or India.

It has now been decided to make a modest, but systematic beginning with the world-wide distribution of the book. The Dayaka-Sabha or the "Island Hermitage", the "Sasanadhara Kantha Samitiya" ("Ladies' Association for Promoting the Sasana") at Colombo, has formed a "WORD OF THE BUDDHA Publishing Committee" which will print, as a first beginning, 5–10,000 copies, but the first target should be 100,000 copies.

The idea is that of an intensive propaganda and distribution, e.g. by the following measures:

Regional and local committees should see to it that the book is stocked by leading book sellers. This is to be supported by advertisements (with a uniform attractive block) in daily papers and magazines. Introducing it as text book in Colleges, Buddhist study circles, etc; as a gift book on private festive occasion s, at school prize-giving, etc. Free distribution to Public libraries, schools, hospitals, prisons, etc. and beyond that in the measure of donations made for free distribution of the book.

For the purpose of that scheme, a fully revised edition of the book has been prepared. It will have an enlarged introduction (containing the Refuges and the Five Precepts), additional explanatory notes and a list of Buddhist literature. It will be neatly printed in a handy pocket size, with an attractive cover. The sale price will be kept as low as possible. Ten percent of the edition will be reserved for free distribution.

As India is a particularly fertile field for Buddhist mission, a special Indian edition is planned if support from India is forthcoming. This edition will contain a "directory" of the Buddhist societies, temples, institutions and magazines in India; a list of Buddhist literature published in the various Indian languages, etc.

This scheme bids fir to bring far-reaching results in the propagation of the Dhamma. It may well become the nucleus for a Buddhist counterpart to the big "Bible Societies". In 1948, 1 million and 80 thousand Bibles were distributed in India, Pakistan and Ceylon. This is certainly a challenge to us Buddhists to start, at least in a small scale, with systematic literary propaganda.

The scheme had the advantage that it can be extended gradually, and that a considerable part of the printing costs will be returned through the sale or the book. For the beginning, however, a propaganda fund, for advertisements, etc. will be required. After a start has been made, the scheme is sure to attract co-workers, and the demand for the book will grow in many countries.

207. Published as "Message of the Ven. Nyanatiloka Mahāthera, (read by Ven. Nyanaponika Thera)," *The Chaṭṭha Sangāyanā Souvenir Album*, Rangoon, 1956.

208. The article "Begegnung im Lande des Wohlbehagens," by Alexander Sosso and Pitt Severin, was published in the magazine *Stern*, Nr. 21, v. 22.5.1955, pp. 12–16.

209. Lord Soulbury, the governor of Ceylon from 1949 to 1954.

210. See Sam Wickramasinghe "German Swami Gauribala: Walking the Razor's Edge of Liberation," and "German Swami Gauribala: the Bohemian Swami of Jaffna" at http://kataragama.org/sages/razors-edge.htm; and "From 'Secret Germany' to Secret Lanka–The life and times of German Swami," by Patrick Harrigan at http://sundaytimes.lk/070916/Plus/ plus00011.html. Not all details in these articles, such as Schönfeldt's first coming to Sri Lanka from India and escaping to Tibet, are reliable. The Swami talked very little about his early life to his disciples.

211. In the archives of the German Dharmaduta Society there is the transcript of the following message by Ñāṇatiloka delivered at a German Dharmaduta Society meeting on May 25, 1953:

> It was just 50 years ago, in 1903, that I came first to this Island which, since then, I have considered my spiritual home, and I am therefore happy to be now a citizen of Sri Lanka. Yet, it will be understood that it was the great wish of my heart to give the country of my origin the best I possessed, i.e. the Dhamma. And to that end I have devoted the greatest part of my 50 years in the Sangha. I did so in the firm conviction that the Dhamma will take root in my home country, Germany, and may have a great future there. Now it has been a very great pleasure to me to hear that Mr. Weeraratna returned from Germany with the very same conviction, and was able to report on lively Buddhist activities there. I believe that the chances for Buddhist mission work in Germany are now greater than ever before. I am therefore very happy that the Lanka Dharmaduta Society has undertaken that great task of sending a well-prepared mission to Germany and to support Buddhist work there, in general.
>
> I greatly appreciate the initial work done by the Society up to now, and particularly the sacrificing labour, devotion and energy shown by the Founder and Secretary of the Lanka Dharmaduta Society, Mr. Asoka Weeraratna. I should, indeed, regard it as a happy culmination of my life if Vesak 1956, i.e. the year 2500, will see a well-established mission in Germany, which will not fail to have a far-reaching influence on the other Western countries, too. I wish

the Society full success in their great and noble enterprise. Selfless effort to give the Dhamma to those who are most in need of it will be of great blessing to those who give and receive.

Nyanatiloka

212. Earlier published in Bhikkhu Bodhi, *Nyanaponika: A Farewell Tribute*, BPS, Kandy 1995.

213. Francis Story (1910–1972), a.k.a. Anāgārika Sugatananda) became acquainted with Buddhist teachings early in life. For 25 years he lived in India, Burma, and Sri Lanka, studying Buddhism. He produced a considerable body of writings, collected and published in three volumes by the Buddhist Publication Society.

214. Earlier published in *Nyanatiloka Centenary Volume*; see Bibiography.

215. As said in the Introduction, see p. 10, these have been found at the archives of the Forest Hermitage in 2006.

216. In bibliographies prepared by Nyanaponika and in his introduction to his *Abhidhamma Studies*, this unpublished translation into German is mentioned, however, despite having been searched for in Sri Lanka and Germany, the manuscript has not been traced and appears to be irretrievably lost.

Of Related Interest from the BPS

THE WORD OF THE BUDDHA
An Outline of the Buddha's Teaching in the Words of the Pali Canon
Nyanatiloka Mahāthera

This superb little work by the eminent German scholar-monk is probably the best compact sourcebook in English on the Buddha's basic teachings, all expounded in his own words. Translated into a dozen languages, it is now in its 16th English edition, yet still reads as fresh, clear, and vigorous as if it were just written.

BP 201S 100 pp.

THE BUDDHA'S PATH TO DELIVERANCE
A Systematic Exposition in the Words of the Sutta Piṭaka
Nyanatiloka Mahāthera

Larger in size and more advanced in treatment than The Word of the Buddha, this book arranges the Buddha's discourses into the threefold framework of morality, concentration, and wisdom, and the seven stages of purity. The selections, giving full coverage to both serenity and insight meditation, gain further light from the translator's own authoritative explanations.

BP 202S 232 pp.

THE FUNDAMENTALS OF BUDDHISM
Nyanatiloka Mahāthera

Four lectures by the German monk on the Four Noble Truths, kamma and rebirth, dependent origination and meditation.

WH394/396 88 pp.

Middle Land, Middle Way
A Pilgrim's Guide to the Buddha's India
Ven. S. Dhammika

A comprehensive guidebook to the places in India made sacred by the Buddha's presence. Beginning with an inspiring account of Buddhist pilgrimage, the author then covers sixteen places in detail. With maps & colour photos, an essential companion for pilgrim and traveller.

BP 609S 192 pp.

Sacred Island
Ven. S. Dhammika

This guidebook is meant primarily for Buddhists or those interested in Buddhism who wish to explore Sri Lanka's rich cultural and spiritual heritage. Drawing on his extensive knowledge of the Island, the author weaves together archaeological findings, art history and the stories and legends of the Theravadin tradition to bring to life thirty three places of religious significance. He also offers practical advice to how to travel in Sri Lanka and what the visitor can do to learn more about Buddhism and meditation.

BP612 237 pp.

A Comprehensive Manual of Abhidhamma
Bhikkhu Bodhi, General Editor

This is the classical introduction to the study of Abhidhamma, the Buddhist philosophy of mind and mental processes. The work contains a translation of Ācariya Anuruddha's *Abhidhammattha-sangaha* along with the Pali text and a detailed explanatory guide to this ancient philosophical psychology. A long introduction explains the basic principles of the Abhidhamma. Includes 48 charts and tables.

BP 304S 426 pp.

All prices as in latest catalogue: http://www.bps.lk

THE BUDDHIST PUBLICATION SOCIETY

The BPS is an approved charity dedicated to making known the Teaching of the Buddha, which has a vital message for all people. Founded in 1958, the BPS has published a wide variety of books and booklets covering a great range of topics. Its publications include accurate annotated translations of the Buddha's discourses, standard reference works, as well as original contemporary expositions of Buddhist thought and practice. These works present Buddhism as it truly is—a dynamic force which has influenced receptive minds for the past 2500 years and is still as relevant today as it was when it first arose. For more information about the BPS and our publications, please visit our website, or contact:

Administrative Secretary
Buddhist Publication Society
P.O. Box 61
54 Sangharaja Mawatha
Kandy • Sri Lanka

E-mail: bps@bps.lk
web site: http://www.bps.lk
Tel: 0094 81 223 7283 • Fax: 0094 81 222 3679